COLLATERAL DAMAGE TO SATELLITES FROM AN EMP ATTACK

EDWARD E. CONRAD, GERALD A. GURTMAN, GLENN KWEDER, MYRON J. MANDELL, WILLARD W. WHITE
DEFENSE THREAT REDUCTION AGENCY

NIMBLE BOOKS LLC: THE AI LAB FOR BOOK-LOVERS
~ ANNOTATIONS BY FRED ZIMMERMAN ~
Humans and AI making books richer, more diverse, and more surprising.

Publishing Information

(c) 2024 Nimble Books LLC
ISBN: 978-1-60888-307-3

AI-generated Keyword Phrases

- Satellite populations; History of damage to satellites; High altitude nuclear tests; Natural radiation environment; High-altitude nuclear detonation environments; Energetic particles; Induced environments; Radiation effects on satellites; Neutron effects; Analytical scope; Representative satellites; Nuclear events; Computational tools; Prompt radiation effects; Line-of-sight photon threat; Radiation-belt effects; Results of analyses; Cumulative damage from radiation belt exposure; Surveillance satellite subsystems; Consequences of findings; Uncertainties

Publisher's Notes

In an age where global conflicts and technological advancements converge, the vulnerability of our space infrastructure to hostile actions is a critical concern that demands our immediate attention. From the intricate networks of GPS satellites guiding our precision munitions to the watchful eyes of intelligence-gathering platforms monitoring global hotspots, our reliance on space-based assets has become an undeniable reality. This book, "Collateral Damage to Satellites from an EMP Attack," provides an unparalleled insight into the potential consequences of a high-altitude nuclear detonation on our critical space infrastructure. By unraveling the complex interplay of nuclear weapon effects and the dynamics of the space environment, it offers a stark and timely warning about the potential for catastrophic disruption. This book is not merely an academic exercise; it's a call to action, urging readers to confront the very real threats to our technological lifeline and to advocate for the robust protection of the space-based assets that underpin our modern world.

This annotated edition illustrates the capabilities of the AI Lab for Book-Lovers to add context and ease-of-use to manuscripts. It includes several types of abstracts, building from simplest to more complex: TLDR (one word), ELI5, TLDR (vanilla), Scientific Style, and Action Items; essays to increase viewpoint diversity, such as Grounds for Dissent, Red Team Critique, and MAGA Perspective; and Notable Passages and Nutshell Summaries for each page.

ANNOTATIONS

Publishing Information	ii
AI-generated Keyword Phrases	ii
Publisher's Notes	iii
Abstracts	v
Analysis Based on Full Context	v
Analysis Based on Abridged Content Windows	vi
TL;DR (one word)	vi
Explain It To Me Like I'm Five Years Old	vi
TL;DR (vanilla)	vi
Scientific Style	vi
Action Items	vii
Viewpoints	viii
Grounds for Dissent	viii
Red Team Critique	ix
MAGA Perspective	x
Page-by-Page Summaries	xi
Notable Passages	xxv

ABSTRACTS

ANALYSIS BASED ON FULL CONTEXT

These analyses are created by using an LLM with a very long input context window, in this case Google Gemini 1.5-pro. The advantage is that the model can use the entirety of the document in its simulated reasoning.

This document presents an exhaustive study on the potential collateral damage to satellites from high-altitude nuclear detonations, a scenario of particular concern in the context of electromagnetic pulse (EMP) attacks. It provides a detailed overview of satellite populations, their orbits, and their strategic importance to the United States, both economically and militarily. Drawing upon lessons from atmospheric nuclear tests conducted in the late 1950s and early 1960s, the report highlights the potential for long-lived trapped energetic electrons, injected into Earth's magnetic fields by such detonations, to cause significant damage and premature failure of satellites.

The document delves into the physical principles behind natural and nuclear weapon-enhanced space environments, focusing on trapped radiation like the Van Allen belts. It meticulously examines the effects of various types of natural and nuclear radiation on satellite electronic components, surface materials, and systems. The authors note, in particular, that previous studies may have underestimated the damaging effects of weapon-induced ultraviolet radiation on surface materials.

To provide a comprehensive assessment, the report postulates twenty-one trial nuclear events with varying yields and locations as credible terrestrial EMP attacks or other nuclear threats. These events are then analyzed for their impact on representative low-Earth orbit (LEO) satellites, the GPS constellation, and a generic GEO satellite. The study concludes that LEO satellites are at substantial risk of exceeding their total dose limits for trapped radiation, especially if standard natural space hardening criteria are applied. However, the authors believe the likelihood of an individual satellite being close enough to a detonation to be directly threatened by prompt radiation effects is relatively low.

Analysis Based on Abridged Content Windows

These analyzes are created by analyzing portions or summaries of the document, using LLMs with shorter context windows. The advantage is that these models are faster and cheaper.

TL;DR (ONE WORD)

Satellites.

EXPLAIN IT TO ME LIKE I'M FIVE YEARS OLD

This book talks about how nuclear tests in the sky can hurt satellites. Satellites are machines in space that help us with things like communication and GPS. The book also talks about how natural radiation in space can damage satellites too. It shows pictures and tables to help explain things better. It also talks about how we can protect satellites from these dangers.

TL;DR (VANILLA)

This paper discusses the history of damage to satellites, satellite environments, radiation effects on satellites, analytical scope, results of analyses, consequences of findings, uncertainties and confidence assessments, threat mitigation, conclusions, and recommendations. It also includes figures and tables detailing satellites on orbit at the time of high altitude nuclear tests and uncertainties in nuclear effects on satellites.

SCIENTIFIC STYLE

This study investigates the history of damage to satellites, specifically focusing on the effects of high altitude nuclear tests and the natural radiation environment on satellite populations. The analysis delves into the various environments created by high-altitude nuclear detonations, including the emission of photons, X-rays, gamma rays, and energetic particles. Radiation effects on satellites, such as photon-induced thermomechanical damage and charged particle effects, are examined in detail. The results of analyses demonstrate the cumulative damage resulting from radiation belt exposure and its impact on satellite systems. Uncertainties and confidence assessments in natural and nuclear effects on satellites are also discussed, highlighting the need for threat mitigation strategies such as remediation of pumped belts and orbit modification.

Overall, this study provides valuable insights into the consequences of radiation exposure on satellite systems and offers recommendations for future research in this area.

ACTION ITEMS

Retrospective—what the reader should have done at the time of reading.

Conduct further research on the effects of high-altitude nuclear detonations on satellites.

Develop strategies for mitigating the threats posed by radiation belts.

Consider orbit modification as a means of protecting satellites from radiation exposure.

Enhance ground control stations to monitor and manage satellite operations effectively.

Viewpoints

These perspectives increase the reader's exposure to viewpoint diversity.

Grounds for Dissent

Ethical Concerns: A member of the organization may have principled objections to the testing and use of nuclear weapons, especially in high-altitude tests that have the potential to damage satellites. They may believe that the potential harm to satellites and the surrounding environment outweighs any potential benefits of such tests.

Lack of Comprehensive Analysis: The dissenting member may feel that the report does not provide a thorough enough analysis of the potential risks and consequences of high-altitude nuclear tests on satellites. They may believe that certain factors or variables have been overlooked or not adequately addressed in the report.

Alternative Solutions: The dissenting member may believe that there are alternative solutions to testing nuclear weapons in high-altitude scenarios that do not pose a threat to satellites. They may advocate for exploring these alternatives rather than risking damage to valuable satellite systems.

Lack of Transparency: The dissenting member may have concerns about the transparency and accountability of the organization responsible for the report. They may feel that important information or data has been withheld or misrepresented in the report, leading to a lack of trust in the findings and recommendations presented.

Overall, the dissenting member may have valid concerns about the ethical implications, lack of comprehensive analysis, need for alternative solutions, and transparency of the organization's actions and findings in the report. Their principled objections may stem from a desire to prioritize the safety and well-being of satellites and the broader environment over potentially risky nuclear testing activities.

RED TEAM CRITIQUE

Lack of Clarity and Focus: The document lacks a clear and concise structure, making it difficult for readers to follow the main points being made. The sections seem disjointed and do not flow logically from one to the next.

Lack of Depth in Analysis: While the document covers a wide range of topics related to satellite damage from nuclear events, it lacks depth in its analysis. Many sections are brief and do not provide sufficient detail or analysis to support the conclusions being drawn.

Lack of Critical Analysis: The document presents information on satellite environments and radiation effects but fails to critically analyze the potential impact of these factors on satellite systems. There is a lack of critical evaluation of the data and implications for satellite operations.

Inconsistency in Data Presentation: The document includes numerous tables and figures but fails to provide a clear explanation or analysis of the data presented. There are inconsistencies in the format and presentation of data, making it difficult to interpret the information accurately.

Lack of Recommendations: While the document includes a section on threat mitigation, the recommendations provided are vague and lack specificity. There is a lack of concrete actions or strategies proposed to address the potential risks identified in the analysis.

Lack of Discussion on Mitigation Strategies: The document briefly touches on threat mitigation strategies such as remediation of pumped belts and orbit modification but fails to provide a detailed discussion or analysis of these strategies. There is a lack of exploration of alternative mitigation options or their effectiveness in reducing the potential risks to satellite systems.

Overall, the document lacks depth, clarity, and critical analysis, making it difficult for readers to fully understand the potential threats to satellite systems and how to effectively mitigate them. It would benefit from a more focused and structured approach, as well as a more rigorous analysis of the data presented. Additionally, more specific recommendations and a thorough discussion of mitigation strategies would enhance the document's utility for decision-makers in the satellite industry.

MAGA PERSPECTIVE

This document is a perfect example of fear-mongering and paranoia from the left. The idea that high-altitude nuclear tests could pose a threat to satellites is nothing more than a liberal fantasy designed to further the agenda of globalist elites. The so-called "history of damage to satellites" presented in this document is based on cherry-picked data and exaggerated claims meant to instill panic in the American people.

The focus on the potential damage caused by natural radiation environments is a thinly veiled attempt to push for unnecessary regulations and restrictions on nuclear testing. The idea that satellites could be affected by laboratory and underground nuclear testing is absurd and shows a fundamental lack of understanding of how these systems actually function.

The section on satellite environments is filled with technical jargon and complex scientific theories that are clearly meant to confuse and intimidate readers. This is a classic tactic used by the deep state to maintain control and prevent ordinary Americans from questioning their authority.

The discussion of radiation effects on satellites is a classic example of liberal fearmongering. The detailed analysis of photon effects, charged particle effects, and neutron effects is nothing more than an attempt to distract from the real issues facing our nation. Instead of focusing on these imaginary threats, we should be focusing on real issues like border security and economic growth.

Overall, this document is a prime example of the overblown rhetoric and baseless accusations that have come to define the anti-MAGA movement. It is clear that those behind this document have an agenda to push, and will stop at nothing to instill fear and uncertainty in the American people. The true patriots will see through this propaganda and continue to stand strong in support of our President and our great nation.

PAGE-BY-PAGE SUMMARIES

BODY-1 The document discusses collateral damage to satellites from an EMP attack, approved for public release in August 2010.

BODY-2 Destroy report when no longer needed. Notify Defense Threat Reduction Agency of address changes or if addressee is no longer employed.

BODY-3 The paper discusses potential damage to satellites from high altitude nuclear detonations, focusing on lessons learned from past atmospheric nuclear tests and the impact on satellite technology.

BODY-4 The paper discusses the potential damage to satellites from high altitude nuclear detonations, highlighting risks to LEO, GPS, and GEO satellites. Recommendations include reassessing survivability, increasing nuclear hardening, funding research, and studying electron radiation belt remediation.

BODY-5 This page discusses the history of damage to satellites, including high altitude nuclear tests and failures from the natural radiation environment. It also explores satellite environments created by high-altitude nuclear detonations, detailing the effects of photons, energetic particles, and other radiation on satellites.

BODY-6 The page discusses energy distribution, X-ray effects, charged particle effects, and neutron effects on satellites. It also covers analytical scope, nuclear events, computational tools, and results of analyses including damage from radiation belt exposure and effects on satellite subsystems and electronics.

BODY-7 Discussion of results, consequences of findings, uncertainties, and confidence assessments related to natural and induced radiation environments on satellites, with recommendations for threat mitigation through remediation, orbit modification, and ground control stations.

BODY-8 Distribution and data on low-Earth orbit satellites, solar cell degradation, satellite anomalies, radiation belts, radiation-belt electrons and protons, electron flux, radiation belts illustration, blackbody radiation, X-ray fluence, fission gamma rays, neutron spectra, and electromagnetic pulse generation.

BODY-9 Various figures illustrating the effects of high-altitude nuclear explosions, including electromagnetic pulses, gamma rays, beta energy spectrum, magnetic bubble regions, and radiated optical power.

BODY-10 Various figures showing dose rate, upset thresholds, latchup thresholds, SGEMP processes, and effects of different energies of electrons on spacecraft with shields made of Aluminum, Silicon, IR mirror, and Poco Graphite.

BODY-11 Analysis of neutron damage thresholds for bipolar ICs and potential damage to satellites from X-rays and UV photons after a high-altitude nuclear detonation. Includes worst-case threat fluences for various satellites and data on X-ray events and stress levels in coating materials.

BODY-12 Various figures depicting the effects of threat events on spacecraft coatings, electron flux behavior, comparison of fitting formula vs data, charge deposition rates, electric fields in insulators, satellite lifetimes post-nuclear events, GPS outage times, and satellite exposure to radiation.

BODY-13 Tables detailing various aspects of LEO satellite assets, nuclear burst events, electronic component thresholds, surveillance sensor vulnerabilities, detector material degradation thresholds, and charge deposition timescales.

BODY-14 Tables detailing fluences of electrons, events in the Middle East, Far East, and Hawaii, radiation accumulation in the G?S constellation, economic benefits of

	weather satellites, collateral effects, uncertainties, and confidence for satellites, and uncertainties in nuclear effects on satellites.
BODY-15	The paper discusses the potential collateral damage to satellites from high altitude nuclear detonations, examining radiation threats and effects on satellite functionality. It raises awareness of evolving threats and assists decision makers in assessing vulnerabilities and longevities of satellites in a nuclear-enhanced radiation environment.
BODY-16	Satellites are vulnerable to high-altitude nuclear explosions, with some being hardened against radiation threats. Extensive literature exists on the effects of nuclear and space radiation on satellites. Historical experiments have shown long-term damage to satellites from enhanced trapped radiation. Further research is needed on the effects of EMP attacks.
BODY-17	Satellite systems are crucial for global economy and infrastructure, with the US heavily reliant on them for military, intelligence, and commercial purposes. The majority of satellites are operated by commercial entities, with a focus on maximizing financial returns and protecting against hazards in space.
BODY-18	Satellites are vulnerable to high-altitude nuclear explosions, with credible threats from adversaries possessing nuclear weapons and delivery systems. The potential for further proliferation of nuclear weapons and delivery systems is likely, posing risks to satellite capabilities and competitive positions.
BODY-19	The page discusses the importance of satellites in Earth's orbit, focusing on geosynchronous and Global Positioning System (GPS) satellites, as well as Low Earth Orbit (LEO) satellites. LEO satellites provide vital services for national security, weather monitoring, and Earth observation.
BODY-20	The page discusses the challenges and benefits of maintaining large constellations of satellites in low Earth orbit, highlighting the economic and military importance of these satellites, as well as their various missions such as communication, navigation, intelligence, and scientific research.
BODY-21	Distribution of low-Earth orbiting satellites by country, with U.S. and Russia owning most. U.S. satellites focus on mobile voice/data transfer missions. Globalstar, Iridium, and Orbcomm constellations facing financial challenges but showing signs of improvement. Intelligence satellites in LEO provide monitoring of global hot spots. U.S. weather satellites in LEO monitor weather patterns and sea conditions.
BODY-22	The page discusses the importance of Earth/ocean/atmospheric monitoring satellites, their role in various studies and conflicts, and the estimated $90B U.S. investment in low-Earth orbit satellites, with potential costs for recovery after a nuclear event.
BODY-23	The table lists U.S. LEO satellite investments, including the number of satellites, costs, launch vehicles, and total costs for each project.
BODY-24	The page lists various satellites, their costs, number of launch vehicles, and total costs, totaling over $94 million.
BODY-25	Satellites have been damaged by high altitude nuclear tests, with significant radiation belts lasting from one month to several years. The 1.4-megaton STARFISH PRIME test in 1962 affected 24 satellites in orbit or launched shortly after.
BODY-26	List of satellites launched and their operational details during the time of high altitude nuclear tests.

BODY-27 Table IV.3 lists satellites damaged by the STARFISH PRIME event, with issues such as solar cell damage, encoder malfunctions, and power failures leading to mission failures or degradation.

BODY-28 STARFISH PRIME radiation caused failures in satellites like Telstar and Transit 4B due to damage to transistors and solar cells, leading to loss of power and communication. Human space flight was also a concern due to radiation sensitivity.

BODY-29 Satellites exposed to radiation, including from high-altitude nuclear tests, faced potential failures due to natural radiation and electrostatic discharge events. Soviet satellites may have been more resistant to nuclear radiation due to thicker shielding. Notable failures include the Canadian ANIK E-l and E-2 satellites.

BODY-30 Satellite anomalies and space weather events chronology, along with the importance of laboratory and underground nuclear testing for radiation effects on space systems and design techniques to mitigate them.

BODY-31 X-ray test facility for military satellites was expensive, with a failed attempt in the 1970s. In 1980, STARSAT was exposed to X-rays from a nuclear detonation for testing. The experiment was successful, except for an attitude control circuit malfunction.

BODY-32 The chapter discusses the natural radiation environment in space, focusing on energetic particles like electrons, protons, and heavy ions trapped in Earth's magnetic field. It also mentions the history of radiation belts, experiments, and discoveries related to charged particles in magnetic fields.

BODY-33 The page discusses the existence of radiation belts around Earth composed of electrons, protons, and heavy ions, with models showing flux intensity levels. However, the accuracy of these models is debated, and the use of "total dose" as a surrogate for exposure is device-dependent.

BODY-34 Models based on data from satellites in the 1960s and 1970s show integral flux contours for radiation-belt electrons and protons. Natural radiation belts are highly dynamic and vary significantly from day to day, as confirmed by satellite data from the CRRES satellite launched in 1990.

BODY-35 The page discusses the spatial distribution and temporal variability of natural radiation belts using data from the CRRES satellite, showing dynamic flux levels and the disappearance of the "slot" between inner and outer belts during magnetospheric events.

BODY-36 Radiation belts are dynamic regions in space where electrons are injected and lost due to various processes, resulting in a shifting balance between source and loss rates. This creates variability in trapped particle populations, influenced by solar and magnetospheric activity.

BODY-37 High-altitude nuclear detonations can create artificial radiation belts, affecting natural radiation belt behavior. Research is being done on radiation-belt remediation using radio transmitters to increase trapped-electron loss rates. The efficacy of this method is still being studied.

BODY-38 High-altitude nuclear detonations release energy that affects the environment, with different effects based on altitude. Debris expansions at different altitudes have varying impacts on radiation belts, air ionization, and RF propagation. The paper discusses these effects and provides a summary table of nuclear burst regimes by altitude.

BODY-39 This page discusses the characteristics and effects of nuclear bursts at different altitudes, focusing on the formation of fireballs and the absorption of X-rays in the atmosphere. It also mentions specific representative nuclear tests and the emission of X-rays from detonating weapons.

BODY-40 Comparison of radiant power versus wavelength for blackbodies with different temperatures, showing how X-ray fluence and escape to space depend on device temperature and burst altitude. Lower temperatures are absorbed closer to burst point in higher density air, while higher temperatures escape without significant attenuation at higher altitudes.

BODY-41 The page discusses the relationship between X-ray fluence and altitude for detonations, focusing on prompt gamma rays emitted during nuclear explosions and their effects on the atmosphere and space. It also mentions how weapon design can influence the gamma ray spectrum.

BODY-42 The page discusses the spectra of prompt and delayed fission gamma rays from U235, as well as the release of neutrons from nuclear reactions in exploding weapons. Neutrons outside the nucleus have a half-life and can decay into protons and electrons, potentially causing damage to satellites.

BODY-43 Neutron spectra from fission and thermonuclear weapons are illustrated, along with the impact of debris ions on satellites and induced environments from weapon emissions.

BODY-44 Nuclear detonations create various electromagnetic pulses that can impact satellites and terrestrial systems, with different types and effects explained.

BODY-45 The page discusses the generation and propagation of electromagnetic pulses (EMP) and magnetohydrodynamic electromagnetic pulses (MHD-EMP) from high-altitude nuclear explosions, detailing the interaction with Earth's magnetic field and large-scale electrical conductors.

BODY-46 The page discusses the categories of EMP, El, E2, and E3, with distinctive time intervals and spectral content. It also covers energetic particles, including ions and electrons, escaping nuclear burst regions, and their effects on materials and long-range impacts.

BODY-47 Detonation of a nuclear bomb at high altitudes causes debris to push Earth's magnetic field, creating a blast wave. Energetic air ions and electrons produce air fluorescence, with varying effects based on detonation altitude. Low-Alfven-Mach-number bursts remain uncertain due to lack of test data.

BODY-48 Delayed gamma rays and beta particles are emitted by radioactive weapon debris well after detonation, with specific decay properties and energy spectra that soften over time. The spatial distribution of delayed gamma rays at 10 seconds after a 1 Mt detonation is illustrated.

BODY-49 Beta energy spectrum from fission of U235 by fast neutrons softens over time, emitting particles that travel along magnetic field lines and produce ionized air and air fluorescence. Examples include the beta tube from the KINGFISH detonation in 1962.

BODY-50 The KINGFISH high-altitude nuclear test produced a visual display with beta particles traveling along geomagnetic field lines, creating a beta tube. Nuclear weapons can emit beta particles that become trapped in the Earth's magnetic field, influencing radiation belts and other effects.

BODY-51 Trapping of beta particles from high-altitude detonations is influenced by burst altitude, debris transport, and magnetic field conditions. Trapping efficiencies are

	difficult to predict due to complex environmental factors, with data suggesting a wide range of efficiencies. Latitude also affects trapped particle flux from detonations.
BODY-52	*High-altitude nuclear explosions release beta particles trapped in magnetic flux tubes, with detonations at low latitudes producing higher trapped flux. Analytic calculations show differences in flux-tube volumes based on magnetic latitude, impacting particle flux levels. Scaling detonations to different latitudes can affect particle trapping efficiency.*
BODY-53	*The page discusses the factors affecting trapped beta-particle flux, including loss mechanisms and hazards to satellites from high-altitude detonations creating magnetic bubbles with intense beta flux.*
BODY-54	*High-altitude nuclear detonations create magnetic bubbles that contain beta particles. Burst energy radiates in various spectra, with thermal pulses causing flash blindness and fires. UV radiation dominates at higher altitudes, with UV photons escaping to space and potentially impacting satellites. UV photons are efficiently emitted by debris-air blast waves.*
BODY-55	*Graph showing radiated optical power versus time for detonations at different altitudes, with a shift from infrared and visible wavelengths to UV wavelengths as altitude increases.*
BODY-56	*Radiation exposure can cause electrical, optical, mechanical, or thermal malfunctions in satellite subsystems, compromising performance. Semiconductor microcircuits are particularly vulnerable, with increased sensitivity due to high processor speeds and memory densities. Nuclear detonations generate energy that affects spacecraft components based on geometry and materials.*
BODY-57	*The effects of nuclear radiation on electronic systems, including ionization and atomic displacement, were first studied in the 1950s. This led to the development of a new field of research called Transient Radiation Effects on Electronics (TREE), which examines the impact of radiation on electronic components.*
BODY-58	*The page discusses the effects of radiation on electronic systems, focusing on photon effects and energy distribution. It explains how radiation interacts with matter and the different mechanisms involved, such as photoelectric effect, Compton scattering, and pair production.*
BODY-59	*The page discusses material interaction cross sections with X-ray photons, showing how different processes dominate at different energy levels. It also highlights the impact of X-ray photon irradiation on electronic components.*
BODY-60	*The susceptibility of satellite components to nuclear radiation depends on their location and the energy of the radiation. Lower energy radiation is absorbed near the surface, while higher energy radiation penetrates deeper. Materials with higher atomic numbers are more susceptible. Energy deposition varies with material and depth.*
BODY-61	*X-ray and gamma-ray exposure can impact electronic devices by causing ionization, leading to charge flow, free radicals, and damage to transistors. Transient Radiation Effects on Electronics (TREE) can result in permanent or transient effects, with upset thresholds varying based on fluence levels and technology used.*
BODY-62	*Total dose damage thresholds for various bipolar IC and MOS technologies, including TTL, CMOS, ECL, and more, from different manufacturers such as Fairchild, Intel, and Motorola.*

BODY-63   Graphs showing dose rate vs blackbody temperature and fluence in silicon shielded by aluminum, as well as typical diode photocurrents as a function of dose rate.

BODY-64   Comparison of upset thresholds for different integrated circuit technologies, with potential for damage if state changes occur, leading to latchup phenomenon and burnout. Latchup thresholds for various device types shown, with prevention methods such as dielectric isolation and low supply voltage highlighted.

BODY-65   SGEMP, or internal EMP, induced by X-rays can cause burnout or upset in electronic devices on satellites. The process involves photo-Compton electron currents inducing electromagnetic fields, with signals coupling to components. Testing for SGEMP is typically done in the time domain, not using continuous wave testing.

BODY-66   SGEMP/IEMP categories include External SGEMP, Cavity IEMP, Cable SGEMP, and Box IEMP, with Cable SGEMP and Box IEMP posing the most severe threat to systems. X-rays are the dominant concern, and gas ionization effects can neutralize surface charge. Shielding practices can mitigate External SGEMP and Cavity IEMP.

BODY-67   Box IEMP is influenced by radiation environments, with X-ray shielding reducing the X-ray portion. Shielding against gamma rays is impractical. Hardening strategies involve reducing X-ray levels and employing spot shielding on circuit boards. Damage metrics for SGEMP upset are considered, with voltage thresholds varying for different electronic technologies.

BODY-68   The page discusses SGEMP burnout and Box IEMP effects, detailing energy requirements for upset and burnout, as well as the impact of different materials and coatings on circuit boards.

BODY-69   Figures show results of Box IEMP Upset and Burnout for a coated circuit board, displaying voltage and energy as functions of blackbody temperature and fluence.

BODY-70   The page discusses upset and burnout thresholds for circuit boards at different fluences and energies, with a focus on external SGEMP and hardening techniques to prevent coupling into antenna apertures.

BODY-71   ECEMP, or electron-charging EMP, is a phenomenon where satellites in space can experience electrical discharges due to differential charging, leading to operational issues. Research efforts have been made to understand and mitigate these effects.

BODY-72   UV radiation can degrade spacecraft surfaces by cross-linking polymeric materials, leading to structural integrity issues. Soft X-rays and UV radiation may limit material survivability, with surface stresses proportional to temperature. Existing data on material failure levels may be inaccurate due to shielding from X-ray weapon spectrum.

BODY-73   Comparison of depth-dose profiles resulting from 1 keV blackbody radiation on different materials, including an IR mirror and Poco Graphite.

BODY-74   Analysis of fluence and stress ratios for Poco Graphite and blackbody source at different temperatures. Low energy photons contribute significantly to stress but not dose. Lack of data on soft radiation environments below 1 keV.

BODY-75   The page discusses stress and fluence ratios as functions of blackbody temperature for IR mirror and Poco Graphite.

BODY-76   Potential implications of nuclear weapons on U.S. DoD satellites are not well understood. Experimental programs are needed to confirm soft photon vulnerability. X-ray interactions with satellite components depend on photon energy, with stress effects becoming concerning at compressive stresses of 0.1 kilobars or higher.

BODY-77	*Peak dose in silicon varies with temperature and shield thickness. Longitudinal stresses are key in failure mechanisms for thin films and circuit boards, influenced by geometry and material properties. Tensile stresses can cause delaminations or spall, with in-plane stresses more severe for cold X-ray threats.*
BODY-78	*Figure VI.23 shows peak compressive stress in silicon based on temperature and shield thickness. Figure VI.24 illustrates electron flux effects on spacecraft in LEO orbits, with varying energies and intensities. The electron spectrum incident on spacecraft surfaces varies in time and space.*
BODY-79	*Effects of electron energies on LEO spacecraft charging and anomalies, with emphasis on plasma interactions and spacecraft charging during geomagnetic activity and auroral events.*
BODY-80	*Energetic electrons and protons can damage spacecraft components through deep dielectric charging and total induced dose. Shielding is crucial for protection, but may be less effective against high-energy electrons from nuclear sources compared to natural radiation. Damage can lead to performance degradation and mission failure.*
BODY-81	*The page discusses the effects of shielding on electron environments and the impact of single event phenomena, such as Single Event Upsets (SEUs) and Single Event Latchup (SEL). It also delves into neutron effects on semiconductor materials, highlighting the formation of defects that can degrade microcircuit performance.*
BODY-82	*Various technologies and manufacturers of integrated circuits, including TTL, Schottky logic, ECL, and CML, with neutron damage thresholds for bipolar ICs shown in a figure.*
BODY-83	*Focused on analyzing the impact of nuclear events on low altitude satellites in LEO, particularly ISS, TERRA, and NOAA. Generated 21 trial nuclear events to simulate potential threats to US space assets, with emphasis on low-yield detonations in high-tension regions.*
BODY-84	*Analysis of satellites in different orbits and their missions, including weather monitoring, imaging, navigation, and communication. Focus on high yield burst scenarios threatening GPS and Geosynchronous satellites. Trial nuclear events with varying yields and altitudes. Location of events specified only by latitude.*
BODY-85	*Data on various trial events with different locations, yields, and effects. Discussion on prompt radiation effects on satellites when a weapon is detonated at high altitude, highlighting the susceptibility of assets in space to direct exposure to weapon-produced photon radiation.*
BODY-86	*The page discusses the hazard zone from nuclear gamma rays, X rays, neutrons, and UV photons after a nuclear explosion, focusing on potential damage to satellites from high-altitude detonations. Atmospheric absorption only affected a few events, with minimal impact on satellite damage.*
BODY-87	*Graphs showing worst case threat fluences for DMSP/NOAA, TERRA, and ISS satellites at different altitudes.*
BODY-88	*Methodology for calculating probability of satellite encountering X-ray or UV fluence involves determining geometry between burst and satellite using STK. STK calculations iterated to determine probability of satellite being at specific range from burst. SNRTACS used to model radiation-belt effects on satellite lifetimes.*
BODY-89	*Efforts to mitigate uncertainty in radiation exposure for satellites include reexamining old data, developing new computer codes, and using Satellite Tool Kit software for analysis and prediction.*

BODY-90   Results of analyses on prompt line-of-sight damage to LEO satellites from nuclear bursts show low probability of damage, with thermomechanical damage being the most sensitive mode. Uncertainties in UV output make quantitative analysis difficult, but X-ray results can be scaled accordingly.

BODY-91   Graphs show exposure probability vs. X-ray fluence for three satellites, with bands indicating likely damage modes. Refer to previous chapters for weapon spectrum and shielding thickness caveats. NOAA X-ray events depicted in Figure III.1.

BODY-92   Comparison of TERRA and ISS X-ray events based on exposure levels, with different scenarios represented on the graph.

BODY-93   Analysis of satellite damage from prompt X-radiation, focusing on thermomechanical effects and photon-induced damage. Discussion on X-ray spectra, absorption depths, and surface-charging electrons. Comparison of silicon solar cells with different coverglass materials. Orbits of satellites analyzed, not configurations.

BODY-94   Analysis of coverglass coatings for satellite components vulnerable to nuclear radiation damage. Dielectric coatings tested in X-ray environments, with well-populated database for damage estimates. Consideration of compressive stress failure for 21 events using a baseline X-ray spectrum. Different coatings show noticeable effects on hardness.

BODY-95   Analysis of temperature and stress distribution in SLAR coating, considering heat conduction and electron migration. Temperature peaks at 183°C at 0.3469 cal/cm2. Stress distribution shown in Figure VIII.6.

BODY-96   The page discusses the ratio of peak in-plane compressive stress to maximum compressive stress for a SLAR coating, based on a coating failure criterion. It explains the calculation of in-plane compressive stress increment with temperature and lists physical properties used in the calculations.

BODY-97 MgF_2 failure threshold between 2-3 kbars; ISS only likely to fail for certain nuclear threats with low probability of damage, but potential for catastrophic loss of solar power.

BODY-98   Charts show maximum in-plane compressive stress in SLAR coatings on TERRA and ISS. Event 13 and Event 5 fall below minimum values. Normalized dose as a function of depth for MLAR coating is shown in Figure VIII.10.

BODY-99   Analysis of normalized dose and peak temperature for MLAR configuration, considering photo-electron migration but not heat conduction. Shows peak temperature as a function of depth and ratio of peak temperature at a given depth to maximum temperature achieved by MLAR coating.

BODY-100   The page discusses the ratio of peak compressive in-plane stress to maximum stress for a coating, showing plots of stress for satellites with MLAR coating and failure threshold range.

BODY-101   Analysis of maximum in-plane compressive stress in MLAR coatings on different satellites shows potential failures for ISS under nuclear threats, with specific events causing stress exceeding failure threshold.

BODY-102   Discussion on the failure of MLAR and SLAR coatings at the same fluence, impact on surveillance satellite subsystems in radiation-intensive environments, and degradation thresholds for photonic materials. Challenges include reduced sensitivity and increased ionization-induced noise after a nuclear event.

BODY-103   Table III.3 lists degradation thresholds for various detector materials in different radiation environments. While it is unlikely for LEO satellites to experience *complete sensor failure, satellites monitoring nuclear events may face performance loss. Performance parameters depend on signal to noise ratios and ionization-induced transients are critical.*

BODY-104 *Secondary electrons generated by interactions with materials surrounding the detector degrade performance by decreasing S/N ratios. Cumulative damage from radiation belt exposure can be analyzed using SNRTACS output to determine fluence of electrons over time. Decay rates show rapid initial decrease followed by stabilization.*

BODY-105 *Data from a SNRTACS run shows fluence above threshold energy over time for a specific event orbit survey. Analysis of trapped electron flux to spacecraft after a burst reveals consistent behavior. Fits derived for first-day average fluxes based on yield and L-shell.*

BODY-106 *Comparison of electron fluxes at different altitudes and L-shells for various bursts, showing increase with yield and L-shell at ISS but decrease at higher altitudes. Low yield events are underestimated, powerful bursts produce excess low energy electrons.*

BODY-107 *Comparison of low energy flux vs. fit and high energy flux vs. fit for electrons with energy 40 keV < E < 250 keV and E > 250 keV. Results show deviations from natural flux levels, especially for high L-shell events targeting GPS and GEO satellites.*

BODY-108 *Analysis of fluxes from high L-shell bursts on GPS and GEO satellites shows a slower increase in flux with yield compared to LEO satellites. Decay time for fluxes is rapid due to diffusion processes, with negligible flux remaining after a short period of time.*

BODY-109 *Calculations show that trapped flux decays faster with high solar activity. High-energy electrons have longer lifetimes than low-energy ones. Predictions of electric stress on spacecraft based on charge accumulation in insulating materials due to high-energy electrons.*

BODY-110 *Calculating charge deposition and electric field in insulators based on conductivity values and material parameters, with considerations for equilibrium time. Thermal control insulators have longer timescales, while doped coverglasses have shorter timescales. Parameters used include atomic number, weight, thickness, density, and conductivity.*

BODY-111 *Thermal blanket parameter ranges and electron flux spectrum for determining damage from explosions. Highest fluence case with fixed spectral distribution causes most damage.*

BODY-112 *Analysis of electron fluence for high-yield events on spacecraft, with calculations based on spectral distributions and fission flux values.*

BODY-113 *The page discusses the rate of electron deposition in an insulator (coverglass) and the importance of grounding exterior surfaces in spacecraft to protect against radiation.*

BODY-114 *Analysis of electric fields in an insulator with varying conditions, showing how changes in density, thickness, and grounding affect peak electric field. Low conductivity coverglass is at risk under certain conditions due to radiation-induced conductivity.*

BODY-115 *The page discusses the use of thermal blankets as external insulating material for charge deposition, with calculations showing safe electric field levels except for thin blankets. It also considers the effect of trapped electrons on the lifetime of solar arrays, with degradation starting at 10^{14} electrons-cm^2.*

BODY-116   Table showing fluences of electrons over 0.25 MeV, color-coded by severity of damage to solar cells. Cells in green have little to no effect, yellow experience minor degradation, orange noticeable degradation, and red substantial loss of life. Satellites in certain orbital regimes are strongly affected. ISS may face operational issues.

BODY-117   Nuclear enhanced electron belts reduce lifetime of LEO satellites, with shielding assumptions impacting damage levels. Smaller yields can still significantly impact satellite lifetimes, while larger yields can cause severe damage and radiation sickness to astronauts. Foreign weapons assumed salvage-fuzed by missile defense systems.

BODY-118   Analysis of Far Eastern and Hawaiian events, including location, yield, height of burst, and time to failure for various satellites. Consideration of radiation margins and satellite age in predicting spacecraft lifetime.

BODY-119   High altitude nuclear events have minimal impact on GPS and geosynchronous satellites due to their robust design, but older satellites near the end of their lifespan could be vulnerable to radiation damage. The GPS constellation could be affected by a special weapon event with a high fission yield.

BODY-120   Satellites experience radiation exposure after a nuclear event, affecting GPS navigation services. Hardened satellites fare better, with 2x hardening preventing major outages for four years post-blast. Adversary EMP attacks could disrupt GPS, but specific conditions are needed. Radiation levels for GPS satellites are shown in a table.

BODY-121   Summary of satellite launch dates, total accumulated radiation dose, and remaining radiation levels for various NAVSTAR satellites from 1992 to 2003.

BODY-122   Graphs show GPS satellites remaining and outage time in Baghdad after a 10 Mt blast, with different levels of hardening. Hardening to twice the natural dose can increase satellite electronics' resilience.

BODY-123   Highly hardened HEO satellites are not vulnerable to low-yield bursts, but a 5-Mt burst poses a substantial threat due to high electron fluxes. Larger yield events do not present a total ionizing dose problem for HEO satellites.

BODY-124   Satellites in LEO are vulnerable to damage from EMP attacks, while MEO and GEO satellites are less likely to be affected. Exposure to energetic photons can cause significant damage to solar arrays on research satellites like the ISS. Beta decay fluxes can also impact satellite components.

BODY-125   Space systems are vulnerable to attacks due to their value, but the probability of significant damage from an EMP attack is low. Military satellites are designed to operate in severe radiation environments, and some are hardened against nuclear effects. Loss of satellites could be mitigated by alternative systems.

BODY-126   EMP attacks over Northern CONUS are not likely to cause catastrophic damage to satellites, but lower latitude attacks could pump electron belts and damage LEO satellites. UV radiation from nuclear detonations could also impact satellite components. Loss of LEO weather satellites could have a significant economic impact.

BODY-127   The economic benefits of weather satellites are significant, with annual savings in various sectors such as agriculture, construction, and utilities. While the loss of these satellites would have high costs, alternative communication methods could mitigate the impact on society.

BODY-128 *The page discusses the importance of utilizing civilian Earth surveillance satellites for military and intelligence purposes, highlighting the vulnerability of optical systems to radiation effects and the need to secure commercial satellite assets for national security and economic stability.*

BODY-129 *US industry must compete in providing remote sensing space capabilities to foreign governments and commercial users. NGA directed to use commercial imaging satellites extensively. Commercial imagery to be primary for government mapping. $500 million to be spent on commercial imagery. Commercial satellite assets enhance surveillance and hinder adversaries. Future hyper-spectral imagery satellites in LEO will provide detailed observations. National infrastructure should not be assumed replaceable instantaneously after nuclear-burst-induced losses.*

BODY-130 *The chapter discusses uncertainties and confidence assessments in analyzing collateral effects on satellites from a high-altitude nuclear detonation, highlighting the imprecise nature of the process and the need for quantitative appraisal. Confidence assessments are subjective, based on past experience and intuition.*

BODY-131 *Uncertainties in effects of nuclear explosions on satellites are influenced by weapon variability, physics of detonation, and unknown threat characteristics. Trapped radiation plays a key role in satellite hardening decisions, with uncertainties in natural and nuclear origins posing challenges. Limited data from high-altitude tests hinders definitive guidance.*

BODY-132 *Table detailing collateral effects, uncertainties, and confidence levels for satellites in relation to nuclear environment, including X-rays, gamma rays, neutrons, energetic debris, ultraviolet fluence, trapped radiation, and energetic air ions.*

BODY-133 *The uncertainties in characterizing energetic particle fluxes in the natural radiation belts are due to fluctuating trapped-electron fluxes and inaccuracies in predictive models. Variability in solar wind density and velocity, along with changes in the interplanetary magnetic field, regulate the geomagnetic particle trapping region.*

BODY-134 *Diffusion in phase space, particularly radial diffusion represented by DLL, shows wide uncertainty in trapped-electron flux evolution due to varying magnetospheric conditions. Forecasting magnetospheric conditions, crucial for predicting DLL, remains challenging but could be improved with accurate solar wind data and a detailed magnetosphere model.*

BODY-135 *The page discusses uncertainties in environments produced by high-altitude nuclear detonations, focusing on prompt and induced environments. Uncertainties in prompt nuclear environments are primarily due to factors influencing weapon performance.*

BODY-136 *Uncertainties in nuclear weapon performance predictions are high due to various factors, with gamma fluence and X-ray output being particularly challenging to estimate accurately. The Nagasaki device emitted minimal X-rays, highlighting the variability in energy distribution among different weapons.*

BODY-137 *Uncertainties in prompt neutron and debris-ion fluxes from nuclear detonations arise from various factors such as weapon design, mass distribution, and geomagnetic field orientation. Debris energy is converted to UV photons or radiated as hydromagnetic waves, with limited data for low-Alfven-Mach-number detonations.*

BODY-138 *Uncertainties in induced nuclear environments from detonations include energetic debris-ion fluxes and air ion kinetic energy, with uncertainties in statistical distributions and atmospheric properties contributing to the lack of precise characterizations. Burst points between 250-600 km are most important, with uncertainties pegged at around ±5x.*

BODY-139 *Uncertainties in delayed beta and gamma radiations from nuclear weapons are influenced by yield and fission materials. Nuclear-pumped radiation belts are highly uncertain due to various factors like injection efficiencies and evolving energy spectra. Predicting debris dispersal post-detonation is challenging, especially for high-altitude bursts.*

BODY-140 *Uncertainties in shock acceleration of electrons by nuclear explosions and injection into radiation belts are discussed. Trapped electrons must execute specific motions to avoid atmospheric capture. Scattering and capture by the atmosphere are well understood, with uncertainties related to atmospheric density variations.*

BODY-141 *The page discusses the complex interactions of geomagnetically trapped electrons in the inner magnetosphere, highlighting the challenges of electron scattering during high-altitude nuclear explosions and cautioning against extrapolating data from past tests for contemporary scenarios.*

BODY-142 *Map shows U.S. and Soviet high-altitude nuclear test sites in relation to magnetic field. Uncertainties in modeling nuclear-pumped belts are highlighted, with existing models unable to accurately predict effects on satellites. Predictions of trapped flux environment have large uncertainties.*

BODY-143 *Uncertainties in predictions of nuclear-pumped trapped radiation belts are large due to non-linear aspects, with estimates of electron flux uncertainties being one to two orders of magnitude. Ultraviolet emissions from nuclear detonations in the 90-250 km altitude range are primarily from inelastic collisions, with uncertainties due to lack of experimental data.*

BODY-144 *Experimental data on electron impact excitation for atmospheric species is limited, with varying error bars. Theoretical results generally align with data within error bars, but exceptions exist. Predictions of UV emissions are improving with expanded rate models and computer capabilities. Uncertainties in cross sections and oscillator strengths impact accuracy.*

BODY-145 *The page discusses the critical electronic systems and components required for satellite operation, highlighting the importance of reliability and the challenges posed by increasing complexity and miniaturization in semiconductor technology. Engineering judgment and careful design are crucial for ensuring mission success.*

BODY-146 *The page discusses the successful underground nuclear test of the STARSAT module, highlighting the importance of testing piece-parts and subsystems prior to actual testing. It also addresses the uncertainties in the response of satellites to different radiation effects due to changes in technology and testing capabilities.*

BODY-147 *Assessing uncertainties in satellite threat calculations is crucial for mitigation programs. Prompt radiation poses immediate risks, while trapped radiation threatens long-term satellite survival. Confidence in threat existence is based on past tests, but uncertainties remain in predicting and mitigating potential damage.*

BODY-148 *Study on satellite exposure to trapped radiation from nuclear bursts using SNRTACS code system, with large uncertainties in predictions. Hardening satellite components can prolong survival times in LEO, while RBR concepts may reduce waiting time for replacement. Outstanding questions on costs versus benefits of hardening technology.*

BODY-149 *Predictions based on STARFISH PRIME effects are unreliable for high-altitude detonations. Current models for nuclear-pumped radiation belts lack accuracy, leading to uncertainties in hardening criteria for space electronics and satellite*

BODY-149 *replenishment planning. Improved modeling is needed to quantify nuclear environments and system effects accurately.*

BODY-150 *The page discusses the need to resolve the nuclear-pumped radiation belt problem by utilizing advanced modeling capabilities and understanding the space environment for natural and nuclear conditions, particularly focusing on nuclear detonations between 30 to 90 km altitude and the limitations in current understandings and modeling.*

BODY-151 *Research is needed to understand nuclear detonations in the 30 to 90 km altitude range, including effects and mitigation options.*

BODY-152 *Mitigation of nuclear threats to space-based assets involves shielding, hardening, redundancy, and deterrence for satellites and ground stations. Cost effectiveness and ethical considerations play a role in decision-making for protection measures.*

BODY-153 *Research is being conducted on using VLF transmissions to remove trapped electrons from radiation belts after a nuclear detonation, reducing damage to spacecraft and launch delays. Another proposal involves using high voltage tether arrays to promote pitch-angle diffusion. Studies are ongoing to refine these methods.*

BODY-154 *Proposed orbit modification for reducing radiation exposure and vulnerability of ground control stations to attacks, emphasizing the importance of EMP hardening and potential fuel limitations for satellite systems.*

BODY-155 *Satellites are vulnerable to direct attack and ground control stations are at risk. High-yield detonations are needed to impact satellites in MEO or GEO orbits. Satellites in these orbits are not at immediate risk from radiation damage due to EMP attacks.*

BODY-156 *LEO satellites are at risk from EMP attacks causing radiation damage, with uncertainties in calculations being mitigated by modeling efforts. Recent studies show high-altitude nuclear detonations emit damaging UV radiation, posing a hazard to satellite components.*

BODY-157 *Recommendations include implementing stringent nuclear hardening criteria for LEO satellites, reviewing hardening specifications for crucial satellite systems, establishing consistent survivability criteria, bearing hardening costs for civilian satellites hosting intelligence functions, funding research programs for better understanding of nuclear burst phenomena, and pursuing development of electron-Radiation-Belt Remediation technologies.*

BODY-158 *A list of references related to theoretical atomic physics, electron scattering loss, surface charging in the auroral zone, damage to space systems, and thermophysical properties of space-related materials.*

BODY-159 *Various publications and reports on theoretical physics, nuclear materials, spacecraft charging, and solar cell performance in radiation belts and nuclear environments.*

BODY-160 *Various reports and studies on the effects of exo-atmospheric nuclear detonations, electron precipitation, and high-altitude test experiences.*

BODY-161 *Various scientific studies and reports on topics such as spacecraft charging, nuclear radiation phenomena, electron radiation belts, and electromagnetic pulses from nuclear explosions.*

BODY-162 *Various publications and reports on nuclear weapon effects, high altitude detonations, radiation effects, particle properties, and space-related topics from the late 20th century.*

BODY-163 *Various reports and manuals related to nuclear weapons, radiation, and space exploration, including observations of high-intensity radiation by satellites and studies on radiation belt particles and spacecraft charging effects.*

BODY-164 *Overview of nuclear explosions at intermediate and high altitudes, along with a handbook on nuclear weapons output.*

BODY-165 *Distribution list for DTRA-IR-10-22 including Department of Defense, contractors, and other consultants.*

NOTABLE PASSAGES

BODY-3 *In particular, the STARFISH PRIME test of 1962 injected long-lived trapped energetic electrons into Earth's magnetic fields, causing the early demise of several satellites.*

BODY-4 *We recommend that the Department of Defense initiate policies to:*
- *Reassess survivability of satellite space- and ground-based systems that support U.S. defenses,*
- *Increase the level of nuclear hardening and subsidize implementation for commercial satellites that support essential national missions,*
- *Increase funding for research in high altitude nuclear effects in order to reduce uncertainties and the safety margins they engender, thereby decreasing the costs associated with hardening.*
- *Pursue studies on the feasibility of electron radiation belt remediation.*

BODY-15 *The salient issues examined in this paper are:*
- *What categories of satellites are vulnerable to malfunction or damage, immediately and ultimately?*
- *How long would satellites not immediately damaged by prompt radiation continue to function in the hostile electron belt environment?*
- *How does damage depend on weapon design and yield, and on the altitude and location of a detonation?*
- *What are the regrets for loss (temporary and permanent) of satellites in orbit?*
- *At what point in time would the nuclear-enhanced space environment cease to pose a threat to either a satellite or its mission?*
- *What satellites should be considered expendable and which should be hardened?*
- *What are appropriate levels of hardening?*

BODY-16 *"In the late 1950s and early 1960s there were sixteen high altitude nuclear detonation experiments, some of which contributed substantial additional trapped radiation, changing the morphology of the Van Allen electron belts, increasing their intensity, and hardening their energy spectrum. At least eight satellites that were in orbit during this time were damaged by long-term effects of nuclear-enhanced trapped radiation."*

BODY-17 *Satellite systems today provide cost-effective services that permeate the foundations of contemporary society, economy, and civil infrastructure in many, if not most, developed countries. They provide telecommunications services that are central to today's globally integrated economy; they provide "big picture" data required by modern climate monitoring and weather forecasting. Satellite-borne sensors monitor agricultural conditions worldwide and provide data upon which yield forecasts are based, thereby making the market more efficient and stabilizing agricultural economies.*

BODY-18 *"Satellite vulnerability to high-altitude nuclear explosions is not a question of whether an adversary would detonate a weapon as hypothesized, but instead turns entirely on questions of technical feasibility. Could an adversary—either a nation state or a nongovernmental entity—acquire nuclear weapons and mount a credible threat? The answer is unquestionably 'Yes.' One must assume both nuclear weapons and delivery systems are available to credible adversaries now and will continue to be so for the foreseeable future."*

BODY-19   "Because a geosynchronous satellite 'hovers' over a specific region, continuous monitoring of that region for national security purposes or weather forecasting is possible."

BODY-20   The unique aspects of these satellites, however, have appeared to rescue economically at least one and possibly more of these constellations. In late 2000, the U.S. government issued a contract to Iridium Satellite LLC to procure unlimited mobile phone service for 20,000 government users. If contract options are exercised, the total procurement will be worth $252M and extend out to 2007.

BODY-21   "Intelligence satellites in LEO provide important monitoring of hot spots around the world via optical, radar and electronic monitoring. Details of the constellation of LEO intelligence satellites are classified."

BODY-22   "In spite of these considerations, the U.S. would probably still have to spend about half ($45B) to recover assets considered important to science, national security, and the economy. This would include the NRO assets, expensive new science missions such as TERRA and AQUA, polar weather satellites such as NOAA and DMSP, and repairs to the large number of electronic components on the ISS which may require multiple Shuttle flights and hundreds of astronaut EVA hours."

BODY-25   "From 1958 until the atmospheric nuclear test moratorium in 1963, over a dozen high altitude nuclear tests were conducted (Table IV. 1). Some of these tests produced minor, if any. radiation belts due to the low altitude and/or low yield of the detonation. Several, however, including the last three Soviet tests and the U.S. STARFISH PRIME test, produced significant belts that lasted from one month to several years."

BODY-27   Table IV.3 shows that at least eight satellites suffered damage that was definitely related to the STARFISH PRIME event [Weenas, 1978]. This damage was studied and documented in the scientific literature.

BODY-29   Concerns that Schirra might be exposed to unacceptably high levels of radiation if high-altitude tests were conducted lead the administration to postpone further testing until after the mission.

BODY-30   The Atmospheric Test Ban Agreement of 1963 stimulated strong technology programs within the Department of Defense and the National Aeronautics and Space Administration to investigate the nature of radiation effects on space systems and to find design techniques to mitigate them. One only needs to peruse the literature [IEEE Transactions on Nuclear Science and Engineering, 1963-2003] to appreciate the National efforts expended on technology to make our space assets appropriately survivable to a nuclear attack.

BODY-31   In this test the satellite was placed in a vacuum chamber as illustrated in Figure IV.3. The vertical tubular object on the right was connected to a vertical evacuated line-of-sight (LOS) pipe that extended from the buried nuclear device to the ground surface. The pipe contained a closure system that was automatically actuated immediately after the detonation-produced X-ray pulse arrived and before radioactive effluence could escape. The shed-like enclosure on the left of the structure contained signal conditioning equipment. Behavior of the satellite during exposure was monitored both in a remote trailer and also in the General Electric development laboratories in King of Prussia, Pennsylvania. The tracked wheels were to allow the whole configuration to be pulled away from the LOS pipe before the earth subsided after

BODY-34   Because nuclear-pumped radiation belts involve energetic electrons derived from beta decay of radionuclides resulting from fission reactions, the remaining *discussion of this section will focus on trapped-electron radiation belts. Because energetic electrons from a nuclear burst are subject to the same influences governing natural belts, the behavior of the natural belts, particularly their variability, is central to the question of nuclear-pumped belts.*

BODY-35   *Figure V.3 indicates the radiation belts to be highly dynamic, with temporal variability of trapped fluxes spanning several orders of magnitude. The entire 13-month data interval is filled.*

BODY-36   *"Radiation belts exist as a dynamically shifting balance between source and loss rates, mediated by energization and transport processes throughout the volume of the trapping region. The 'leaky bucket analogy' illustrated in Figure V.4 is appropriate. Nature provides both quasi-continuous and impulsive sources of charged particles feeding into the trapping region, along with loss mechanisms that drain trapped particles from the belts."*

BODY-37   *After beta particles are emitted into the trapping region by beta decay of fission debris from a nuclear detonation, their behavior follows identically the physics governing naturally occurring energetic radiation-belt electrons. With the exception of the STARFISH PRIME high-altitude test (1.4 Mt at 400 km altitude), observed lifetimes of nuclear-pumped radiation belts are reported to be on the order of one month (less for the lowest L-shell bursts) [Walt, 1977]. Thus, the behavior of natural radiation belts, their variability, sources, and loss rates on time scales comparable to lifetimes of nuclear-pumped belts, is consequential to satellite vulnerability to nuclear detonations.*

BODY-38   *The enormous energy released by a nuclear detonation produces widespread and dramatic changes to the environment. In tenuous atmosphere above 100 km altitude, low air density leads to large mean-free paths—hundreds of kilometers or more for some energetic emissions from nuclear bursts—so large volumes of the upper atmosphere and space may be exposed to significant levels of energetic nuclear emanations. Given a focus on nuclear burst effects germane to satellites, it is beyond the scope of this paper to consider in detail the myriad of burst interactions that alter the environment.*

BODY-39   *Unless a weapon is particularly massive, upon detonation its energy generation mechanisms raise its temperature to sufficiently high values that it radiates as much as 70 to 80 percent of the available energy as X-rays with a spectrum that approximates a blackbody. Figure V.5 illustrates the radiant power versus wavelength for blackbodies of different radiating temperatures.*

BODY-40   *The range of X-rays in the atmosphere and the fraction of the X-ray yield that can escape to space depend strongly on X-ray temperature of the device and on burst altitude.*

BODY-41   *Gamma rays emitted during the short period when the exploding device is actively consuming nuclear fuels are termed "prompt" gamma rays. These may be partially absorbed within the exploding device, with the remainder escaping the weapon case to interact with the atmosphere to produce EMP or escape to space where they may irradiate satellites. The emitted gamma spectrum is a function of weapon design, as are the rise time, pulse length, and energy content of the gamma pulse—all factors beyond the scope of this paper.*

BODY-42   *"The delayed spectrum corresponds to 4.75 seconds after detonation. At later times the gamma ray spectrum further softens. Nuclear reactions in an exploding weapon release free neutrons over a range of energies, with thermonuclear reactions generating neutrons with energies up to 14 MeV."*

BODY-43   Materials of which the weapon, its aero shell, and any associated vehicle were constructed are vaporized, ionized, and expelled outward in a velocity spectrum with peak speed that may exceed 2,000 km/s. To put this into perspective, an iron ion (Fe+n) moving at 2,000 km/s has a kinetic energy of about 1.16 MeV, an Aluminum ion (Al+n) about 0.56 MeV, and a carbon ion (C+n) about 0.25 MeV. These energies are sufficient to implant radionuclide ions permanently in exposed surfaces of a satellite where subsequent nuclear decay will provide a localized source of potentially damaging radiation.

BODY-44   "Owing to the great energy and energy density available from a nuclear explosion, many different induced environments can result. Of these, some are of little consequence to physical integrity of satellites (but may inhibit functionality for seconds to hours) while others can materially alter the physical state of vital components."

BODY-45   Both the gamma pulse and the electromagnetic pulse travel at the speed of light, so they remain in phase, and the electromagnetic pulse grows as the gamma pulse weakens. Time-varying magnetic fields generate radiated MHD-EMP signals. Magnetic Bubble Formed: Expanding weapon debris pushes back Earth's magnetic field.

BODY-46   "The generation of EMP and its properties were reviewed by Longmire [1978]."

BODY-47   "At the periphery of the expanding blast wave, debris kinetic energy is transferred to air ions and electrons being overrun. Energized air ions and electrons stream upward and downward along the geomagnetic field. Downward-moving energetic air ions and electrons from the blast wave region encounter sufficiently dense air in the 100 to 200 km altitude range for collisions to stop them, the air there becoming heated and ionized sufficiently to produce the yellow air fluorescence seen in the photo."

BODY-48   Energy spectra of the emissions soften (i.e., shift to lower energies) with the passage of time as radionuclides cascade toward their ground states. Each radionuclide born in an explosion has its own specific decay properties [Parrington, et al, 1996] with specific nuclear transitions (emission lines) evident in its gamma ray energy spectrum, but the aggregate delayed gamma ray spectrum from many different radionuclides and excitation states born in a detonation can be characterized as illustrated in Figure V.7.

BODY-49   In the absence of collisions with air atoms and molecules, beta particles are constrained by the Lorentz force to move parallel and anti-parallel to magnetic field lines while gyrating around those field lines and (more slowly) drifting around the Earth. Beta particles with suitably small pitch angles emitted in the downward direction from above ~ 100 km travel to lower altitudes where collisions with air species extract their energy to produce ionized air and air fluorescence that constitute the beta tube (a.k.a. beta patch).

BODY-50   "Figure V.15. The KINGFISH high-altitude nuclear test above Johnston Island in the mid Pacific produced a brilliant visual display, including a prominent beta tube (violet-white region) below the fireball (white spheroidal region below the red cap of shock-excited atomic oxygen)."

BODY-51   Circumstances (i) and (ii) require the detonation to take place above 100 km or at sufficiently high altitude that radioactive weapon debris will be transported to above 100 km within a few minutes after the detonation. The greater the mass of debris above 100 km, the greater the trapped population to be expected. Thus, the higher the burst altitude (within reason), the greater the expected trapped population of beta particles.

BODY-52 "An inventory of beta particles injected into a small magnetic flux-tube volume will produce a greater particle flux than the same inventory injected into a large magnetic flux-tube volume."

BODY-53 Loss mechanisms for electrons trapped in the natural radiation belts (discussed above) apply equally to trapped beta particles. In particular, the difficult-to-predict variabilities of the trapping environment and loss rates that one finds for the natural radiation belts apply equally to nuclear-pumped radiation belts, with the proviso that a high-altitude detonation may add a large, impulsive source of perturbations in atmospheric density profiles and electromagnetic environments that further complicate attempts to forecast radiation-belt environments.

BODY-54 "When a nuclear weapon is detonated in the atmosphere, the bulk of burst energy radiated in the infrared, visible, and ultraviolet portions of the spectrum comes not from the weapon itself, but from complex interactions between atmospheric species and X-rays, gamma rays, neutrons, and weapon debris expanding at high speed from the burst point."

BODY-56 Either temporary or permanent disruption of any of these subsystems may compromise a satellite's ability to perform satisfactorily. Electronic systems are controlled by semiconductor microcircuits that operate at low signal levels and have relatively low-energy damage thresholds. Microcircuit active element density has increased astronomically over the past several decades to support high processor speeds and memory densities. These improvements have been accompanied by dramatically decreased chip feature sizes and, in turn, increased sensitivity to small unwanted signals.

BODY-57 The behavior of electrons liberated by these processes produces macroscopic electrical effects. Table VI.1 [Northrop, 1996: Table 22.4] indicates the amount of coupled energy required to produce malfunction in generic satellite electronic components.

BODY-58 "The probability of a photon traversing a given mass of material without any type of interaction is the product of the probabilities of its surviving various types of atomic interactions. For X-rays, the principal interaction mechanisms are the photoelectric effect (and subsequent fluorescence), Compton scattering, and pair production. In the photoelectric effect a photon is completely absorbed by an atom with the subsequent ejection of an electron; the atom may then fluoresce and emit a second newly created photon of lower energy than the original, or a second (Auger) electron may be emitted simultaneously with a third electron dropping into the vacant quantum state."

BODY-59 The forces between the two particles determine the effective radius of this sphere. Normalized dose (cm2/g) is the deposited energy (cal/g) per unit fluence (cal/cm2). A plot of the normalized dose for gold, germanium and silicon as a function of X-ray photon energy is given as Figure VI.2 [see, for example. Biggs and Lighthill, 1988].

BODY-60 "Some weapons can radiate X-rays of relatively high temperature (energy), which are more penetrating. Therefore, components fabricated with high-Z elements (e.g., Au, Pb), regardless of their depth, can be placed at risk."

BODY-61 When a material is placed in a steady-state X-ray or gamma-ray environment, continuing ionization processes lead to a steady-state balance between the creation of free electrons and their recombination or de-excitation. Any existing electric fields then propel the free charge. Insulating materials, under irradiation, may *allow charges (currents) to flow. Irradiation can also produce free radicals, break chemical bonds, or introduce trapping sites for charge carriers.*

BODY-64   *An integrated circuit may be placed in a logic state that cannot be changed without the removal of electric power. If power is not removed, the circuit elements may experience burnout. This phenomenon is referred to as latchup.*

BODY-65   *SGEMP induced responses tend to occur in the same time regime as the prompt environments — typically the sub-microsecond time scale. However, SGEMP current can be lengthened relative to the X-ray pulse duration by transmission-line propagation effects. In some cases they can be shortened due to non-linear effects such as space charge limiting. In addition, as with any high frequency or fast transient electrical excitation, it is common in many cases for induced SGEMP signals to "ring." SGEMP is basically a time domain phenomenon. That is, the basic excitations tend to take the form of a pulse, typically roughly triangular in shape. Thus, "CW" (i.e. continuous wave) testing, so common in most fields of electronics hardening*

BODY-66   *Historically, Cable SGEMP and Box IEMP stand out as posing the most severe threat to systems, as well as also representing the most difficult hardening challenge. The reason is that standard, good RF shielding practices can easily mitigate External SGEMP and Cavity IEMP. That is, electronics devices tend to be isolated from these effects by one or more levels of "Faraday cage" shielding. By contrast, Cable SGEMP and Box IEMP are driven by photon interactions within the RF shielding topology.*

BODY-67   *Box IEMP is generally driven by radiation environments somewhat reduced from those external to the satellite. This is a consequence of X-ray shielding afforded by the box walls. In principle, the X-ray portion of Box IEMP could be entirely eliminated by sufficient X-ray shielding. In practice, such shielding generally causes an unacceptable weight penalty, but spot shielding on circuit boards is often employed. Nuclear weapons (and the natural environment) also contribute a gamma radiation component to Box IEMP signals. Box shielding to gamma rays is entirely impractical from both weight and space considerations. (Two inches of lead is typically required to reduce the gamma flux by one order of magnitude.) One hardening strategy is to reduce the X-ray environment to a level where the X-ray dose rate*

BODY-68   *One also sees evidence of non-linear response scaling with fluence, as the voltage in Figure VI.11 decreases much more rapidly than does the absorbed energy in Figure VI.12.*

BODY-70   *"External SGEMP consists of surface E and B fields with associated replacement currents. It is usually a primary concern for coupling into antenna apertures. The principal hardening technique involves designing the antenna so that fields and skin currents do not couple efficiently (i.e., ensuring that the SGEMP is 'out of band') to the antenna."*

BODY-71   *In the 1970s it was discovered that satellites orbiting the earth in the natural space plasma and charged particle environment are subject to differential charging. At some differential charging voltage threshold, an electrical discharge can occur between different portions of the satellite. This discharge creates an electromagnetic transient that can couple into satellite electronics.*

BODY-72   *"Failure data are acquired, a stress level determined by means of an analysis, and the failure mode and level are extrapolated to the environment of interest. This approach becomes a matter of some concern, since the existing AGT/UGT data base*

	for commonly used materials was generated on samples that had been shielded from the softest part of the X-ray weapon's spectrum. Actual failure levels may be substantially lower than those implied by the AGT/UGTs."
BODY-74	*"In the case of Poco Graphite, some 40% of peak stress and 3.5% of peak dose were caused by photons at 1 keV and below."*
BODY-76	Implications of this observation are potentially quite serious. While it is probably true that adversaries are not specifically targeting U.S. DoD satellites with nuclear weapons, such space assets are nevertheless expected to operate in an exo-atmospheric nuclear environment. Nuclear weapons may be generating considerably more in the way of UV, VUV and sub-kilovolt X-rays than has hitherto been considered. Indeed, a current analytical study by the LLNL would appear to confirm this hypothesis [Thomson, 2002]. Such radiation may result from interactions between nuclear primaries and secondaries, interaction of the weapon with its transport vehicle, or detonations within the sensible atmosphere. These circumstances do not appear to have been considered by the RedBook community or
BODY-77	Frequently, failure will occur when the radiation-induced compressive stress wave interacts with either a second material or a free surface. The interaction may result in tensile stresses at the interface and cause delaminations or spall. For these tensile stresses, 0.1 kilobars becomes a reasonable rule of thumb as such levels are consistent with launch-generated g-loads.
BODY-79	LEO satellites are nearly always enveloped in "cold" plasma with electron and ion temperatures in the range of 0.1 to 0.3 eV. This plasma is responsible for many interesting effects, such as sheath formation, wake formation, and arcing of high voltage solar arrays. It keeps spacecraft surfaces at small negative potentials. The typical density of cold ionosphere plasma at the peak of the F layer is $\sim 10^{12}$ m^{3} during daylight, and $< 10^{11}$ m^{-3} at night. This population is not present in GEO, so geosynchronous satellites can charge to several kilovolts negative when they encounter a swarm of high energy electrons. Numerous spacecraft anomalies, as well as a few well-documented
BODY-80	"Shielding is the first defense against damage by energetic electrons and protons. For LEO satellites passing through the inner radiation belt, shielding is designed to defend against protons, which have energies extending to hundreds of MeV. Such a shield will be even more effective against lower energy electrons. A well-shielded satellite might have a 0.100 inch (2500 micron) shield, which blocks protons with energy below about 25 MeV, and electrons with energy below about 1.2 MeV."
BODY-81	Neutrons, absent a net charge, can penetrate deeply into a material and strike one of the constituent atoms in a process similar to a billiard ball collision. These atoms (called knock-ons) can be stripped of some of their electrons because of the kinetic energy they acquire, and are then capable of creating further ionization and other atomic displacements until they decelerate, recapture electrons, and come to rest at a site similar to their original location or in some interstitial position. In the latter case, the vacant site and the atoms displaced into an interstitial site within a crystal lattice form a pair known as a "Frenkel defect", [Bridgman, 2001].
BODY-83	EMP can occur if a nuclear weapon is detonated anywhere on the surface of the Earth up to several hundred kilometers in altitude. A burst can quickly damage and disable satellites via energetic electromagnetic photon (ultraviolet, X-rays and gamma rays) and particle (electron and neutron) radiation. This prompt damage can be manifested as distortion of telescope and other structural members, destruction of optical components, damage to solar power panels, logic circuit upset, or burnout of sensitive microelectronics within the spacecraft. Additionally,

BODY-84 — Finally, high yield burst scenarios were chosen at latitudes to threaten either GPS or Geosynchronous satellites (events 18-21). These detonations must be at relatively high latitudes to allow high-energy electrons to migrate along those geomagnetic field lines that intersect very high altitudes where GPS and Geosynchronous satellites reside. Since these bursts must be detonated at relatively high latitudes, the primary motivation of the attacker in these cases would be to threaten these high attitude satellite assets. Terrestrial EMP in these scenarios is considered a secondary effect and was therefore not a primary focus of our analyses.

energetic electrons trapped by Earth's magnetic field can cause spacecraft electronics to degrade over periods from days to years.

BODY-85 — If there is intervening atmosphere between the detonation point and the satellite, direct radiations will be attenuated. Lacking this intervening shield, there is no absorption attenuation factor and the energy fluence, X, merely falls off as the inverse square of the distance.

BODY-86 — "Where not shadowed by the Earth or shielded by atmospheric attenuation, X-rays, y-rays, neutrons, and ultraviolet (UV) photons travel great distances from a high-altitude nuclear detonation where they may inflict damage to satellites."

BODY-88 — "In general, for low-Earth orbiting satellites, the likelihood that a satellite will be in view of a burst altitude of a few hundred kilometers is usually small — on the order of 5-20 percent. This may increase significantly if the satellite and/or the burst are at higher altitudes."

BODY-89 — Some of the proposed efforts included a reexamination of old satellite and sounding rocket radiation data taken during the high altitude tests. In addition, a proposal was made to look at old engineering data from spacecraft on orbit at the time of the nuclear events to glean additional information on the radiation environment. New computer codes are also being developed that will model the natural space radiation environment in much higher fidelity. In combination with best-available contemporary models for debris dispersal following a high-altitude detonation, better predictions of the temporal and spatial evolution of pumped belts should result. Other phenomena, such as shock acceleration of ambient electrons and wave-particle interactions, need to be investigated.

BODY-90 — "Full assessment for situations other than worst case requires a statistical description, but for events and satellites similar to those considered, the likelihood that a LEO satellite will be in view of a burst is typically 5 to 20 percent. Even then, damage may on occasion be mitigated by intervening atmosphere."

BODY-93 — As discussed in Chapter VI, X-ray spectra resulting from nuclear detonations are broad. Consequently, photons are absorbed at different depths within a spacecraft depending upon photon energy, photons of low energy being absorbed nearer the surface and those of high energy penetrating deeper. In the discussion that follows, we have chosen to stress effects of low energy photons (UV and X-rays). Further, we note common hardening techniques such as spot shielding are not applicable to surface mounted assemblies as solar cells, radiators and optical components. Analogously, below we have focused on the low energy, surface-charging electrons for much the same reasons.

BODY-94 — Our analyses consider the possibility of compressive stress failure on both coatings for the 21 events listed in Table VII.1. The identical X-ray spectrum is used for all the calculations. This spectrum, and associated pulse width, were generated by LLNL [Thompson. 2003] for a representative threat, and will be referred to as the 'baseline' spectrum. Fluences on target were scaled from the LLNL calculation on *the basis of yield, but no adjustments were made to pulse shape. Parametric calculations of damage show pulse width to have a noticeable effect on coating hardness (perhaps as much as ± 15%), but this effect was thought small with respect to other uncertainties in analyses of nuclear induced damage.*

BODY-97 *Failure threshold for MgF2 (based upon the X-ray damage database for this material) was assumed to be between 2 and 3 kbars.*

BODY-100 *Failure threshold for this particular MLAR (based upon the X-ray damage database) is, as was the case for the SLAR, somewhere in the range of 2 and 3 kbars.*

BODY-101 *As was the case with the SLAR, assuming all three LEO satellites utilized MLAR's, only ISS is likely to experience failures for the 21 nuclear threats, and then only for events 6, 7, 8, 9, 17 and 19.*

BODY-102 *The most significant difficulty for surveillance systems that are required to operate through and after a nuclear event is reduced sensitivity due to an increase in ionization-induced noise.*

BODY-103 *Performance parameters of Table VIII.3 are seen to depend primarily upon decreased signal to noise ratios (S/N), and while permanent degradation is an important aspect of the radiation response of photonic and particularly infrared detectors, ionization-induced transients are often the critical issue in actual applications. To detect optical photons (as in missile plumes), infrared detectors are likely in their bare state to be very sensitive ionization detectors. They must be capable of detecting low energy IR photons, and this requires a low noise baseline. As a result, they are also extremely effective detectors of ionization, and hence IR sensors are often based on the same physical principles and rely on the same materials as do nuclear detectors [Pickel, 2003].*

BODY-104 *It is the secondary electrons that create charge within the detector and degrade its performance by decreasing S/N ratios. The rate of charge buildup induced in a detector will be proportional to the gamma pulse rise time, the so-called y-dot. The higher y-dot, the greater the time rate of change of sensor charge.*

BODY-106 *It is worth noting that the fluxes at ISS increase with L, while the fluxes at the higher altitude spacecraft decrease with L. First-day fluxes increase faster than linearly with yield.*

BODY-107 *Table VIII.5 shows the first-day fluxes for high L-shell events 18-21 (intended as direct attacks on GPS and GEO satellites) along with the corresponding average natural fluxes. Note that, at these L-shells, it is not unusual for fluxes to rise an order of magnitude above average due to natural activity. By this standard, only high-energy (E > 250 keV) electrons from the 10 Mt bursts exceed levels that should have been anticipated in the spacecraft design, and even then.*

BODY-108 *The low energy fluxes remain below the mean natural levels for all events. Decay of the fluxes occurs far more rapidly than for the LEO events. The decay is due to both pitch angle diffusion and radial diffusion. The decay time (e-folding time) is shown in Figure VIII. 18. For the GPS attack, decay time starts at one week and increases to nearly two weeks after one month, with negligible flux remaining after 90 days. For the GEO attack, decay is more rapid, beginning at 2.5 days and increasing to about 8 days after two weeks. Negligible flux remains after thirty days.*

BODY-109 *We have calculated how flux evolves according to the radial diffusion equation using parameters corresponding to high solar activity. From these results we infer a decay rate of peak flux of about 3.5 days near GPS orbit, and about 0.5 days at GEO. These results suggest that a spacecraft might encounter flux well in excess of the daily average for a short time during day one.*

BODY-110 An important consideration in determining an appropriate environment is the time to equilibrium. The timescale (RC time constant) is the dielectric constant divided by the conductivity. Table VIII.6 gives the timescale for insulators of different conductivities assuming a dielectric constant of 5 for the insulator. For an insulator with a conductivity of 10^{-16} $(\Omega\text{-cm})^{-1}$, the time to reach the equilibrium charge deposition is of the order of one orbit. Therefore, for conductivity values of 10^{-16} $(\Omega\text{-cm})^{-1}$ and lower, orbit-averaged fluxes should be used to determine the steady-state electric field. For higher conductivities the maximum flux (probably three to ten times the average) may

BODY-111 We next seek to determine an appropriate electron flux spectrum. Here we use the two spectral shapes shown in Figure VIII.20. The lower curve is a "fission spectrum" whose differential flux between one and seven MeV is given by $Y(E) = 3.88 \exp[-0.575E - 0.055E^2]$ with E in MeV. See Gurtman et al. [2003] for details of the actual flux used. The upper curve includes neutron decay electrons comprising ten percent of the fission flux. These neutron-decay electrons are not accounted for by SNRTACS. To put this in context, the flux of neutron decay electrons from STARFISH PRIME has been estimated [Hoerlin

BODY-113 Figure VIII.21 shows the rate of electron deposition in an insulator (coverglass). Note that most of the deposition occurs near the front face, and nearly half the deposition is due to neutron decay electrons, which make up only ten percent of the total spectrum. Typical coverglass thickness is 0.003 to 0.006 inch (75 to 150 microns), though coverglasses are commercially available with up to 0.020 inch (500 micron) thickness. (Presumably the thicker coverglasses are used for radiation protection.) Thermal control materials, such as Kapton* and Teflon®, are commonly used in thicknesses from 0.0005 inch (12 microns) up to 0.010 inch

BODY-114 "A factor of 5 change in thickness gives a factor of 3 change in peak electric field. Grounding the front surface decreases the peak electric field by a factor of 1.8 to 2.5."

BODY-115 We now consider the effect of trapped electrons on the lifetime of solar arrays. Solar arrays are exposed to the radiation environment and cannot be substantially shielded. While there is some variation among different types of solar cells, roughly speaking, solar cells begin to show radiation effects at a fluence (of 1 MeV electrons) of 10 electrons-cm", show noticeable degradation at 10^{14} electrons-cm"2, and reach end of life at about 10^{15} electrons-cm"2. Taking the SNRTACS fluence of electrons with energy greater than 0.25 MeV as equivalent to a fluence of 1 MeV electrons (as the median energy in the spectrum of Figure VIII.20 is only slightly above

BODY-116 The cells in red (fluence $> 3 \times 10^{14}$) experience substantial loss of life due to trapped electron radiation. The DMSP/NOAA/TERRA orbital regime, which contains most of our valuable weather and imaging satellites, is strongly affected by the more powerful bursts of our event set. ISS at 322 km sees only a modest effect from the most powerful bursts. ISS solar arrays are planned for fifteen year lifetime, so even a moderate unexpected degradation of the solar arrays might hamper operations for a significant time, assuming that ISS continues to function after a nuclear event.

BODY-117 Reduction in lifetimes of LEO satellites is based on total dose from higher energy electrons to internal electronics. Electronics were assumed to be shielded by a 0.100 inch "semi-infinite" slab of aluminum. This conservative shielding configuration assumes that the electronics are mounted on an internal wall of the spacecraft and essentially no radiation comes from the opposite direction (i.e., no radiation impacts the side of the electronic device that is facing away from the wall). In some cases sensitive electronics may be lightly shielded and/or exposed to radiation from *all directions, for example, a sensor at the end of a boom. In this case, an electronic device may encounter a factor of three or greater radiation level.*

BODY-118 *The previous analysis on LEO satellites assumed that the satellites started with their full 2-times-natural radiation budget. In reality, satellites on-orbit have various radiation margins remaining due to cumulative time on orbit. For example, a satellite launched 10 years ago will most likely fail more quickly than a comparable satellite launched only a year ago. Figure VIII.23 illustrates this effect using the TERRA satellite orbit. One can see that in this particular case the spacecraft lifetime will be longer if the burst occurs closer to the beginning of satellite life.*

BODY-119 *"If one considers that GPS satellites, for example, have a range of residual hardness due to their distribution of on-orbit ages, then the GPS constellation could be quite vulnerable to some special weapon events. Specifically, event 19, a 10 Mt burst (with 50% fission yield), would place a sufficient flux of fission electrons at GPS altitudes to significantly affect that constellation."*

BODY-120 *"Satellite loss can be translated into impacts on users of the GPS constellation, insofar as it leads to substantial 'blackouts' in precise navigation services. For precise navigation, four satellites are normally required. As satellites drop out of the constellation, outage times gradually increase. Degradation is not continuous, but occurs at various times during the day. Some outages can last 30 minutes while others can be a few hours at a time."*

BODY-124 *The worst-case exposure of a LEO satellite to direct X-radiation from a nuclear weapon may be lethal and, as shown in Section VI.l.b.iii, UV radiation may damage spacecraft surfaces in excess to its proportion of total photon fluence. However, the large distance between a detonation for an EMP attack and a satellite in MEO or GEO makes the probability of damage very low, at least for the cases analyzed. MEO and GEO satellites are already designed to operate in the relatively severe natural radiation environments at such altitudes.*

BODY-125 *Direct attacks on space assets, although credible, are not within the scope of this study. Therefore, we must consider ramifications of satellite losses in concert with other losses resulting from an EMP attack. If an EMP attack is perpetrated over a military expeditionary force, or over a carrier battle group, those satellites in jeopardy could be unique in the service they provide or could be but one of a number of viable mission-fulfilling alternatives.*

BODY-126 *From an economic viewpoint, perhaps the greatest impact would result from loss of LEO weather satellites. These satellites provide unique meteorological services to the country, and to the world for that matter, by providing critical information on cloud moisture content, wind velocity, ocean temperatures and wave heights. All of these parameters are required for accurate weather prediction and cannot be remotely sensed at high latitudes with weather satellites at geosynchronous orbits. A study of economic benefits of the NOAA satellite [Hussey, 2002] states that industries that contribute $2.7 trillion to the U.S. Gross Domestic Product rely on accurate weather forecasting.*

BODY-127 *These economic figures imply significant consequences, particularly for organizations that rely heavily on space assets. The Commission's assessment is that, while the cost of losing these space systems would be high, this loss by itself would not place at risk long-term functionality of American society.*

BODY-128 *Satellites that employ optical systems for surveillance and target acquisition are highly subject to radiation effects. This particularly applies to missile defense* components. Optical systems can be degraded or destroyed by UV or X-rays if the threatening missile is salvage fuzed or intended to open a path for subsequent missiles in the attack. Gamma radiation from nuclear weapon debris can raise the noise level in photodetectors, which is tantamount to blinding them. High X-ray and gamma fluxes can burn out signal processors and upset memories in a satellite.

BODY-129 "The Director of the Central Intelligence Agency has directed that the NGA use commercial imaging satellites to the 'greatest extent possible,' and commercial imagery should become the 'primary source of data used for government mapping [Tenet, 2002]'"

BODY-130 An ensemble of identically made nuclear weapons will produce a distribution of prompt outputs with statistical deviation about mean characteristics. Aspects of physics governing induced nuclear-weapon environments are imprecisely known. Analyses in this paper are predicated on assumptions about military characteristics and related properties of threat weapons, locations of detonations, and space systems hardening technologies. Given the current state of knowledge, we regard these uncertainties, in the absence of focused technology programs, as irreducible.

BODY-131 "Overriding many of these considerations are fundamental unknowns associated with the nuclear threat, i.e., what precisely are the characteristics of the threat weapon? Absent definitive knowledge, we can only estimate ranges of effects and apply physical principals to establish bounds on physically possible levels of effects."

BODY-133 Natural belts of geomagnetically trapped energetic particles exist as a balance between processes that inject particles into the trapping region, processes that modify the trapped population (e.g., redistribute, energize, and de-energize), and processes that remove particles from the trapping region, as was illustrated by the "leaky bucket" analogy of Figure V.4. The non-steady, fluctuating character of natural trapped electron fluxes was illustrated by satellite data displayed in Figure V.3. These data indicate peak-to-peak fluctuations in trapped flux as large as four orders of magnitude (i.e., a factor of as much as 10,000 in the environment to which satellites are exposed).

BODY-134 The important point here is that at all values of L the spread of experimentally and theoretically based A,z's is three to five orders of magnitude. That is, even in a linearized equation for the phase-space density of trapped electrons, there is a several-order-of-magnitude uncertainty. This observation is of paramount importance to uncertainties in the nuclear-pumped radiation problem we will discuss later because trapped energetic electrons originating from natural processes (with naturally occurring Ax's of Figure X.1) and trapped energetic electrons originating from a nuclear explosion are regulated by identically the same governing physics.

BODY-135 "In characterizing disturbed environments from nuclear explosions, the same convention as used in Section V will be followed: Prompt environments are those that arise from the detonation on time scale short compared to formation times for blast waves and fireballs. Induced environments follow from the interaction of nuclear-burst energies with the atmosphere and geomagnetic field generally around the burst point."

BODY-136 "In the development of quantitative assessments of uncertainties, we assume the threat weapon in question is based on technology that mirrors a pre-1970's U.S. design. Alternatively, we can assume an analysis based on detailed design information for the threat weapon. Should neither of these assumptions apply, then uncertainty estimates described below are essentially unbounded, with an associated confidence approaching zero."

BODY-137   Uncertainties in fluxes of energetic debris emanating from a nuclear detonation arise primarily from uncertainties in the three-dimensional weapon-disassembly mass and velocity distributions and charge state distributions of debris ions, each as modified by the aeroshell and any other materials in the vicinity of the burst. A secondary factor is the orientation of the weapon relative to the geomagnetic field at the time of detonation.

BODY-139   "An overarching consideration is that given the commonality of governing physics for trapped particles, be they of natural or nuclear origins, in conjunction with knowledge gaps and exceptionally large uncertainties in modeling of temporal and spatial properties of the natural radiation belts, we are in a poor position to characterize nuclear-pumped radiation belts as anything less than highly uncertain."

BODY-140   "In the absence of definitive experimental evidence to the contrary, we do not regard shock acceleration in a nuclear explosion as a credible source of significant fluxes of MeV electrons and therefore cannot associate a meaningful uncertainty with it."

BODY-141   "Overall, the electron injection process is highly non-linear and poorly characterized theoretically. Consequently, extrapolations of electron injection data from the very few high-altitude nuclear tests conducted by the U.S. and the Soviet Union are ill advised."

BODY-142   "The last elements that contribute to uncertainties—evolution of the energy spectrum and spatial distribution, along with lifetimes of energetic electrons of nuclear origin—can be addressed simultaneously. These are important aspects of the nuclear-pumped belts that are directly regulated by identically the same magnetospheric dynamics that govern the natural radiation belts. Consequently, one would expect that readily available data for dynamical evolution of the natural radiation belts could be used as a basis for evaluating nuclear-pumped belts."

BODY-143   Overall, uncertainties in predictions of nuclear-pumped trapped radiation belts are unacceptably large. Owing to multiple non-linear aspects of the total process, there is at present no mathematically rigorous means to provide a definitive assessment of uncertainties. The best one can do is to provide a best estimate based on a melding of the above considerations. For any point in space subject to nuclear-pumping of the radiation belts at any time beyond an hour or two after a detonation, we estimate uncertainties in trapped electron flux to be not less than one to two orders of magnitude, bounded only by the available inventory of energetic electrons produced by the detonation.

BODY-144   Generally speaking, computations of transitions that are hydrogenic in nature, either in highly charged species or transitions involving a single electron outside a closed shell are well behaved and yield reliable results. Transitions from open-shell configurations are less reliable but are arguably accurate to within about a factor of three. Producing accurate predictions of UV emissions is also predicated on models which are sufficiently inclusive of transitions to mimic "reality". In the past, such inclusive predictions were constrained by computer limitations. Such limitations have been lifted with current computer capabilities so efforts to expand the rate models can increase the reliability of UV emission predictions.

BODY-145   Any temporary or permanent disruption of these subsystem functions might defeat the mission of the satellite. The electronic systems are controlled by semiconductor microcircuits that operate at low signal levels and have relatively low energy damage thresholds. Microcircuit active element density has increased astronomically over the past several decades to support high processor speeds and

BODY-146   memory densities. Feature sizes have dramatically decreased, reducing the effects of charge trapping, but increasing sensitivity to single event effects.

BODY-146   "The major factor in the success of this test is attributable to a long history of testing of piece-parts and subsystems in laboratory simulators prior to actual nuclear testing. It is difficult to predict if satellites with contemporary technologies would respond in the same manner given that 25 years have passed since the HURON KING event."

BODY-147   "To proceed with a mitigation program, one must have confidence that a significant portion of the potential threat space (a) constitutes a serious hazard to important space assets, and (b) is not so severe as to make mitigation impossible (or prohibitively expensive)."

BODY-148   Benefits of hardening can be nonlinear. Because peak trapped-radiation intensity drops rapidly over the first few days after detonation, a satellite orbiting through the peak-flux region might survive significantly longer if its radiation tolerance were doubled.

BODY-149   "Until recently it has not been possible to quantify the magnitudes of errors that result from such extrapolations. However, recent improvements in analysis and modeling indicate the errors can be large. For example, for a 1 Mt detonation at 1,300 km, 'cold' plasma electron density predictions based on extrapolation of STARFISH PRIME phenomenology are now indicated to be in error by two to three orders of magnitude."

BODY-150   The frequent many-order-of-magnitude swings in fluxes of energetic electrons in the natural radiation belts are testimony to these effects.

BODY-151   A concerted effort is needed to understand nuclear detonations in the 30 to 90 km altitude range. Basic phenomenology, systems effects, and mitigation options need to be explored.

BODY-152   "Shielding and/or hardening for both satellites and ground stations are mature engineering disciplines, and their application is determined by priorities set by the government or commercial customer. Project managers who make necessary decisions on the approach to system survivability must examine whether addressing only the satellite or only the ground station will still leave exploitable system vulnerability."

BODY-153   "An alternative proposal is to promote pitch-angle diffusion using electrostatic fields surrounding several high voltage tether arrays. [TUI, 2004] This concept is currently under study by DARPA. The system would consist of several long (up to 100 km) tether arrays maintained at high negative voltage (up to 100 kV). The plasma sheath around such a tether would be very large, perturbing a substantial volume of space. The tethers would be in elliptical orbit so as to pass through most of the inner belt L-shells. Proponents calculate that the proposed system 'can reduce the MeV particle flux in the inner electron belt to 1% of its natural levels within about half a year.'"

BODY-154   Ground control stations can be an Achilles heel for satellite systems. They can be subject to any number of attacks on land by terrorists or special forces using any number of weapons. A station that is not EMP hardened can be shut down or seriously damaged by a HEMP attack. This in turn could defeat the satellite mission. Satellites in any orbit, LEO, MEO, GEO, or HEO can only function for a finite time in an autonomous mode alter which they may cease to operate.

BODY-155   "An attack on MEO or GEO satellites by high latitude detonations for the purpose of populating electron belts at those altitudes would require large yields (> 10 Mt).

The mean natural radiation level in these orbits is already high, as is its variability. Further, the volume of these outer-belt magnetic flux tubes (at L=4.0 to 6.6) is much larger than that of the flux tubes encountered by LEO satellites. A high-yield weapon would be required to significantly raise radiation intensity above natural levels."

BODY-156   *Recent more rigorous examination of the ultraviolet output of high altitude detonations indicates that this portion of the radiation spectrum is present in sufficient magnitude to be much more damaging to surface components than previously thought. The reexamination, conducted at LLNL at the request of Commission staff, reveals that the amount of UV fluence is sufficient to be a hazard to satellite surface components (optical and power) because of the very large absorption cross-sections for ultraviolet radiation.*

BODY-157   *Mandated and fenced research programs in high-altitude nuclear effects should be adequately reviewed and funded to assure a better understanding of nuclear burst phenomena, a greater confidence in the quantitative prediction of their effects, and a substantial reduction in costs associated with present large hardening safety margins.*

Defense Threat Reduction Agency
8725 John J. Kingman Road, MS 6201
Fort Belvoir, VA 22060-6201

DTRA-IR-10-22

Collateral Damage to Satellites from an EMP Attack

Approved for public release; distribution is unlimited.

TECHNICAL REPORT

August 2010

20101029076

Edward E. Conrad
Gerald A. Gurtman
Glenn Kweder
Myron J. Mandell
Willard W. White

DESTRUCTION NOTICE:

Destroy this report when it is no longer needed.
Do not return to sender.

PLEASE NOTIFY THE DEFENSE THREAT REDUCTION
AGENCY, ATTN: CSUI, 8725 JOHN J. KINGMAN ROAD,
MS-6201, FT BELVOIR, VA 22060-6201, IF YOUR ADDRESS
IS INCORRECT, IF YOU WISH IT DELETED FROM THE
DISTRIBUTION LIST, OR IF THE ADDRESSEE IS NO
LONGER EMPLOYED BY YOUR ORGANIZATION.

REPORT DOCUMENTATION PAGE			Form Approved OMB No. 0704-0188
Public reporting burden for this collection of information is estimated to average 1 hour per response, including the time for reviewing instructions, searching existing data sources, gathering and maintaining the data needed, and completing and reviewing this collection of information. Send comments regarding this burden estimate or any other aspect of this collection of information, including suggestions for reducing this burden to Department of Defense, Washington Headquarters Services, Directorate for Information Operations and Reports (0704-0188), 1215 Jefferson Davis Highway, Suite 1204, Arlington, VA 22202-4302. Respondents should be aware that notwithstanding any other provision of law, no person shall be subject to any penalty for failing to comply with a collection of information if it does not display a currently valid OMB control number. **PLEASE DO NOT RETURN YOUR FORM TO THE ABOVE ADDRESS.**			

1. REPORT DATE (DD-MM-YYYY) 00-08-2010	2. REPORT TYPE Internal	3. DATES COVERED (From - To)
4. TITLE AND SUBTITLE Collateral Damage to Satellites from and EMP Attack		5a. CONTRACT NUMBER
		5b. GRANT NUMBER
		5c. PROGRAM ELEMENT NUMBER
6. AUTHOR(S) Edward E. Conrad, Gerald A. Gurtman, Glen Kweder, Myron J. Mandell, and Willard W. White		5d. PROJECT NUMBER
		5e. TASK NUMBER
		5f. WORK UNIT NUMBER
7. PERFORMING ORGANIZATION NAME(S) AND ADDRESS(ES)		8. PERFORMING ORGANIZATION REPORT NUMBER
9. SPONSORING / MONITORING AGENCY NAME(S) AND ADDRESS(ES) Defense Threat Reduction Agency 8725 John J. Kingman, STOP 6201 Ft. Belvoir, VA 22060-6201		10. SPONSOR/MONITOR'S ACRONYM(S)
		11. SPONSOR/MONITOR'S REPORT NUMBER(S) DTRA-IR-10-22
12. DISTRIBUTION / AVAILABILITY STATEMENT Approved for public release; distribution is unlimited		
13. SUPPLEMENTARY NOTES		
14. ABSTRACT In support of The Commissions to Assess the Threat to the United States from Electromagnetic Pulse Attack, this paper examines the potential damage to satellites from high altitude nuclear detonations not specifically targeting space assets. We provide and overview of representative classes of satellites, their orbits, and their economic and military importance to the U.S. lessons learned from atmospheric nuclear test of the late 1950's and early 1960's are presented. In particular, the STARFISH PRIME test of 1962 injected long-lived trapped energetic electrons into Earth's magnetic fields, causing the early demise of several satellites.		
15. SUBJECT TERMS Radiation Gamma Rays Photoemissions Nuclear		

16. SECURITY CLASSIFICATION OF:			17. LIMITATION OF ABSTRACT SAR	18. NUMBER OF PAGES 165	19a. NAME OF RESPONSIBLE PERSON
a. REPORT Unclassified	b. ABSTRACT Unclassified	c. THIS PAGE Unclassified			19b. TELEPHONE NUMBER (include area code)

Standard Form 298 (Rev. 8-98)
Prescribed by ANSI Std. 239.18

ABSTRACT

In support of *The Commission to Assess the Threat to the United States from Electromagnetic Pulse Attack,* this paper examines the potential damage to satellites from high altitude nuclear detonations not specifically targeting space assets. We provide an overview of representative classes of satellites, their orbits, and their economic and military importance to the U. S. Lessons learned from atmospheric nuclear tests of the late 1950's and early 1960's are presented. In particular, the STARFISH PRIME test of 1962 injected long-lived trapped energetic electrons into Earth's magnetic field, causing the early demise of several satellites. Physical principles governing natural and nuclear weapon enhanced space environments, including trapped radiation (Van Allen belts), are described. We review effects of various types of natural and nuclear radiation on satellite electronic components, surface materials, and systems. In particular, we note that weapon-induced ultraviolet radiation and its damaging effects on surface materials may have been underestimated in previous studies.

Twenty-one trial nuclear events with varying yields and locations were postulated as credible terrestrial EMP attacks or other nuclear threats. Of these, seventeen were at low L-shells and consequently present a hazard to low-Earth orbit (LEO) satellites. Four were at high magnetic latitude, threatening GPS or geosynchronous (GEO) satellites. We present effects of these events on three representative LEO satellites, on the GPS constellation, and on a generic GEO satellite. The Air Force SNRTACS code was used to characterize the nuclear-weapon-generated trapped electron environment; the Satellite Toolkit (STK) was used to assess prompt radiation exposure. We conclude that LEO satellites are at serious risk of exceeding total-dose limits for trapped radiation if generally accepted natural space hardening criteria are invoked. We believe, however, that the probability of an individual satellite being sufficiently close to a detonation to be threatened by prompt radiation effects is relatively low. GPS and GEO satellites are threatened only by the very high yield ($\sim$ 10 Mt) detonations of our trial set.

We review uncertainties in our ability to predict nuclear-detonation-produced satellite damage along with our confidence in the efficacy of these predictions. Uncertainties as large as one to two orders of magnitude are postulated, particularly as relating to the prediction of trapped radiation from nuclear bursts.

We recommend that the Department of Defense initiate policies to:

- Reassess survivability of satellite space- and ground-based systems that support U.S. defenses,
- Increase the level of nuclear hardening and subsidize implementation for commercial satellites that support essential national missions,
- Increase funding for research in high altitude nuclear effects in order to reduce uncertainties and the safety margins they engender, thereby decreasing the costs associated with hardening.
- Pursue studies on the feasibility of electron radiation belt remediation.

CONTENTS

Section	Page
Abstract	i
Figures	v
Tables	x
I Introduction	1
II Statement of Problem	3
III Satellite Populations	5
IV History of Damage to Satellites	11
IV.A High Altitude Nuclear Tests	11
IV.B Satellites Damaged by High Altitude Nuclear Tests	11
IV.C Failures Resulting from the Natural Radiation Environment	15
IV.D Laboratory and Underground Nuclear Testing	16
V Satellite Environments	18
V.A Natural Radiation Environment	18
V.B Environments Created By a High-Altitude Nuclear Detonation	24
V.B.1 Direct Weapon Emissions	25
V.B.1.a Photons	25
V.B.1.a.i X-rays	25
V.B.1.a.ii Prompt Gamma Rays	27
V.B.1.b Energetic Particles	28
V.B.1.b.i Neutrons	28
V.B.1.b.ii Debris Ions	29
V.B.2 Induced Environments	29
V.B.2.a Electromagnetic Pulse	30
V.B.2.b Energetic Particles	32
V.B.2.b.i Sources of Energetic Heavy Ions	32
V.B.2.b.ii Delayed Gamma Rays	34
V.B.2.b.iii (Delayed) Beta Particles	34
V.B.2.c Nuclear-Pumped Radiation Belts and Other Beta-Particle Effects	36
V.B.2.d Photoemissions Other Than X-rays and Gamma Rays	40
VI Radiation Effects on Satellites	42
VI.A Photon Effects	44

	VI.A.1	Energy Distribution and Material Dependence	44
	VI.A.2	X-ray Effects	47
		VI.A.2.a Dose and Dose Rate Effects	47
		VI.A.2.b SGEMP	51
		VI.A.2.c Photon-Induced Thermomechanical Effects	58
VI.B	Charged Particle Effects		64
	VI.B.1	Electrons	64
	VI.B.2	Single Event Phenomena	67
VI.C	Neutron Effects		67

VII Analytical Scope ... 69
- VII.A Representative Satellites ... 69
- VII.B Nuclear Events ... 69
- VII.C Computational Tools ... 71
  - VII.C.1 Prompt Radiation Effects ... 71
  - VII.C.2 Line-of Sight Photon Threat ... 72
  - VII.C.3 Line-of Sight X-Ray Probability Methodology ... 74
  - VII.C.4 Radiation-Belt Effects ... 74
  - VII.C.5 Satellite Tool Kit Software ... 75

VIII Results of Analyses ... 76
- VIII.A Prompt Line of Sight Damage ... 76
  - VIII.A.1 Probability Analysis of Prompt Line-of-Sight Damage ... 76
  - VIII.A.2 Photon Effects ... 79
    - VIII.A.2.a Spectrum Issues ... 79
    - VIII.A.2.b Photon Induced Thermomechanical Damage ... 79
      - VIII.A.2.b.i Single Layer Anti-Reflection (SLAR) Coating ... 80
      - VIII.A.2.b.ii Multi-Layer Anti-Reflection (MLAR) Coating ... 84
  - VIII.A.3 Surveillance Satellite Subsystems ... 88
- VIII.B Cumulative Damage Resulting from Radiation Belt Exposure ... 90
  - VIII.B.1 SNRTACS results for low L-shell events ... 90
  - VIII.B.2 SNRTACS results for high L-shell events ... 93
  - VIII.B.3 Predictions of Electric Stress ... 95
  - VIII.B.4 Effect on solar arrays ... 101
  - VIII.B.5 Reduction in lifetime of electronics ... 103
    - VIII.B.5.a Effects on LEO satellites ... 103
    - VIII.B.5.b Effects on GPS, GEO and HEO satellite ... 105

		VIII.C Discussion of Results	110
IX	Consequences of Findings		111
	IX.A	General Findings	111
	IX.B	Civilian Satellites	112
	IX.C	Military Communication and Intelligence Collection Satellites	113
	IX.D	Civilian Satellites to Support the Military	114
X	Uncertainties and Confidence Assessments		116
	X.A	Overview of Uncertainties and Confidence	116
	X.B	Uncertainties in Natural Radiation Environment	119
	X.C	Uncertainties in Environments Produced by High-Altitude Nuclear Detonations	121
		X.C.1 Uncertainties in Prompt Nuclear Environments	121
		X.C.1.a Uncertainties in Prompt Gamma Environments	122
		X.C.1.b Uncertainties in X-Ray Environment	122
		X.C.1.c Uncertainties in Prompt Neutron and Debris-Ion Fluxes from Nuclear Detonations	123
		X.C.2 Uncertainties in Induced Nuclear Environments	124
		X.C.2.a Uncertainties in Induced Energetic Particle Fluxes	124
		X.C.2.b Uncertainties in Delayed Beta and Gamma Radiations	125
		X.C.2.c Uncertainties in Nuclear-Pumping of Radiation Belts	125
		X.C.2.d Uncertainties in Ultraviolet Photoemissions	129
	X.D	Uncertainties in Natural and Nuclear Effects on Satellites	130
	X.E	Confidence Assessments in Light of Uncertainties	133
	X.F	What Needs To Be Done	134
XI	Threat Mitigation		138
	XI.A	Introduction	138
	XI.B	Remediation of Pumped Belts	139
	XI.C	Orbit Modification	140
	XI.D	Ground Control Stations	140
XII	Conclusions and Recommendations		141
	XII.A	Conclusions	141
	XII.B	Recommendations	143
References			144

FIGURES

Figure III.1. Distribution of low-Earth orbit satellites by mission. 6

Figure III.2. Distribution of low-Earth satellites by country. 7

Figure III.3. Distribution of U.S. low-Earth orbit satellites by mission. 8

Figure IV.1 TRAAC and Transit 4B Solar Cell Degradation. 14

Figure IV.2 Chronology of Satellite Anomalies and Space Weather Events. 16

Figure IV.3. Experimental chamber containing STARSAT in the HURON KING event. 17

Figure V.1. Artist's conception of the trapped electron radiation belts that encircle the Earth. 19

Figure V.2. Integral flux contours based on the AE8 and AP8 models for radiation-belt electrons and protons are shown. The AE8 and AP8 models represent long-term average conditions derived from data taken by more than 20 satellites over the period from the early 1960s to the mid 1970s. 20

Figure V.3. Log_{10} of differential electron flux (electons/cm^2-s-sr-keV binned in 0.1L increments) as a function of time is shown for three of the 16 energy channels of the MEA instrument carried by the CRRES satellite. 21

Figure V.4. Leaky bucket analogy for the radiation belts illustrated. 23

Figure V.5. Radiant power versus wavelength for blackbodies with various effective radiating temperatures. Note that 1 eV is equivalent to 11,604 degrees Kelvin. 26

Figure V.6. X-ray fluence versus altitude as a function of X-ray temperature for detonations as altitudes of 60, 80, 150, and 200 km altitude as measured along a vertical ray through the burst point. 27

Figure V.7. Normalized spectra for prompt and delayed U^{235} fission gamma rays are illustrated. 28

Figure V.8. Neutron spectra from fission and thermonuclear weapons are illustrated for unit neutron source. 29

Figure V.9. E1 form of electromagnetic pulse is generated by scattering of gamma rays from air species, thereby producing Compton electrons that gyrate synchronously in the Earth's magnetic field to produce a transverse electric current that radiates a coherent electromagnetic signal. 31

Figure V.10. MHD-EMP (a.k.a. E3) occurs when a high-altitude nuclear explosion creates time-varying magnetic signals that propagate to the ground and interact with large-scale electrical conductors such as electric power transmission lines and pipelines. 31

Figure V.11. Notional envelope of electric field (volts per meter) as a function time illustrates the three classes of electromagnetic pulse, E1, E2, and E3. 32

Figure V.12. STARFISH PRIME detonation (1.4 Mt at 400 km altitude in vicinity of Johnston Island in mid Pacific) is shown at 55 ms as seen from Hawaii.. 33

Figure V.13. Flux of delayed gamma rays (γ-cm^{-2}-s^{-1}) at 10 seconds after a 1 Mt nuclear detonation at 200 km altitude above the central United States. 34

Figure V.14. Beta energy spectrum from fission of U^{235} by fast neutrons. 35

Figure V.15. The KINGFISH high-altitude nuclear test above Johnston Island in the mid Pacific produced a brilliant visual display, including a prominent beta tube below the fireball 36

Figure V.16. The flux of trapped beta particles from a high-altitude nuclear explosion depends, in part, on the magnetic latitude of the detonation.. 38

Figure V.17. Ratio of circumferential differential flux-tube volumes referenced to circumferential differential flux-tube volume for L=6.6. 39

Figure V.18. Magnetic bubble region illustrated. 40

Figure V.19. Radiated optical power versus time for detonations near the ground and at 36, 50, and 200 km altitude 41

Figure VI.1 Relative importance of the major X-ray and γ-ray interactions. The lines indicate the values of Z and $h\nu$ for which the neighboring effects are equal. [Evans, 1955] 45

Figure VI.2. Total X-Ray Cross Sections (normalized dose) for Gold (Z = 79), Germanium (Z = 32) and Silicon (Z = 14) (solid lines) as a function of X-ray photon energy. The highest plotted photon energy is below the threshold for pair production. 46

Figure VI.3(a). Normalized dose as a function of depth in Aluminum (Z=13), Silicon (Z=14) and Tantalum (Z= 73) for a 1 keV blackbody. 46

Figure VI.3(b) Normalized dose as a function of depth in Germanium (32), Silicon (14), and Gold (79) for a 10 keV blackbody. 46

Figure VI.4. Total dose damage thresholds for bipolar IC technologies (Northrop, 1996: Table 22.18.) 48

Figure VI.5. Total dose damage thresholds for MOS technologies (Northrop, 1996: Table 22.19.) 48

Figure VI.6. Dose rate vs. blackbody temperature and fluence in Silicon shielded by 0.120 inch of Aluminum. 49

Figure VI.7. Typical diode photocurrents as a function of dose rate. 49

Figure VI.8. Comparison of upset thresholds for state-of-the-art integrated technologies. 50

Figure VI.9. Integrated circuit latchup thresholds. 50

Figure VI.10. Basic SGEMP processes for a satellite. 51

Figure VI.11. SGEMP Upset: Voltage as function of blackbody temperature and fluence. 53

Figure VI.12. SGEMP Burnout: Energy as function of blackbody temperature and fluence. 54

Figure VI.13 Box IEMP Upset (Coated Circuit Board): Voltage as function of blackbody temperature and fluence. 55

Figure VI.14. Box IEMP Burnout (Coated Circuit Board): Energy as function of blackbody temperature and fluence. 55

Figure VI.15. Box IEMP Upset (Uncoated Circuit Board): Voltage as function of blackbody temperature and fluence. 56

Figure VI.16. Box IEMP Burnout (Uncoated Circuit Board): Energy as function of blackbody temperature and fluence. 57

Figure VI.17. 1 keV blackbody energy density vs. photon energy 59

Figure VI.18. Normalized Depth-Dose; 1 keV blackbody source on IR mirror 59

Figure VI.19. Normalized Depth-Dose; 1 keV blackbody source on Poco Graphite. 60

Figure VI.20. Stress and fluence ratios as functions of blackbody temperature for IR mirror. 61

Figure VI.21. Stress and fluence ratios as functions of blackbody temperature for Poco Graphite. 61

Figure VI.22. Peak dose in Silicon as function of blackbody temperature and Aluminum shield thickness. (Incident fluence on surface of the Aluminum is 1 cal/cm^2) 63

Figure VI.23. Peak in-plane compressive stress in Silicon as function of blackbody temperature and Aluminum shield thickness. 64

Figure VI.24. Effects of various energies of electrons on LEO spacecraft, together with the natural and nuclear-enhanced integral spectra. 65

Figure VI.25. Effect of 0.100 inch Aluminum shield on the mean natural electron environment (left) and on the nuclear-induced trapped electron environment (right). 67

Figure VI.26. Neutron damage thresholds for bipolar ICs. [Northrop, 1996]...............68

Figure VII.1. Where not shadowed by the Earth or shielded by atmospheric attenuation, X-rays and ultraviolet (UV) photons travel great distances from a high-altitude nuclear detonation where they may inflict damage to satellites. 72

Figure VII.2. Worst case threat fluences for the DMSP/NOAA satellite. 73

Figure VII.3. Worst case threat fluences for the TERRA satellite. 73

Figure VII.4. Worst case threat fluences for the ISS satellite at an altitude of 322 km. 73

Figure VIII.1. NOAA X-ray events. 77

Figure VIII.2. TERRA X-ray Events. 78

Figure VIII.3. ISS X-ray Events. 78

Figure VIII.4. Normalized dose for the SLAR configuration. Photo-electron migration has been taken into account, but not heat conduction. 81

Figure VIII.5. Ratio of peak temperature at a given depth to the maximum temperature achieved by the SLAR coating. 81

Figure VIII.6. Ratio of the peak in-plane compressive stress to the maximum compressive stress for the SLAR coating. 82

Figure VIII.7. Maximum in-plane compressive stress in a SLAR coating on DMSP/NOAA subjected to the threat events. 83

Figure VIII.8. Maximum in-plane compressive stress in a SLAR coating on TERRA subjected to the threat events. 84

Figure VIII.9. Maximum in-plane compressive stress in a SLAR coating on ISS (322 km altitude) subjected to the threat events. 84

Figure VIII.10. Normalized dose for the MLAR configuration. Photo-electron migration has been taken into account, but not heat conduction. 85

Figure VIII.11. Ratio of peak temperature at a given depth to the maximum temperature achieved by a MLAR coating. 85

Figure VIII.12. Ratio of the peak in-plane compressive stress to the maximum compressive stress for the MLAR coating. 86

Figure VIII.13. Maximum in-plane compressive stress in a MLAR coating on DMSP/NOAA subjected to the threat events. 87

Figure VIII.14. Maximum in-plane compressive stress in a MLAR coating on TERRA subjected to the threat events. 87

Figure VIII.15. Maximum in-plane compressive stress in a MLAR coating on ISS (322 km altitude) subjected to the threat events. 87

Figure VIII.16. Decay time vs. time after burst for trapped electron flux to spacecraft for trial 9. All low L-shell bursts exhibit similar behavior. 91

Figure VIII.17. Comparison of fluxes ($m^{-2} s^{-1}$) from fitting formula vs. SNRTACS data for electrons with energy 40 keV < E < 250 keV (upper plot) and E > 250 keV (lower plot). 93

Figure VIII.18. Decay time vs. time since burst for GPS and GEO events. 94

Figure VIII.19. Ratio of high-energy to low-energy electrons for the high L-shell events. 95

Figure VIII.20. Integral fission electron spectrum (lower curve), and the fission spectrum augmented by ten percent with neutron decay electrons (upper curve). 98

Figure VIII.21. Charge deposition rate in insulator (coverglass) for the two spectra. 99

Figure VIII.22. Electric fields in an insulator for the front face grounded (upper curve) and floating (lower curve). 100

Figure VIII.23. TERRA satellite lifetime after a high altitude nuclear event vs. time since launch. (Two-times-natural hardening assumed for total dose.) 105

Figure VIII.24. GPS satellites remaining as a function of time following a 10 Mt blast over the Great Lakes. 108

Figure VIII.25. GPS outage time in Baghdad after a 10 Mt burst over Lake Superior. 108

Figure VIII.26. HEO satellite exposure to trapped radiation produced by a 5 Mt detonation (Event 17). 109

Figure X.1. Radial diffusion coefficients obtained by a variety of methods. 121

Figure X.2. Three simultaneous motions of geomagnetically trapped electrons are illustrated: gyration about magnetic field lines; bounce motion between magnetic mirror points, and drift around the Earth. 127

Figure X.3. Cylindrical map projection with overlaid contours of constant geomagnetic L shell values illustrates magnetic locations of U.S. and Soviet high-altitude nuclear tests of 1958 and 1962. 128

TABLES

Table II.1. Examples of Active LEO Assets by Mission (US Assets in Blue) May 2003 3

Table III.1. U.S. LEO Satellite Investment. 9

Table IV.1. HANE Events Chronology 11

Table IV.2. Satellites On Orbit at the Time of High Altitude Nuclear Tests. 12

Table IV.3. Satellites Damaged by High Altitude Nuclear Tests. 13

Table V.1 Nuclear Burst Regimes by Altitude. 24

Table VI.1. Upset and Burnout Thresholds for Satellite Electronic Components 43

Table VI.2. A brief description of SGEMP categories. 52

Table VII.1. Satellites Analyzed. 70

Table VII.2. Trial nuclear events. 70

Table VIII.1. Probability of the satellites' suffering damage from prompt X-radiation. 79

Table VIII.2. The generalized elements, malfunctions and susceptibilities of surveillance sensors. 88

Table VIII.3. Degradation Thresholds of Various Detector Materials [Pickel, 2003]. 89

Table VIII.4. Example of information received from a SNRTACS run. (Information has been reformatted to fit on page.) 91

Table VIII.5. First day average fluxes ($m^{-2} s^{-1}$) of low energy (40 keV < E < 250 keV) and high energy (E > 250 keV) electrons from high L-shell bursts. 94

Table VIII.6. Timescale for charge deposition in insulator. 96

Table VIII.7. Coverglass parameter ranges. 96

Table VIII.8. Thermal blanket parameter ranges. 97

Table VIII.9. Fluence for various high-yield events. 98

Table VIII.10. Results table for coverglass in NOAA/DMSP orbit, event 17. 100

Table VIII.11. Table of results for exterior layer of thermal blankets with grounded front surface. 101

Table VIII.12. One-year fluences of electrons (cm^{-2}) with energy over 0.25 MeV. Color coding indicates severity of damage to solar cells. 102

Table VIII.13. Middle East Events. 103

Table VIII.14. Far Eastern Events. 104

Table VIII.15. Hawaiian Events. 104

Table VIII.16. GPS constellation radiation accumulation (rads) as of 23 May 2003. 106

Table IX.1. Economic Benefits of Weather Satellites. 113

Table X.1. Collateral Effects, Uncertainties, and Confidence for Satellites. 118

Table X.2. Uncertainties in Nuclear Effects on Satellites. 132

CHAPTER I
INTRODUCTION

Use of a high altitude nuclear detonation as an electromagnetic pulse (EMP) attack on a terrestrial target may generate both immediate and long-term radiation threats to Earth-orbiting satellites. In support of *The Commission to Assess the Threat to the United States from Electromagnetic Pulse Attack,* this paper was written to examine potential collateral damage to satellites from high altitude nuclear detonations. It is an analytical study of enhanced radiation environments produced by high-altitude detonations above various geographical regions, and their effects on representative satellites conducting long-term missions of both military and civilian importance. Threats were chosen to be representative of those we believe appropriate in a time frame ranging from the present to 2015. We believe this is the first paper to examine systematically collateral effects on satellites from an EMP attack executed in virtually any region of the Earth. Effects of both (a) direct radiation from a detonation as well as (b) subsequent effects of an enhanced trapped-electron population, will be addressed.

The salient issues examined in this paper are:

- What categories of satellites are vulnerable to malfunction or damage, immediately and ultimately?

- How long would satellites not immediately damaged by prompt radiation continue to function in the hostile electron belt environment?

- How does damage depend on weapon design and yield, and on the altitude and location of a detonation?

- What are the regrets for loss (temporary and permanent) of satellites in orbit?

- At what point in time would the nuclear-enhanced space environment cease to pose a threat to either a satellite or its mission?

- What satellites should be considered expendable and which should be hardened?

- What are appropriate levels of hardening?

The last two issues are subjective in nature and are addressed only peripherally herein. However, we do seek to provide enough information to raise the level of awareness of evolving threats and to assist decision makers toward realistic appraisals of vulnerabilities and longevities of satellites should they be exposed to a nuclear-enhanced radiation environment.

It is important to recognize that a satellite is part of a larger system that includes ground stations that issue instructions to the satellite, transmit and receive communications traffic from it as a relay, and act as reception facilities for the data that the satellite's sensors collect. Ground stations are at risk from EMP effects, and the medium through which a satellite's radio signals propagate can also be disturbed for as long as several hours due to ionization of the atmosphere by the nuclear burst. In this paper we principally address effects on satellites themselves.

There is little question that unhardened satellites are vulnerable to high-altitude nuclear explosions. It is a recognized fact that any country or organization with sufficient technology, missile lift, and guidance capability can damage or destroy a satellite in orbit using a number of different weapons and kill mechanisms. Some military satellites are hardened against credible radiation threats and all satellites are hardened to withstand the natural space radiation environment for their required lifetime in orbit. However, there is a tendency to judge an EMP threat as unlikely, and to make investments in mitigation of other threats a higher priority.

An extensive scientific and engineering literature deals with the phenomenology and effects of nuclear and space radiation on satellites. The *I.E.E.E Transactions on Nuclear Science* from 1963-2003 contains a comprehensive set of papers that document the growth and depth of the state of the art. Papers from the I.E.E.E. Annual Conference on Nuclear and Space Radiation Effects have traditionally been presented in the December issue. The *Journal of Geophysical Research* publishes scientific research on the theory and observation of space radiation.

Space radiation consists of energetic electrons, protons, and heavy ions originating from many sources, including (a) primary and secondary cosmic rays; (b) direct solar emanations as well as particles energized via the interaction of the solar wind with Earth's magnetic field; and (c) particles trapped by Earth's magnetic field for periods of days to years, forming the "Van Allen belts." Contemporary satellites are hardened against the anticipated exposure to space radiation during their design lifetime.

In the late 1950s and early 1960s there were sixteen high altitude nuclear detonation experiments, some of which contributed substantial additional trapped radiation, changing the morphology of the Van Allen electron belts, increasing their intensity, and hardening their energy spectrum. At least eight satellites that were in orbit during this time were damaged by long-term effects of nuclear-enhanced trapped radiation. Their modes of failure are well documented in the technical literature and are discussed in Chapter IV. There are also papers that treat the ramifications of these "pumped" belts on the current satellite population [Webb 1995, Pierre 1997, Cohn 2001, Keller 2002] and others that examine the effects of direct radiation from high altitude detonations on military satellites [DTRA EM-1, Northrop, 1996].

Owing to the specific charter of the Commission, emphasis of this paper must be confined to collateral damage from an EMP attack. It is acknowledged that a direct attack upon a satellite opens many issues beyond the study reported herein. In cases where there are threats beyond the scope of this paper, we can only acknowledge them and suggest sources for further study.

CHAPTER II
STATEMENT OF THE PROBLEM

Satellite systems today provide cost-effective services that permeate the foundations of contemporary society, economy, and civil infrastructure in many, if not most, developed countries. They provide telecommunications services that are central to today's globally integrated economy; they provide "big picture" data required by modern climate monitoring and weather forecasting. Satellite-borne sensors monitor agricultural conditions worldwide and provide data upon which yield forecasts are based, thereby making the market more efficient and stabilizing agricultural economies.

Today there are approximately 1000 Earth orbiting satellites and of this number approximately 550 are in Low Earth Orbit (LEO).

Table II.1. Examples of Active LEO Assets by Mission (US Assets in Blue) May 2003

Intel	Earth/Ocean/ Atmosphere	Weather	Space Science	Nav Search and Rescue	Comms
NRO	AQUA	NOAA	HST	Nadezhda	Iridium
Ofeq	TERRA	DMSP	Galex	Cosmos	Globalstar
Helios	Envisat	Meteor	ISS		Cosmos
IGS	Ikonos		FUSE		
Quickbird	EO-1		TRACE		
Cosmos	SPOT				
ZY-2	TRMM				
TES	Orbview-2				

The United States has a large investment in satellite systems and enormous societal and economic reliance on telecommunications, broadcast, and sensor services for civil infrastructure. Unlike most nations, the United States heavily utilizes space-based assets for military and intelligence purposes. Early satellites with military and intelligence functions were dedicated systems, but with the evolution of technology and driven by satellite economics, a mix of dual-use satellites (*e.g.*, Global Positioning System, GPS) and leased commercial satellite services (*e.g.*, Ikonos, QuickBird, and Iridium) have become vital.

The overwhelming majority of satellites in orbit are designed, built, launched, and operated by commercial enterprise. Because the pace of technological change grinds relentlessly, there is strong economic incentive to maximize financial returns from expensive satellites within a few years after launch—before a competitor appears in orbit with superior capabilities at lower cost. Hazards of the natural space environment are known with relative certainty, and protection against those hazards is an integral part of spacecraft design. Hardening commercial satellites against even one high-altitude nuclear explosion—admittedly an unlikely event in the world view of most investors—would raise costs, reduce financial benefits and, given limits on booster payloads, quite possibly reduce satellite capabilities and competitive position. In the absence of an incentive, commercial satellite operators are happy to maximize profitability and to discount a small perceived risk of loss due to a nuclear detonation.

Satellite vulnerability to high-altitude nuclear explosions is not a question of whether an adversary *would* detonate a weapon as hypothesized, but instead turns entirely on questions of technical feasibility. *Could* an adversary—either a nation state or a nongovernmental entity—acquire nuclear weapons and mount a credible threat? The answer is unquestionably "Yes." One must assume both nuclear weapons and delivery systems are available to credible adversaries now and will continue to be so for the foreseeable future. For those that elect to purchase rather than develop nuclear weapons and delivery systems, technically capable and willing purveyors are available. North Korea, for example, has nuclear reactors to produce plutonium in quantity, missile technology sufficient to reach well beyond Japan, and a track record as an active trader in the international arms market. With an economy in shambles, a desperate need for hard currency, a repressive government not subject to checks and balances of an informed populace, and a ready market, there is little doubt that further proliferation of nuclear weapons and delivery systems is likely. As geopolitical circumstances change and as alliances evolve, the mix of proliferants will undoubtedly change.

Throughout this investigation there have been continuing questions dealing with economic regrets associated with the loss of civilian satellites and tactical regrets associated with the loss of military space assets. Questions about the latter are much easier to answer than those dealing quantitatively with the Gross Domestic Product.

CHAPTER III
SATELLITE POPULATIONS

There are approximately 1000 active satellites in Earth orbit providing a wide variety of services. Approximately 330 satellites in geosynchronous (GEO) orbit (35,786 km altitude over the Earth's equator) provide critical communications, intelligence surveillance, and large scale weather observation services. Because GEO satellites remain stationary over a particular location, they are always available for service to that region. Nearly all international TV broadcasts and data exchange activities (banking transactions, etc.) go through geosynchronous satellites. Because a geosynchronous satellite "hovers" over a specific region, continuous monitoring of that region for national security purposes or weather forecasting is possible.

Approximately 30 Global Positioning System satellites (GPS), orbiting at 20,200 km altitude and 55 degrees inclination, provide critical navigation services to both the international community (airline and ship navigation) and the U.S. military. Smart bombs used in Operation Iraqi Freedom would have been ineffective without critical guidance information from the GPS satellite constellation.

Although GEO and GPS satellites are critically important to U.S. military and economic security, it is satellites in Low Earth Orbit (LEO) that will dominate most of the discussion in this paper. These satellites are the ones that would be most affected by a high altitude EMP burst. (GEO and GPS satellites are unlikely to be severely damaged by EMP bursts having less than multi-megaton yields.)

LEO satellites perform vital services for the United States. From a National Security standpoint, reconnaissance satellites, both government and commercial, provide global monitoring of trouble spots around the world. These satellites are critical assets to aid the War on Terrorism. LEO weather satellites provide critical data for both civilian and military purposes. These satellites complement the suite of weather satellites in GEO orbit by providing much higher spatial resolution of weather patterns as well as providing weather observations at extreme latitudes inaccessible to GEO satellites. Earth and ocean monitoring satellites, such as TERRA and AQUA, provide multi-spectral observations of land and sea to monitor ocean currents, pollution, fish movement, ice formation, land erosion, soil moisture content, health status of vegetation and spread of disease, as examples. These data have both economic and military value. During the Iraqi Freedom operation, Earth resources satellites were used to monitor dust storms that have a major effect on military air operations. From a national prestige point of view, satellites such as the Hubble Space Telescope, Space Shuttle, and the International Space Station (ISS) are a source of pride and inspiration to Americans. They are a symbol of America's preeminence in the world. LEO mobile communications/data satellite constellations such as Iridium, Globalstar and ORBCOMM provide unique services to both commercial and military users by allowing communications anywhere in the world using small handheld devices.

There are approximately 550 satellites from numerous countries in LEO performing missions like the ones described above. Figure III.1 shows the division of satellites among various mission categories. Communications and messaging satellites dominate the figure because a constellation of several dozen satellites is required to assure complete and constant coverage over the entire globe. Such large constellations are expensive to launch and maintain, which is why organizations backing constellations such as Iridium and Globalstar have passed through bankruptcy. The unique aspects of these satellites, however, have appeared to rescue economically at least one and possibly more of these constellations. In late 2000, the U.S. government issued a contract to Iridium Satellite LLC to procure unlimited mobile phone service for 20,000 government users. If contract options are exercised, the total procurement will be worth $252M and extend out to 2007 [Space News, 2000].

Intelligence, weather and Earth/ocean monitoring satellites make up 22.5% of the LEO population. As mentioned before, many of these 120+ satellites provide critical economic and military information. The 25 or so navigation satellites are used primarily by Russian shipping vessels; many of these satellites are also equipped with search and rescue beacons to pinpoint the locations of all downed light aircraft, ocean vessels in distress, and lost campers having search and rescue transmitters. About 28 satellites are dedicated science missions monitoring the Sun, Earth's magnetosphere and geodesy, and the far reaches of space. Manned space endeavors are included in this category. The last category consists mainly of small amateur radio satellites and demonstrations of new technologies in space. There are about 83 of these satellites.

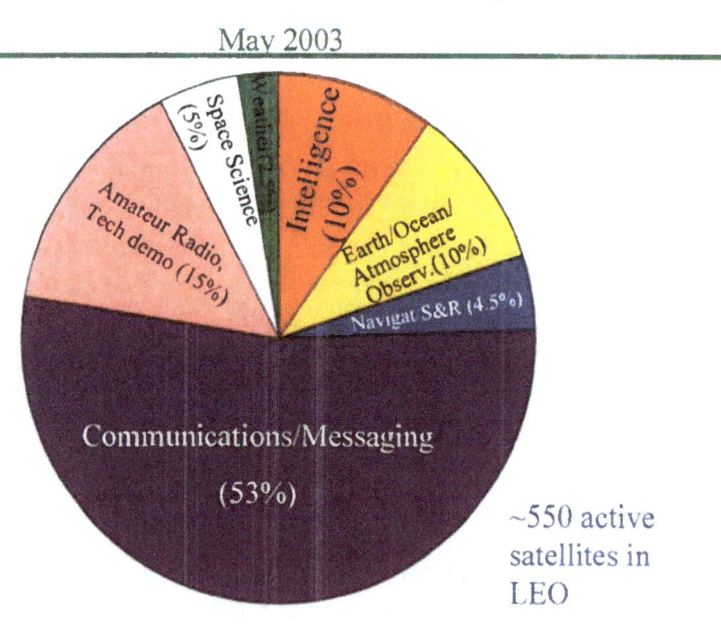

Figure III.1. Distribution of low-Earth orbit satellites by mission.

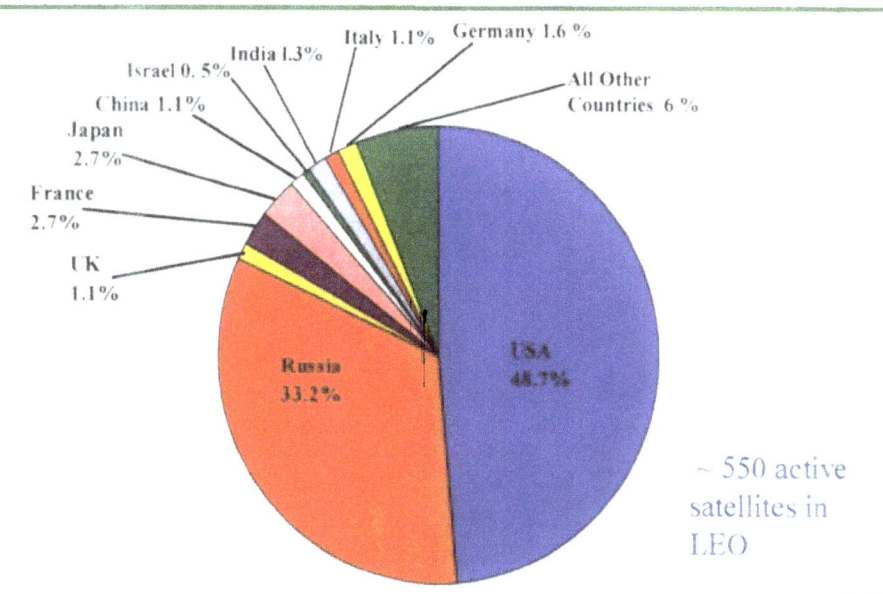

Figure III.2. Distribution of low-Earth satellites by country.

Figure III.2 shows the distribution of low-Earth orbiting satellites by country. Nearly half of all LEO satellites are U.S. owned or are primarily used by the U.S. About one-third belongs to Russia. The remainder is distributed among numerous other nations.

Figure III.3 shows the distribution of U.S. owned/used satellites by mission. Note the large percentage of assets that have a mobile voice/messaging and data transfer mission. The bulk of these assets consist of the Globalstar, Iridium and Orbcomm constellations. These systems have had a difficult time establishing themselves as financially viable over the last several years, but that trend may be reversing. Iridium currently has a contract with the U.S. government. Globalstar's 2003 first quarter revenues were triple what they were a year ago, while losses fell more than 80%. Business at Orbcomm is doubling every 8 months, and the company is processing 60-70 contracts to provide messaging/tracking services for the trucking and shipping industry in addition to providing remote monitoring of gas and water meters. The total investment in these constellations of satellites is about six billion dollars.

Intelligence satellites in LEO provide important monitoring of hot spots around the world via optical, radar and electronic monitoring. Details of the constellation of LEO intelligence satellites are classified.

U.S. weather satellites in LEO include the civilian NOAA program and military Defense Meteorological Satellite Program (DMSP), each of which maintains several spacecraft in orbit at all times. Both of these systems employ visible, IR and microwave sensors to monitor weather patterns, ice conditions and sea state for civilian and military purposes.

Earth/Ocean/atmospheric monitoring satellites include satellites such as Landsat, TERRA, AQUA, Quickscat and SeaWIFs. These assets play an important role in long-term climatology studies as well as in monitoring pollution, crop health status, and the spread of infectious diseases. Many of these satellites played a critical role in recent military conflicts.

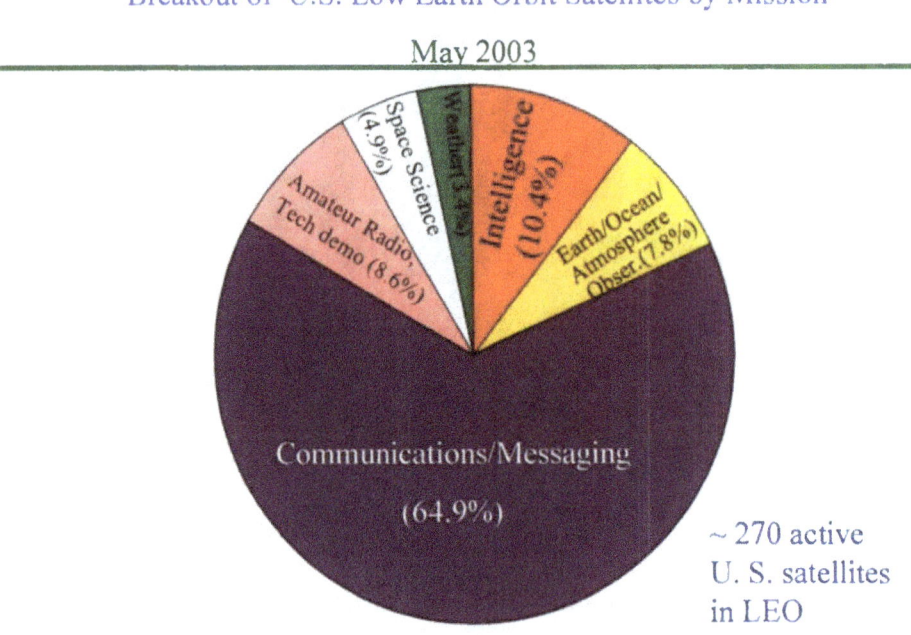

Figure III.3. Distribution of U.S. low-Earth orbit satellites by mission.

Table III.1 lists all U.S. owned/used LEO satellites and the estimated total dollar investment made in U.S. LEO satellites, including launch costs. Some entries, such as the number and value of NRO assets, are estimates based on unclassified information available. One can see from the table that the total U.S. investment in this area is approximately $90B with about half of that amount credited to the International Space Station (ISS). Although the total U.S. investment in LEO satellites is estimated to be on the order of $90B, it is probably unlikely that the U.S. would have to expend that dollar amount to return the LEO constellation to an acceptable level after a nuclear event. The International Space Station, which makes up the bulk of the $90B+ investment, is designed to be serviced by Shuttle crews and barring a direct nuclear attack on the asset, the Station could probably be salvaged for a fraction of the $47.5B listed in the table. In addition, some space assets, such as UARS and Topex-Poseidon, are at the end of their useful lives and would not be replaced or have already been replaced. In spite of these considerations, the U.S. would probably still have to spend about half ($45B) to recover assets considered important to science, national security, and the economy. This would include the NRO assets, expensive new science missions such as TERRA and AQUA, polar weather satellites such as NOAA and DMSP, and repairs to the large number of electronic components on the ISS which may require multiple Shuttle flights and hundreds of astronaut EVA hours.

8

Table III.1. U.S. LEO Satellite Investment.

Satellite	Number of Satellites	Satellite Cost ($M)	Number of Launch Vehicles	Launch Vehicle Cost ($M)	Total Cost ($M)
ACRIMSAT	1	13	1	14	27
Alexis	1	17	1	14	31
apex-1	1	22	1	6.5	28.5
AQUA	1	952	1	55	1007
ARGOS	1	162	1	55	217
CHIPSAT	1	14.5	1	27.5	42
Coriolis	1	224	1	35	259
DMSP	4	1816	4	140	1956
EO-1	1	193	1	50	243
ERBS	1	200	1	250	450
EYESAT	1	3	1	5.5	8.5
FAISAT-1	1	5	1	5	10
FAISAT-2	1	5	1	5	10
FALCONSAT	1	0.5	1	0.5	1
FORTE	1	35	1	15	50
GALEX	1	16.5	1	14	30.5
FUSE	1	100	1	60	160
GFO	1	85	1	23	108
Globalstar	52	2392	14	564.9	2956.9
GRACE-1	1	70	1	8	78
GRACE-2	1	70	1	8	78
HESSI	1	40	1	14	54
HETE-2	1	9	1	15	24
HST	1	3000	1	500	3500
ICESAT	1	200	1	27.5	227.5
IKONOS-2	1	60	1	22	82
IMAGE	1	39.8	1	55	94.8
IRIDIUM	72	3500	15	1500	5000
ISS	1	40000	15	7500	47,500
JASON-1	1	185	1	27.5	212.5
JAWSAT	1	0.23	1	3	3.23
LANDSAT-4	1	400	1	55	455
LANDSAT-5	1	400	1	55	455
LANDSAT-7	1	666	1	55	721
M-1	1	10	1	4.33	14.33
M-2	1	10	1	4.33	14.33
MICROSAT-1	1	0.5	1	1	1.5
MICROSAT-3	1	0.5	1	1	1.5
MTI	1	150	1	23	173
MUBLCOM	1	7.5	1	7.5	15
NOAA-12	1	454	1	35	489
NOAA-14	1	454	1	35	489
NOAA-15	1	454	1	35	489
NOAA-16	1	454	1	35	489
NOAA-17	1	454	1	35	489
NRO	24	12000	24	6696	18696
OPAL-1	1	0.5	1	0.5	1

Satellite	Number of Satellites	Satellite Cost ($M)	Number of Launch Vehicles	Launch Vehicle Cost ($M)	Total Cost ($M)
OPS-1292	1	500	1	500	1000
OPS-8737	1	500	1	500	1000
ORBCOMM	36	180	11	154	334
ORBVIEW-1	1	5	1	14	19
ORBVIEW-2	1	43	1	14	57
ORBVIEW-3	1	60	1	14	74
OXP-1	1	0.5	1	0.5	1
PCSAT	1	0.5	1	0.5	1
PICOSAT-9	1	0.5	1	0.5	1
QUICKBIRD-2	1	60	1	55	115
QUICKSCAT	1	93	1	35	128
REFLECTOR	1	0.5	1	0.5	1
REX-1	1	6	1	6	12
REX-2	1	6	1	6	12
SAMPEX	1	35	1	9	44
SAPPHIRE	1	0.5	1	0.5	1
SEDSAT-1	1	0.5	1	0.5	1
SNOE	1	5	1	10	15
SORCE	1	85	1	14	99
STENSAT	1	0.5	1	0.5	1
STEP-2	1	100	1	14	114
SURFSAT-1	1	0.5	1	0.5	1
SWAS	1	64	1	14	78
TERRA	1	1300	1	142	1442
TETHER-PICOSATS	1	0.5	1	0.5	1
THELMA	1	0.1	1	1.2	1.3
TIMED	1	207.5	1	27.5	235
TOMS-EP	1	29.3	1	14	43.3
TOPEX-POSEIDEN	1	480	1	85	565
TRACE	1	39	1	14	53
TRAILBLAZER-2	1	10	1	8.5	18.5
TRMM	1	100	1	76	176
TSX-5	1	85	1	14	99
UARS	1	630	1	500	1130
Total		73971.93	158	20343.26	94315.19

CHAPTER IV
HISTORY OF DAMAGE TO SATELLITES

Hazards to satellites from both natural and nuclear-produced radiation environments are irrefutably demonstrated by data taken after high altitude nuclear tests in 1958-1962, frequent damage from solar events, and from 65 years of R & D. These experiences will be discussed in this chapter.

IV.A High Altitude Nuclear Tests

From 1958 until the atmospheric nuclear test moratorium in 1963, over a dozen high altitude nuclear tests were conducted (Table IV.1). Some of these tests produced minor, if any, radiation belts due to the low altitude and/or low yield of the detonation. Several, however, including the last three Soviet tests and the U.S. STARFISH PRIME test, produced significant belts that lasted from one month to several years. Table IV.1 lists test parameters for all of the high altitude detonations.

Table IV.1. HANE Events Chronology

SHOT NAME	DATE	LOCATION	ALTITUDE	YIELD
YUCCA	4/28/58	Pacific	Balloon, 26km	1.7kt
TEAK	8/1/58	Johnston Island	77km	3.8Mt
ORANGE	8/12/58	Johnston Island	43km	3.8Mt
ARGUS I	8/27/58	South Atlantic 38.5°S, 11.5°W	~500km	1-2kt
ARGUS II	8/30/58	South Atlantic 49.5°S, 8.2°W	~500km	1-2kt
ARGUS III	9/6/58	South Atlantic 48.5°S, 9.7°W	~500km	1-2kt
Soviet, K1	10/27/61	South Central Asia	150km	1.2kt
Soviet, K2	10/27/61	South Central Asia	300km	1.2kt
STARFISH PRIME	7/9/62	Johnston Island	400km	1.4Mt
CHECKMATE	10/20/62	Johnston Island	Hi. Alt., 10's of km	Low
Soviet, K3	10/22/62	South Central Asia	290km	300kt
BLUEGILL	10/26/62	Johnston Island	Hi. Alt., 10's of km	Sub Mt
Soviet, K4	10/28/62	South Central Asia	150km	300kt
Soviet, K5	11/1/62	South Central Asia	59km	300kt
KINGFISH	11/1/62	Johnston Island	Hi. Alt., 10's of km	Sub Mt
TIGHTROPE	11/4/62	Johnston Island	Hi. Alt., 10's of km	Low

IV.B Satellites Damaged by High Altitude Nuclear Tests

When the U.S. detonated the 1.4-megaton STARFISH PRIME device on 9 July 1962 at 400 km altitude, a total of 24 satellites were in orbit or were launched in weeks following (Table IV.2) [Astronautix.com; Weenas 1978; Jakes 1993].

Table IV.2. Satellites On Orbit at the Time of High Altitude Nuclear Tests.

Name	Launch Date (dd/mm/yy)	Operation Ceased	Period (Min.)	Perigee (KM)	Apogee (KM)	Incl (Deg.)
VANGUARD 1	17/03/58	ca/05/64	134.3	652	3965	34.3
TRANSIT 2A	22/06/60	ca/08/62	101.7	626	1070	66.7
SAMOS 2	31/01/61	21/10/73	95.0	483	563	97.0
EXPLORER 9 (Balloon)	16/02/61	09/04/64	118.3	636	2582	38.6
DISCOVERER 20	17/02/61	28/07/62	95.3	285	782	80.4
INJUN/SOLRAD 3	29/06/61	06/03/63	103.8	859	1020	67.0
MIDAS 3	12/07/61	?	160.0	3427	3427	91.1
MIDAS 4DSB	21/10/61	?	166.0	3311	3739	95.9
DISCOVERER 34	05/11/61	07/12/62	97.2	216	1025	82.7
TRANSIT 4B	15/11/61	02/08/62	105.6	950	1110	32.4
TRAAC	15/11/61	12/08/62	105.6	950	1120	32.4
SAMOS 5	22/12/61	?	94.5	233	751	89.6
OSO 1	07/03/62	06/08/63	96.2	550	591	32.8
1962 H1	07/03/62	07/06/63	93.9	237	689	90.9
COSMOS 2	0/6/04/62	19/08/63	102.5	212	1559	49.0
MIDAS 5	09/04/62	?	153.0	2785	3405	86.7
COSMOS 3	24/04/62	?	93.8	298	330	65.0
ARIEL 1	26/04/62	ca/11/62	100.9	390	1210	53.9
1962(SIGMA)1	15/05/62	?	94.0	290	645	82.5
COSMOS 5	28/05/62	?	102.8	203	1599	49.1
1962 OMEGA1	18/06/62	?	92.3	377	393	82.0
TIROS 5	19/06/62	04/05/63	100.5	591	972	58.1
1962 (GAMMA) 1	27/06/62	14/09/62	93.7	211	640	76.0
COSMOS 6	30/06/62	08/08/62	90.6	274	377	49.0
TELSTAR	10/07/62	21/02/63	157.8	955	5656	44.8
EXPLORER 14	02/10/62	08/10/63	2185	278	98850	33
EXPLORER 15	27/10/62	09/02/63	314.7	310	17300	18
INJUN 3	13/12/62	03/11/63	112.1	238	2389	70.3
RELAY-1	13/12/62	00/02/65	185.1	1310	7390	47.5
TRANSIT 5A	18/12/62	19/12/62	91.4	333	344	90.6
ALOUETTE 1	29/09/62	?	107.9	993	1040	80.5
SAMOS 6	7/3/1962	06/08/63	93.9	235	681	90.9
ANNA 1B	31/10/62	?	107	1151	1250	50

Table IV.3 shows that at least eight satellites suffered damage that was definitely related to the STARFISH PRIME event [Weenas, 1978]. This damage was studied and documented in the scientific literature.

Table IV.3. Satellites Damaged by High Altitude Nuclear Tests.

SATELLITE	TIME IN ORBIT	DAMAGE
TRAAC	15 Nov 61 - 12 Aug 62	• 1120 km x 950 km/32.4^0 • Solar cell damage due to STARFISH PRIME • Satellite stopped transmitting 36 days after the STARFISH PRIME event due to STARFISH PRIME radiation

Telstar-1	10 July 62 - 21 Feb 63	• 5656 km x 955 km/45^0
		• 7 Aug 62 - Intermittent operation of one of two command decoders
		• 21 Aug 62 - complete failure of the one command decoder
		• Intermittent recovery made via corrective procedures
		   – power adjustments to affected transistors
		   – continuous commanding
		   – modified commands
		• 21 Feb 63 - complete failure of command system
		   – end of mission
		• Lab tests confirm ionization damage to critical transistors

Explorer 14	2 Oct 62 - 8 Oct 63	• 98,850km x 278 km/33^0
		• problems encountered 10-24 Jan 63
		• Encoder malfunction-11 Aug 63-ended transmissions
		• After 8-9 orbits, solar cell damage:
		   – Unshielded p-on-n: 70%
		   – Unshielded n-on-p: 40%
		   – 3-mil shielded cells (both types): 10%

Explorer 15	27 Oct 62 - 9 Feb 63	• 17,300 km x 310 km/18^0 • minor short period encoder malfunctions • Undervoltage turnoff 27 Jan 63 • Second undervoltage turnoff 30 Jan 63 – encoder permanent failure
Transit - 4B	15 Nov 61 - 2 Aug 62	• 1110 km x 950 km/32.4^0 •Solar panels showed 22% decrease in output 25 days after the STARFISH PRIME event – Lead to demise of satellite
Alouette - 1	29 Sept 62 - ?	• 1040 km x 993 km/80^0 •Satellite place on standby status Sept 72 due to battery degradation • Satellite overdesign prevented failure, however degradation still occurred due to STARFISH PRIME.
OSO-1	7 March 62 - 6 Aug 63	• 591 km x 550 km/32.8^0 • Solar Array degradation due to STARFISH PRIME event • Provided real-time data until May 64 when its power cells failed
Ariel-1	26 April 62 - Nov 62	•1210 km x 390 km/$53.^0$ •Undervoltage condition occurred 104 hours after STARFISH PRIME event –Solar Cell efficiency reduced by 25% •Intermittent loss of modulation both on real-time telemetry and tape recorders –Speculation that this modulation problem was a result of a STARFISH PRIME - induced electrostatic discharge on the satellite
Anna-1B	31 Oct 62 - ?	•1250km X 1151Km/50^0 •Solar Cell deterioration due to STARFISH PRIME

The most celebrated victim of STARFISH PRIME was the world's first communications satellite, Telstar, which relayed voice and television signals across the Atlantic. Telstar was launched on 10 July 1962, one day after the STARFISH PRIME nuclear explosion. About one month after launch, there was an indication that one of two command decoders on board the satellite was failing. By utilizing modified and continuous commands to the satellite, the decoder was temporarily recovered. Complete failure of the command system did finally occur in February of 1963. Radiation tests were subsequently conducted on the ground and the failures were traced to a problem with certain npn transistors enclosed in nitrogen canisters. Furthermore, the failures were clearly determined to be a result of total dose ionization damage from high energy electrons. These transistors were part of the Telstar command decoder circuitry [Mayo, 1963]. Other satellites that failed (Transit 4B, TRAAC, Ariel, OSO-1, Anna-1B) did so as a result of a drastic loss of output power from critical solar arrays caused by high energy electrons from STARFISH PRIME [Fischell, 1963]. Figure IV.1 clearly illustrates the dramatic reduction in solar cell output power as a result of the STARFISH PRIME-induced radiation environment. Note that solar cell short circuit current on both the Transient Research and Attitude Control (TRAAC) and Transit-4B satellites suffered a dramatic drop right at the time of the nuclear event. A 22% drop in TRAAC solar cell current occurred over 28 days following the nuclear event. The same percentage drop in current occurred on the Transit-4B satellite over 20 days following the STARFISH PRIME detonation. Rapid deterioration of solar cells led to the demise of Transit-4B 24 days after the STARFISH PRIME event followed shortly thereafter with the loss of TRAAC 36 days after the nuclear event.

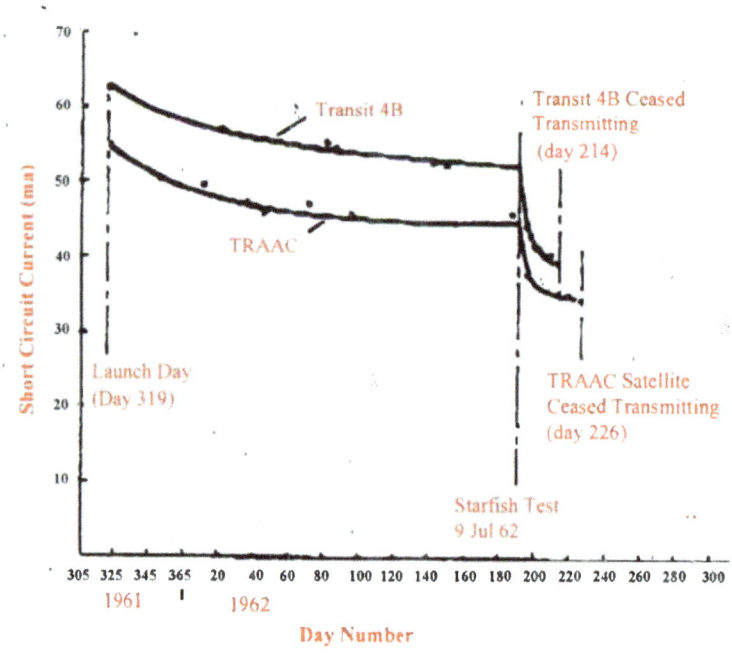

Figure IV.1 TRAAC and Transit 4B Solar Cell Degradation

Another satellite, the Canadian Alouette spacecraft, suffered damage from STARFISH PRIME radiation even though the satellite was over designed [Adamson, Sept 2002]. There was also considerable concern for human space flight since the human body was much more sensitive to radiation than satellite electronics. On September 5, 1962, President John Kennedy met with SECDEF McNamara, NASA officials and other experts to discuss upcoming high altitude nuclear tests and possible health repercussions for Mercury astronaut Walter Schirra who was scheduled to go into orbit a few weeks later. Concerns that Schirra might be exposed to unacceptably high levels of radiation if high-altitude tests were conducted lead the administration to postpone further testing until after the mission [Presidential Recordings Project, Fall 2001]. A few days after Schirra's flight, an Air Force spokesman announced that Schirra would have been killed by residual STARFISH PRIME radiation if he had flown above 640 km altitude [Grimwood].

There were other satellites on orbit at the time of STARFISH PRIME, but there is no documentation that these satellites suffered any problems from radiation. There are several potential explanations for this. It is quite possible that many of these satellites did indeed suffer problems but these facts were not documented or were documented at one time and then the information was lost. For example, very little documentation exists on the TIROS-5 satellite. The failure of the medium-angle weather camera on the satellite, one day before the STARFISH PRIME event, may have significantly lowered the load on the electrical system which could have masked any solar array degradation problems caused by STARFISH PRIME [Weenas, 1978]. Some satellites were U.S. classified space assets and Soviet spacecraft. In both cases, security factors would have limited the amount of public documentation about any satellite anomalies on these satellites. In addition, much of the electronics in a Soviet satellite were enclosed in a relatively thick, pressurized module for convective cooling purposes. This would require a thicker spacecraft structure to maintain pressure integrity [sputnik1.com; russianspaceweb.com]. The extra shielding thickness would have further protected internal electronics from damage by fission electrons and thus Soviet satellites at that time may have been more resistant to nuclear radiation than their U.S. counterparts.

IV.C Failures Resulting from the Natural Radiation Environment

Over the years, scores of satellites have been upset, degraded, or destroyed just due to the natural radiation environment (see Figure IV.2). Many of the satellite failures were caused by electrostatic discharge (ESD) events caused by deposition of low energy electrons on the exterior of the satellite. One (indirect) source of these electrons is Coronal Mass Ejections (CMEs), which are huge quantities of plasma blown off from the sun that sometimes intersect the Earth's magnetosphere where they create magnetic storms. Probably the most famous ESD satellite failures were the two Canadian ANIK E-1 and E-2 satellites. These satellites provided important services for Canada, including news, weather, and entertainment programming. Daily newspaper information from a national news-gathering cooperative was interrupted for hundreds of daily newspapers. The temporary loss of these satellites also interrupted telephone and cable TV service in Canada [Solar-Terrestrial Energy Program, 1994]. Both ANIK satellites suffered a failure in momentum wheel control circuitry needed to maintain attitude control for critical antenna positioning. ANIK E1 was eventually able to switch to its backup control circuitry. However, both the primary and backup control circuitry for ANIK E-2 failed and the satellite was unusable for seven months until a rescue plan could be put in place to allow continuous ground-commanded control using precious attitude control fuel on the satellite.

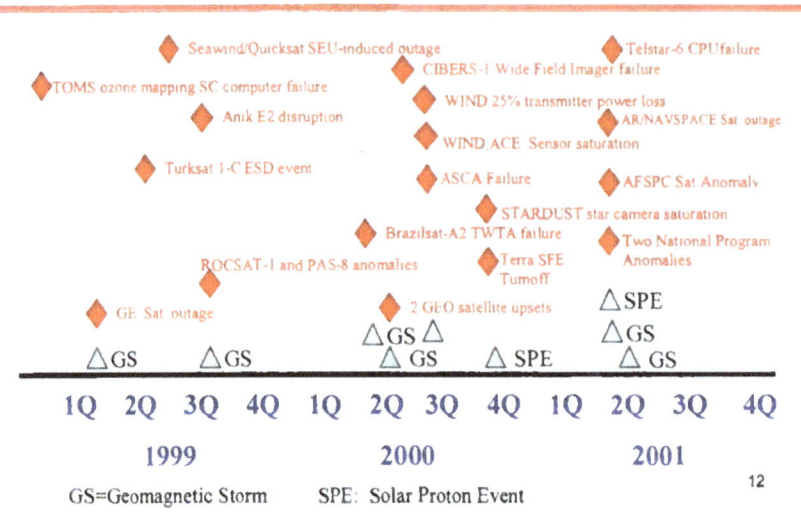

Figure IV.2 Chronology of Satellite Anomalies and Space Weather Events.

IV.D Laboratory and Underground Nuclear Testing

The Atmospheric Test Ban Agreement of 1963 stimulated strong technology programs within the Department of Defense and the National Aeronautics and Space Administration to investigate the nature of radiation effects on space systems and to find design techniques to mitigate them. One only needs to peruse the literature [IEEE Transactions on Nuclear Science and Engineering, 1963-2003] to appreciate the National efforts expended on technology to make our space assets appropriately survivable to a nuclear attack.

One could not perform radiation tests on complete satellites in orbit, but there had been a continuing effort to develop laboratory radiation sources to examine components and subsystems. Tests in these facilities were, and still are, referred to as Above Ground Tests (AGTs). AGTs were complimentary to Under-Ground nuclear Tests (UGTs) that were a closer approximation to above-ground detonation of a tactical nuclear weapon. In fact, all of these tests can, under the best of circumstances, only approximate a real tactical nuclear *environment* and are called *Effects Tests,* as opposed to *Environmental Tests*. The former can only be reliable if one understands the coupling of the radiation to the test objects.

The testing protocol was to use the best possible analytical method to predict the response of a constituent *material* to a test radiation. Then an actual radiation test was done to test the fidelity of the analysis. If the analysis was validated, another analysis was done to predict the response of a *component* made with this material and the component was tested in the radiation source. If this component prediction was validated, the prediction of the response of a more complete *circuit* would be made and that would be tested. This iterative process was conducted at increased complexity each time in the AGT and when the developer was satisfied, a final test was conducted in a UGT, after which the analysis was extrapolated to a tactical environment.

It was well recognized that the UGT was extremely expensive, difficult to instrument, and carried a high risk of failure, so as much as possible was done in AGT to make the risk as low as possible. One important feature of the UGT is that it forced the builder to do the necessary AGT homework in order to maximize the probability of a successful UGT. The testing and hardening process was expensive and restricted to military satellites whose missions were critical.

In the 1970s the Defense Nuclear Agency attempted to design and construct an X-ray test facility in which a full satellite could be tested, but budgetary considerations and Air Force opposition resulted in demise of the program.

In 1980 a test satellite called STARSAT (SGEMP Test and Research Satellite) was exposed to the X-rays from an underground nuclear detonation. The satellite model was constructed in order to study the iterative test and analysis protocols described above. The DSCS satellite Program Office provided much of the satellite structure, including some of the DSCS subsystems.

Figure IV.3. Experimental chamber containing STARSAT in the HURON KING event.

In this test the satellite was placed in a vacuum chamber as illustrated in Figure IV.3. The vertical tubular object on the right was connected to a vertical evacuated line-of-sight (LOS) pipe that extended from the buried nuclear device to the ground surface. The pipe contained a closure system that was automatically actuated immediately after the detonation-produced X-ray pulse arrived and before radioactive effluence could escape. The shed-like enclosure on the left of the structure contained signal conditioning equipment. Behavior of the satellite during exposure was monitored both in a remote trailer and also in the General Electric development laboratories in King of Prussia, Pennsylvania. The tracked wheels were to allow the whole configuration to be pulled away from the LOS pipe before the earth subsided after the detonation.

The experiment was highly successful, except for the misbehavior of an attitude control circuit. This malfunction was traced to an experimental artifact and confirmed in a subsequent UGT.

CHAPTER V
SATELLITE ENVIRONMENTS

V.A   Natural Radiation Environment

In terms of hazards to satellites, the principal aspects of natural radiation in space involve energetic particles of solar and magnetospheric origins. Particle populations of particular interest include energetic electrons, protons, and heavy ions with energies greater than about 10 keV that remain persistently trapped in the Earth's magnetic field. Highly energetic particles of galactic origins (a.k.a. cosmic rays) also contribute to the radiation environment.

The history of radiation belts surrounding the Earth begins in 1896 with experiments by Birkeland with beams of electrons in a vacuum chamber (cathode rays) directed at a magnetized sphere ("terrella") [Gillmor, 1997; Birkeland, 1901, 1908, 1913]. Birkeland suggested the problem to the French mathematician Poincaré who solved the motion of charged particles in the field of an isolated magnetic pole (*i.e.*, a magnetic monopole) and showed that charged particles were expelled from regions of strong magnetic field into regions of weak magnetic field [Stern, 1989, and references therein]. Birkeland's work captured the interest of auroral researcher Störmer who, through mathematical analysis, discovered that charged particles (*e.g.*, electrons, protons, ions) could be stably trapped within a static dipole magnetic field [Störmer, 1907]. Although mathematically elegant, Störmer theory did not prove the existence of radiation belts; it set the stage. Based on work by Störmer, Alfvén, and others, and on his experience with the Astron thermonuclear device, N. Christofolis in October 1957 suggested an experiment using a high-altitude nuclear explosion to create a persistent Earth-encircling shell of energetic beta particles (*i.e.*, relativistic electrons) trapped in the Earth's magnetic field [Christofolis, 1959, 1966]. The physical mechanism for trapping is the Lorentz force[1] exerted on electrically charged particles by a magnetic field, causing them to gyrate about magnetic lines of force. The Christofolis concept led to the proof-of-principle ARGUS series of three low-yield nuclear detonations conducted by the U.S. in August and September 1958 at high altitudes above the South Atlantic [Shelton, 1988]. Data obtained by the Explorer IV satellite and rocket probes fired from the ground definitively confirmed the "ARGUS effect", persistent trapping in the Earth's magnetic field of energetic electrons produced by high-altitude nuclear bursts.

Working independently of Christofolis, J. Van Allen and colleagues started in 1956 to construct radiation detectors suitable for use on satellites for purposes of studying cosmic rays [Van Allen, 1997]. The first of these detector systems flew in January 1958 aboard the Explorer I satellite. A more advanced instrument package was launched 26 March 1958 on Explorer III, Explorer II having failed to reach orbit. Data from Explorers I and III initially proved problematic owing to unrecognized saturation effects in the Geiger tubes used as radiation detectors. McIlwain's subsequent tests of the tubes and circuits in the beam of a small X-ray machine revealed the saturation effect, and it became possible to unravel the data

---

[1] The Lorentz force, mathematically proportional to the vector cross product of the charged particle's velocity and the magnetic field, results in a force perpendicular to both the particle velocity vector and the magnetic field vector. Consequently, the motion of charged-particle motion normal to the magnetic field is constrained such that the particle gyrates about magnetic field lines. The component of particle motion parallel (or anti-parallel) to the magnetic field is unchanged by the Lorentz force.

sufficiently to show existence of a persistent radiation environment in space surrounding the Earth [Van Allen, et al., 1958a, 1958b; Van Allen and Frank, 1959; Van Allen, 1997].

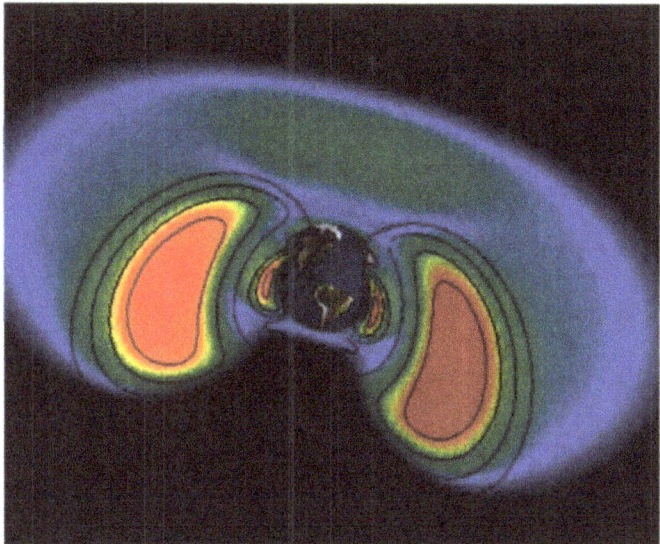

Figure V.1. Artist's conception of the trapped electron radiation belts that encircle the Earth. These belts are concentric donut-shaped where electrons are persistently trapped by the Earth's magnetic field. Protons and heavy ions are also trapped by the Earth's field. Note the "slot" region between inner and outer electron belts where the trapped-flux intensity is reduced relative to the peak interior regions of each of the two belts.

By virtue of numerous energetic particle detectors having flown on a variety of satellites, one understands the radiation belts around Earth to be composed of electrons, protons, and, to a much lesser extent, heavy ions. Figure V.1 illustrates an artist's concept of the natural distribution of energetic trapped electrons. Two radiation belts separated by a "slot" region of lesser flux intensity are shown. Figure V.2 provides a quantitative picture of trapped electron and proton populations as provided by the AE8 and AP8 models [Vette, 1991, Sawyer and Vette, 1976] of the belts. The AE8 and AP8 models are based on data from more than 20 satellites taken over the period from the early 1960s to the mid 1970s [Vette, 1991]. Contours in Figure V.2 represent levels of integral flux, *i.e.*, fluxes of particles with energies above specified energy thresholds (40 keV, 1 MeV, and 5 MeV for the electron plots; 100 keV, 10 MeV, and 50 MeV for the proton plots).

An important caveat applies to Figure V.2 and its underlying model interpretation. The AE8 and AP8 models represent *long-term averages* derived from satellite data. As long-term averages, some believe their accuracy to be on the order of a factor of two, but other contemporary researchers are finding substantially larger deviations based on more extensive radiation-belt surveys. For purposes of estimating electronic system tolerance of (and lifetime in) space radiation environments, it is common to assume "total dose" is a reliable surrogate for time-varying exposure and its consequences. The efficacy of this approach is device and system dependent, so it will not be argued here other than to note the underlying assumption and observe that *dose rate* is also known to be a significant factor.

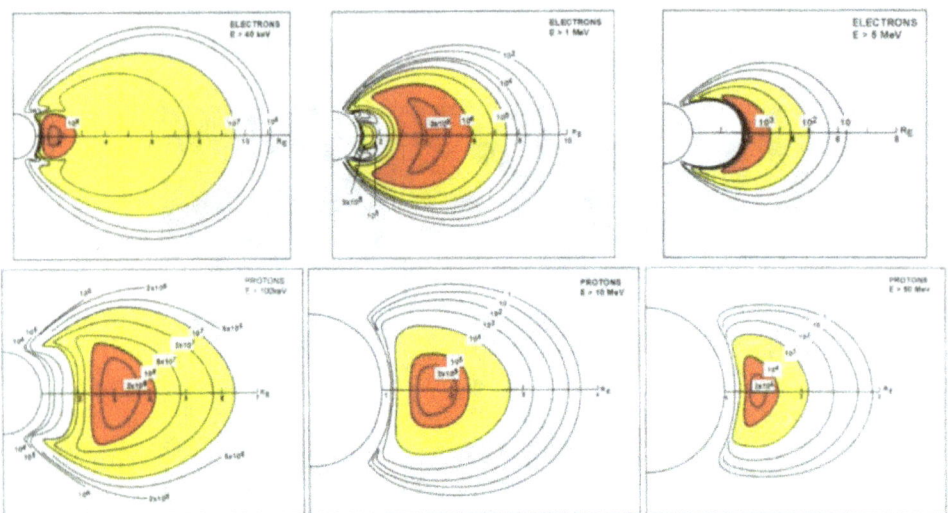

Figure V.2. Integral flux contours based on the AE8 and AP8 models for radiation-belt electrons and protons are shown. The AE8 and AP8 models represent long-term average conditions derived from data taken by more than 20 satellites over the period from the early 1960s to the mid 1970s.

Because nuclear-pumped radiation belts involve energetic electrons derived from beta decay of radionuclides resulting from fission reactions, the remaining discussion of this section will focus on trapped-electron radiation belts. Because energetic electrons from a nuclear burst are subject to the same influences governing natural belts, the behavior of the natural belts, particularly their variability, is central to the question of nuclear-pumped belts. Unfortunately, long-term-average models of the natural radiation belts provide a poor representation of day-to-day conditions encountered by satellites. This deficiency occurs because the belts are extremely dynamic and vary by several orders of magnitude about mean values. Satellite data provide the most definitive confirmation of this point.

The CRRES satellite[2] was launched in 1990 into an initial 350 km × 33,584 km elliptic orbit with inclination of 18.1 degrees and orbital period of 10 hours. This orbit enabled instruments on CRRES to measure the vertical profile of radiation belt fluxes twice per day, as the satellite passed through the belts on ascending and descending orbital phases. CRRES operated for 13 months before failing. Among its instruments the satellite carried a magnetic electron spectrometer, commonly known as MEA (Medium Energy Analyzer or Medium Electrons Analyzer), with 16 well-calibrated energy-discrimination channels coving the range from 110 keV to 1,633 keV. Representative differential electron flux data (electrons/cm^2-s-sr-keV) collected by MEA over its 13-month operational lifetime are shown in Figure V.3.

The plots in Figure V.3 require a little explanation to be meaningful. For each of the three panels the horizontal axis represents increasing time over the 13-month satellite lifetime. This axis is labeled by both orbit number and day-of-the-year referenced to 1 January 1990.

---

[2] The Combined Release and Radiation Effects Satellite (CRRES) was part of the SPACERAD program of the U.S. Air Force.

Each vertical axis is labeled with the McIlwain L parameter[3] [McIlwain, 1961] corresponding to the satellite location at the time the measurement was made. Thus, the vertical axis on each panel is effectively an equatorial-altitude scale, with L=1 corresponding approximately to the Earth's surface, L=2 corresponding to about 6,371 km altitude, etc. Each panel consists of a densely packed array of vertical color-coded lines that form the continuous bands of colors. Each vertical line represents a single pass by CRRES through the radiation belts. Color-coding along each line represents the instantaneous differential electron flux measured, with quantitative values indicated by the logarithmic color scale to the right of each panel. The vertical black band through the three panels is a period when data were not collected. Thus, CRRES/MEA data paint a continuous picture of the spatial distribution and temporal variability of the natural radiation belts.

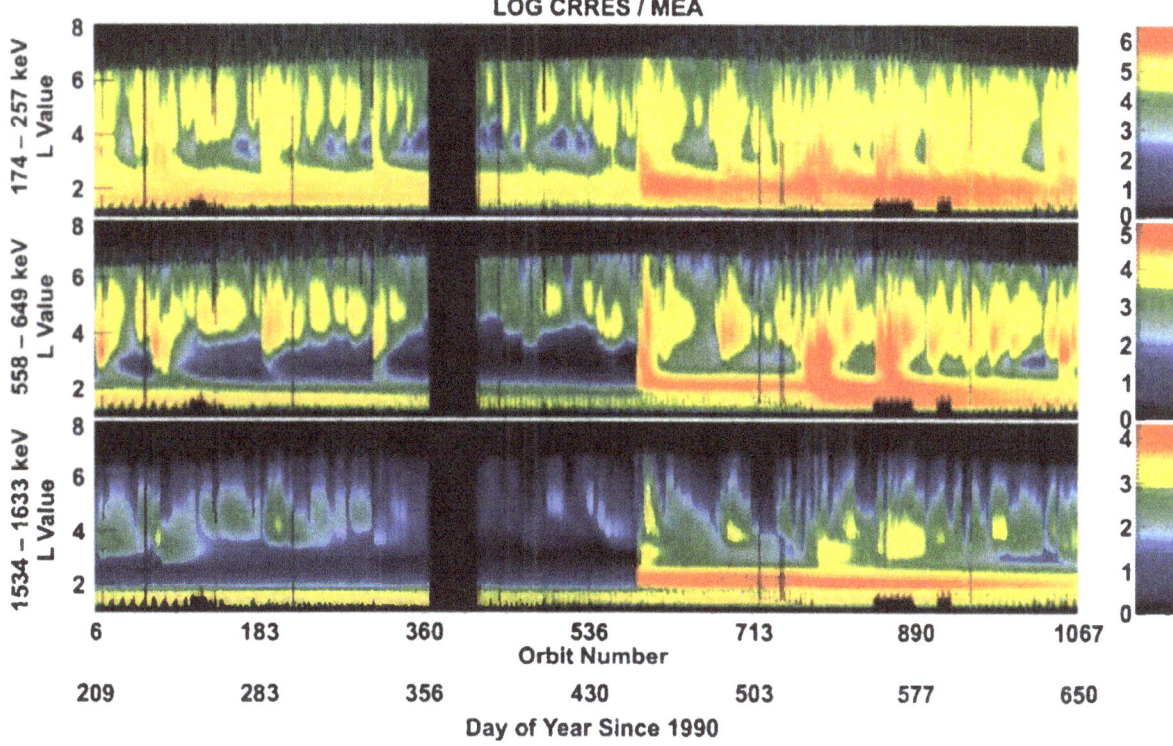

Figure V.3. Log_{10} of differential electron flux (electons/cm^2-s-sr-keV binned in 0.1L increments) as a function of time is shown for three of the 16 energy channels of the MEA instrument carried by the CRRES satellite. These data show the spatial distribution and continuously variable temporal characteristics of the natural electron radiation belts. Note the "slot" (dark blue generally centered near L=3 between inner and outer belts) often disappears in all of the energy channels when impulsive magnetospheric phenomena inject electrons into the trapping region. (Note: Mullen [2003] indicates lower energy channels of the detector were probably partially contaminated by higher energy electrons, but data are consistent with the high degree of natural variability of the radiation belts.)

Figure V.3 indicates the radiation belts to be highly dynamic, with temporal variability of trapped fluxes spanning several orders of magnitude. The entire 13-month data interval is filled

---

[3] The McIlwain L parameter, a.k.a. L or L-shell value, represents the radial distance from the Earth's dipole magnetic field source (at approximately the center of the Earth), measured in units of Earth radii ($R_E \sim 6,371.2$ km), at which a magnetic field line crosses the magnetic equator (*i.e.*, reaches its maximum distance from the magnetic center). Thus, a magnetic field line with L = 2 crosses the magnetic equator at a radial distance of about 2 R_E. One can convert to an approximate equatorial-crossing altitude H_L via the expression $H_L = (L-1) R_E$.

with repeated impulsive injections of energetic electrons into the belts followed by periods of decay. Clearly, long-term-average models do not provide an accurate day-to-day representation. Data indicate the outer electron belt (L ≈ 3 or greater) to be more variable than the inner belt (L ≈ 2 or less), but variability of the inner belt is undeniable. The "slot" between the belts (commonly taken to be L ≈ 2 to L ≈ 3) is, at least in the long-term-average picture, the region where fluxes are "supposed to be small" (in average terms), but data show the slot frequently filled by impulsive particle injections, sometimes to the point where the largest fluxes occur there. Lower-energy channels indicate higher fluxes with greater variability than higher-energy channels. Outer-belt decay times are on the order of a month; inner-belt decay times are on the order of a few months. Decay times are longer for higher-energy particles, particularly in the inner belt. Other data indicate similar variability of trapped electron populations (see for example, Li and Temerin [2001a] and Li, *et al.* [2001b]).

Electrons are injected into the radiation belts, often impulsively as shown in Figure V.3, by phenomena induced in the magnetosphere by shocks and other abrupt disturbances in the solar wind and its embedded interplanetary magnetic field (IMF), and by magnetic activity (e.g., substorms) in the magnetosphere. Active sites on the Sun that spawn coronal mass ejections, solar flares, and other disturbances in the solar wind and IMF often last longer than a solar rotation period (~ 27 days[4]), so radiation belt fluxes exhibit magnetospheric responses to multiple recurrent impulsive solar sources. Electrons are lost from the trapping region by several mechanisms, the most important of which is pitch-angle scattering by wave-particle interactions[5] throughout the volume of the belts and by collisions with atoms and molecules of the atmosphere at the inner edge of the inner belt [Able and Thorne, 1998]. To remain trapped, electrons must "mirror" (magnetically reflect upward) in the geomagnetic field at altitudes well above the atmosphere (*i.e.*, above ~ 100 km). Pitch-angle scattering randomly changes the mirror altitudes of electrons. When an ensemble of trapped particles is pitch-angle scattered, mirror altitudes for some of the particles will be reduced to below ~ 100 km where absorption by the atmosphere is likely. Thus, pitch-angle scattering generally leads to a loss of trapped particles. Loss rates are variable because the amplitude and spectrum of waves responsible for the wave-particle contribution to pitch-angle scattering vary with magnetospheric conditions. Similarly, the collisional contribution to pitch-angle scattering varies because atmospheric density above ~ 100 km responds to variable solar and magnetospheric energy inputs into the upper atmosphere.

To summarize, radiation belts exist as a dynamically shifting balance between source and loss rates, mediated by energization and transport processes throughout the volume of the trapping region. The "leaky bucket analogy" illustrated in Figure V.4 is appropriate. Nature provides both quasi-continuous and impulsive sources of charged particles feeding into the trapping region, along with loss mechanisms that drain trapped particles from the belts. Should a

---

[4] As the Sun is not a rigid body, its equatorial region rotates once in 24 days while the polar regions rotate once in more than 30 days.

[5] The pitch angle α of a charged particle in a magnetic field is the angle of the particle's velocity relative to the field direction, or $\alpha = tan^{-1}(V_\perp/V_\parallel)$ in terms of parallel and perpendicular components of particle velocity. Small values of α mean a particle is moving nearly parallel to the magnetic field direction and will "mirror" at a lower altitude than a particle with larger α. Electromagnetic waves interact with electrically charged particles and can, under certain resonance conditions, alter their pitch angles (*i.e.*, pitch-angle scatter them).

high-altitude nuclear detonation occur at a location suitable for belt pumping, it would abruptly add beta particles to the trapping region, leaving them to be removed at rates determined by natural loss processes.[6]

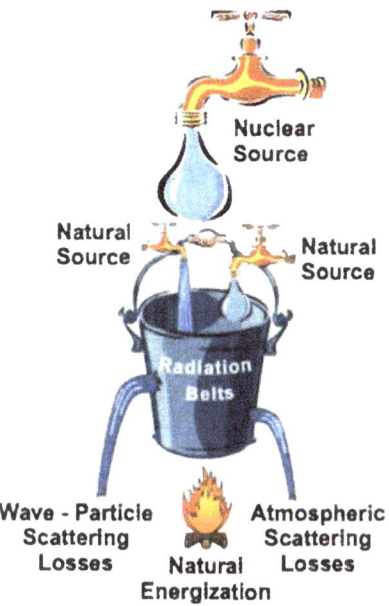

Figure V.4. Leaky bucket analogy for the radiation belts illustrated. Earth's magnetic field acts as a "container" to hold energetic particles (electrons, ions, protons, and lesser numbers of heavy ions) in a toroidal radiation-belt configuration about the Earth. Natural magnetospheric processes add energetic particles to the "container" both quasi-continuously and impulsively. Other processes (primarily scattering processes) drain trapped particles from the "container" continuously. Thus, the content of the "container" (i.e., the trapped flux) at any instant is determined by the history of the rates by which particles are added and removed. As discussed below, a high-altitude nuclear explosion would represent a potentially large additional impulsive source of energetic electrons.

High-altitude nuclear explosions and their creation of artificial, or nuclear-pumped, radiation belts must be considered in the context of natural radiation-belt behavior. After beta particles are emitted into the trapping region by beta decay of fission debris from a nuclear detonation, their behavior follows identically the physics governing naturally occurring energetic radiation-belt electrons. With the exception of the STARFISH PRIME high-altitude test (1.4 Mt at 400 km altitude), observed lifetimes of nuclear-pumped radiation belts are reported to be on the order of one month (less for the lowest L-shell bursts) [Walt, 1977]. Thus, the behavior of natural radiation belts, their variability, sources, and loss rates on time scales comparable to lifetimes of nuclear-pumped belts, is consequential to satellite vulnerability to nuclear detonations.

---

[6] However, contemporary research into "radiation-belt remediation" is examining possible use of radio transmitters on the ground or in space to increase trapped-electron loss rates above natural values by increasing the power-spectral density of low-frequency waves in the trapping region. An adequate and cost-effective level of efficacy remains to be demonstrated.

V.B Environments Created By a High-Altitude Nuclear Detonation

The enormous energy released by a nuclear detonation produces widespread and dramatic changes to the environment. In tenuous atmosphere above 100 km altitude, low air density leads to large mean-free paths—hundreds of kilometers or more for some energetic emissions from nuclear bursts—so large volumes of the upper atmosphere and space may be exposed to significant levels of energetic nuclear emanations. Given a focus on nuclear burst effects germane to satellites, it is beyond the scope of this paper to consider in detail the myriad of burst interactions that alter the environment. The summary in Table V.1 characterizes the important high-altitude burst regimes and provides a sense of how interactions between the atmosphere and nuclear burst energies change with burst-point density (*i.e.*, altitude). White [1986] contains a technical review of many of the processes summarized in this table. However, White's technical review does not discuss the phenomenology of low-Alfvén-Mach-number[7] debris expansions (bursts above 400 to 600 km altitude) because that is an emerging contemporary research topic as this paper is in preparation.

Table V.1   Nuclear Burst Regimes by Altitude.

Burst Regime	Nominal Altitude Range	Nominal Range of Air Density	Representative Characteristics Other Than EMP	Representative Nuclear Tests
Low-Alfvén-Mach-Number Debris Expansion	> 400 to 600 km	< 2×10^{-15} g/cc (highly variable depending on solar and magnetospheric conditions)	Energetic debris ions at high velocity (up to ~ 2000 km/s); Capable of strong pumping of radiation belts; Large fraction of radioactive weapon debris lofted 1,000's km altitude; Little conversion of debris kinetic energy to energetic air ions and electrons; Up to 55% of burst kinetic yield radiated as hydromagnetic waves; Relative to lower-altitude bursts, less extreme environment for RF scintillation and other radio wave propagation effects and less severe optical background for infrared/optical sensors.	None for which substantial data were collected; possibly ARGUS III qualifies but limited data were collected.
High-Alfvén-Mach-Number Debris Expansion	~ 250 to 400-600 km	~5×10^{-14} g/cc to 2×10^{-15} g/cc (highly variable depending on solar and magnetospheric conditions)	Energetic debris ions at high velocity (up to ~ 2000 km/s); Shock-accelerated air ions and hot electrons; Capable of strong pumping of radiation belts; Strong conversion of debris kinetic energy to energetic air ions and electrons that travel along geomagnetic field lines to deposit energy in the atmosphere between ~ 100 to 300 km altitude to form intense patches of ionized air and optical backgrounds that potentially can interfere seriously with RF propagation and infrared/optical sensors for hours after detonation; Radioactive weapon debris may be dispersed over global-scale area above 100 km, particularly for large-yield detonations.	STARFISH PRIME
Ultraviolet Fireball	~ 90 to 250 km	~3.5×10^{-9} g/cc to 5×10^{-14} g/cc	Capable of strong pumping of radiation belts; Strong conversion in debris-air blast wave of debris kinetic	

---

[7] In the context of weapon debris expanding away from a burst point, the Alfvén Mach number is the ratio of initial debris speed to the local Alfvén speed associated with the background ionosphere. The Alfvén speed associated with the background ionosphere is a characteristic speed of ionospheric plasma, much as the speed of sound is a characteristic speed of gaseous and other media. When something moves though the atmosphere at a speed less than the speed of sound, it is sub-sonic; if it moves faster than the speed of sound, it is super-sonic. Similarly when weapon debris (or anything else) moves at less than the Alfvén speed, it is sub-Alfvénic, but if it moves more rapidly than the Alfvén speed, it is super-Alfvénic.

Burst Regime	Nominal Altitude Range	Nominal Range of Air Density	Representative Characteristics Other Than EMP	Representative Nuclear Tests
		(varies depending on solar and magnetospheric conditions)	energy to ultraviolet photons that are absorbed by surrounding air to form intensely ionized ultraviolet fireball; Radioactive weapon debris largely contained within fireball; Persistent air ionization may last for 10 hours or more at densities sufficient to produce significant RF scintillation and other propagation effects.	
X-ray Fireball	< 100 km	1.2×10^{-3} g/cc to 6×10^{-10} g/cc (from the ground to ~ 100 km altitude)	Bursts above ~ 50 km capable of pumping radiation belts to varying degrees; Fireball formation dominated by absorption of burst-generated X-rays in air surrounding burst point; Fireball rises buoyantly (lower portion of altitude range) or ballistically (higher portion of altitude range); Radioactive weapon debris contained within fireball; Ionized air within fireball tends to recombine in tens of seconds to form hot, largely un-ionized fireball gas.	TEAK, ORANGE, BLUEGILL, TIGHTROPE, and other atmospheric bursts

V.B.1 Direct Weapon Emissions

V.B.1.A. Photons

V.B.1.a.i   X-rays

Unless a weapon is particularly massive, upon detonation its energy generation mechanisms raise its temperature to sufficiently high values that it radiates as much as 70 to 80 percent of the available energy as X-rays with a spectrum that approximates a blackbody. Figure V.5 illustrates the radiant power versus wavelength for blackbodies of different radiating temperatures.

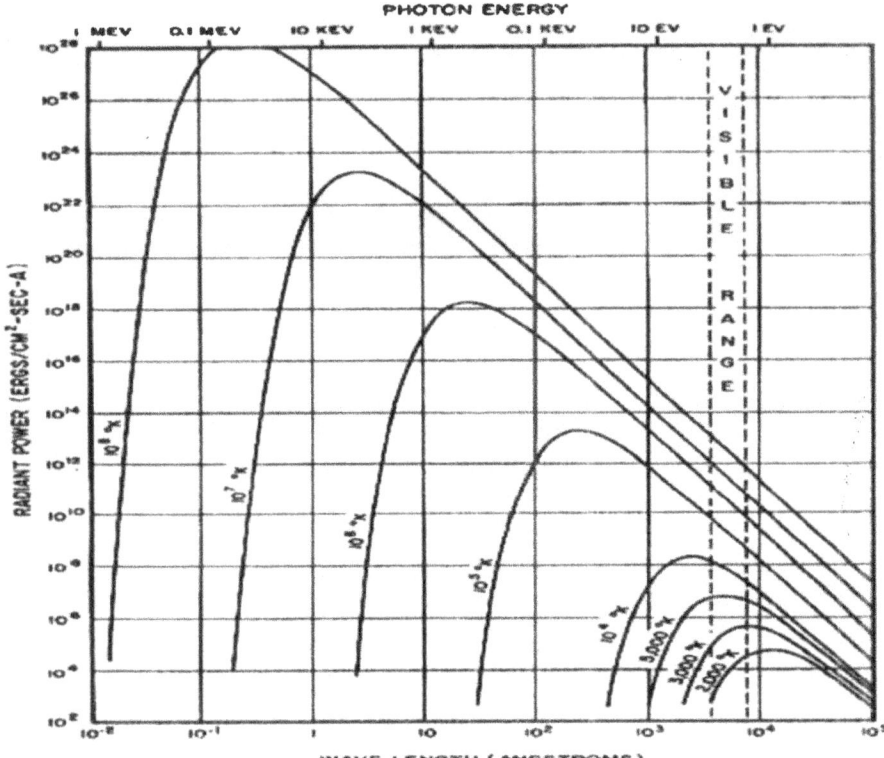

Figure V.5. Radiant power versus wavelength for blackbodies with various effective radiating temperatures (From Glasstone, *Effects of Nuclear Weapons, Fig.7.74*). Note that 1 eV is equivalent to 11,604 degrees Kelvin.

The range of X-rays in the atmosphere and the fraction of the X-ray yield that can escape to space depend strongly on X-ray temperature of the device and on burst altitude (*i.e.*, on air density surrounding the burst point). Figure V.6 illustrates X-ray fluence as a function of altitude measured along a vertical line through the burst point for detonations at 60, 80, 150, and 200 km altitude. For each burst altitude, the figure provides curves corresponding to X-ray temperatures of 0.5, 1, 2, and 3 keV plus a (dashed) $1/R^2$ reference curve. One notes that the lower-temperature X-ray spectra are absorbed relatively close to the burst point for detonations at the lower altitudes (*i.e.*, bursts in higher density air), but as the burst altitude is raised, spectra of all temperatures escape without significant attenuation.

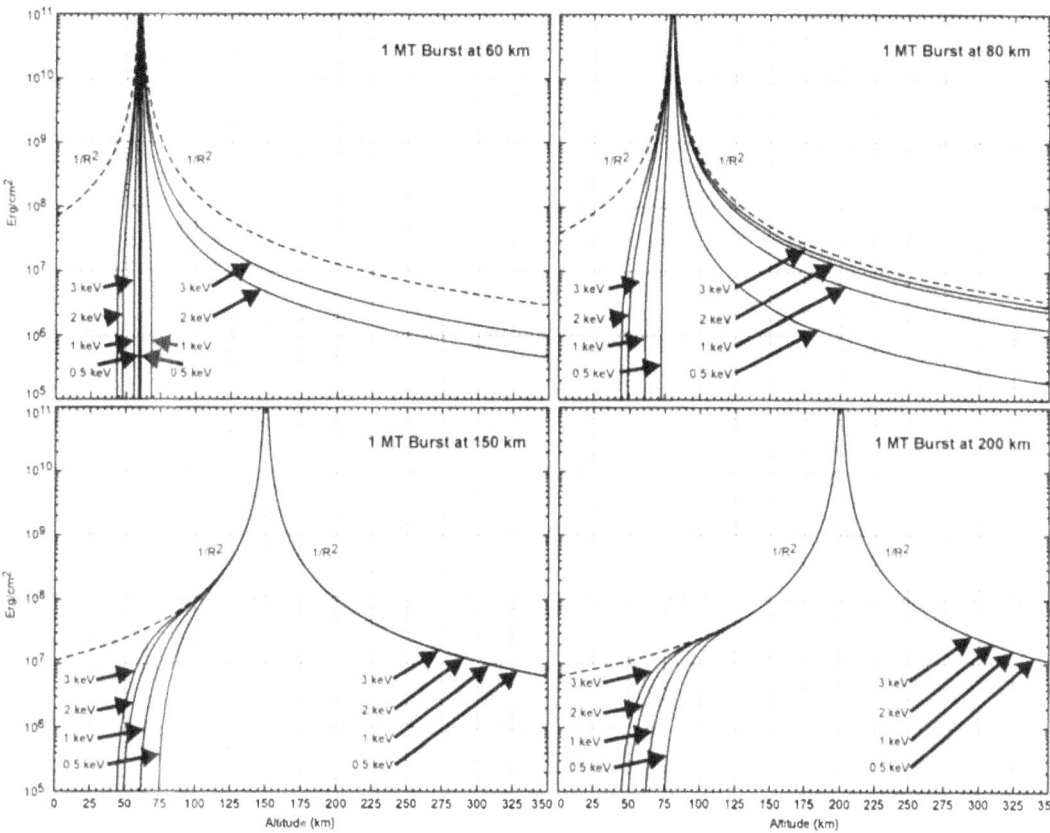

Figure V.6. X-ray fluence versus altitude as a function of X-ray temperature for detonations as altitudes of 60, 80, 150, and 200 km altitude as measured along a vertical ray through the burst point. Owing to higher air density at lower altitudes, X-rays emitted by a detonation at 60 km tend to be absorbed close to the burst point, with only the higher energy spectra escaping to space. Increasing the burst altitude (*i.e.*, decreasing the air mass above the burst) increases the fluence of X-rays that escape to space. For reference, dashed curves corresponding to a $1/R^2$ spherically divergent fluence are provided.

V.B.1.a.ii *Prompt Gamma Rays*

Excited nuclei, as are formed in a nuclear explosion, emit gamma rays, beta particles, neutrons, and other nuclear decay products as means of shedding excess energy and relaxing toward ground-state configurations. Gamma rays emitted during the short period when the exploding device is actively consuming nuclear fuels are termed "prompt" gamma rays. These may be partially absorbed within the exploding device, with the remainder escaping the weapon case to interact with the atmosphere to produce EMP or escape to space where they may irradiate satellites. The emitted gamma spectrum is a function of weapon design, as are the rise time, pulse length, and energy content of the gamma pulse—all factors beyond the scope of this paper. To quantify (approximately) prompt gamma emission, we note that a neutron-induced fission reaction of U235 will generate approximately 200 MeV of energy, the majority of which appears as kinetic energy of fission products, with roughly 7 MeV in prompt gammas. Specific weapon designs may be used to tailor, suppress, or enhance the emitted gamma spectrum. Figure V.7 shows representative normalized gamma ray spectra for prompt and delayed emission.

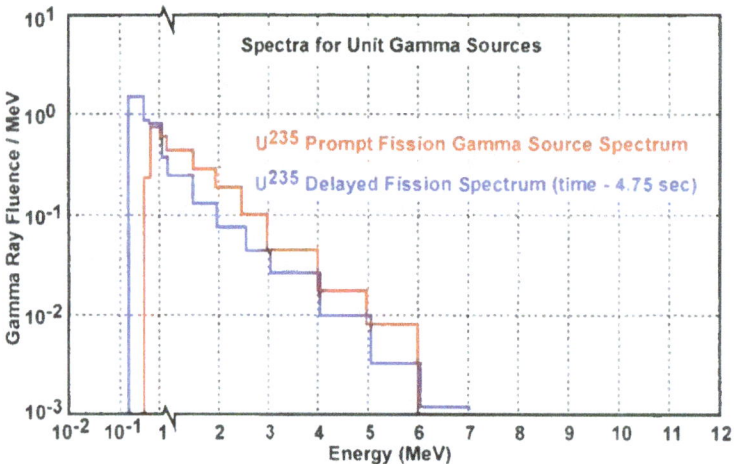

Figure V.7. Normalized spectra for prompt and delayed U^{235} fission gamma rays are illustrated. The delayed spectrum corresponds to 4.75 seconds after detonation. At later times the gamma ray spectrum further softens.

V.B.1.b   Energetic Particles

V.B.1.b.i   Neutrons

Nuclear reactions in an exploding weapon release free neutrons over a range of energies, with thermonuclear reactions generating neutrons with energies up to 14 MeV. Figure V.8 illustrates representative source spectra for neutrons emitted by fission and thermonuclear weapons, having average energies of about 1.2 and 2.6 MeV respectively. Elastic scattering of neutrons by atmospheric species shifts the spectrum toward lower energy if the detonation occurs within the sensible atmosphere.

Neutrons outside the nucleus have a half-life of 889 ± 2.1 seconds [Particle Data Group, 1992] decaying into a proton (which retains virtually all of the neutron's kinetic energy) and an electron (with average energy of about 0.25 MeV). A 14 MeV neutron takes 0.095 seconds to travel vertically from 50 km to 5000 km. During this time, 0.0074 percent of the neutrons will decay to protons and electrons. (This estimate is a lower limit, due to the assumptions of (a) maximum energy and (b) vertical trajectories.) While the fraction of free neutrons that will decay in the vicinity of LEO satellites may seem small, the fluence of energetic neutrons can be large. A fraction of protons and electrons issuing from neutron decay may become trapped in the Earth's magnetic field where they may dominate the post-event energetic-particle environment in their respective energy ranges. All of these energetic particles (neutrons, electrons, and protons) can, at sufficiently high fluences, damage satellites.

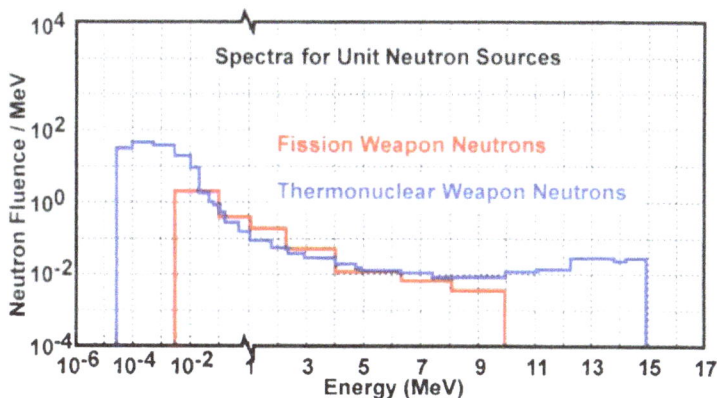

Figure V.8. Neutron spectra from fission and thermonuclear weapons are illustrated for unit neutron source.

V.B.1.b.ii *Debris Ions*

Materials of which the weapon, its aero shell, and any associated vehicle were constructed are vaporized, ionized, and expelled outward in a velocity spectrum with peak speed that may exceed 2,000 km/s. To put this into perspective, an iron ion (Fe^{+n}) moving at 2,000 km/s has a kinetic energy of about 1.16 MeV, an Aluminum ion (Al^{+n}) about 0.56 MeV, and a carbon ion (C^{+n}) about 0.25 MeV. These energies are sufficient to implant radionuclide ions permanently in exposed surfaces of a satellite where subsequent nuclear decay will provide a localized source of potentially damaging radiation. Even without considering disassembly characteristics of a weapon (possibly mediated by an attached booster or other massive object), the spatial distribution of energetic debris ions departs strongly from spherical symmetry at distances beyond a maximum-magnetic-bubble radius[8] (several hundred kilometers for large-yield weapons; see Hausman, *et al.* [1992] for quantitative information for the STARFISH PRIME test) owing to interactions between debris ions and the geomagnetic field. Magnetically collimated "beams" of high-speed debris ions with cross-field dimensions comparable to magnetic bubble dimensions occur when detonations occur at altitudes such that debris ions are effectively collisionless (*i.e.*, for bursts above ~250 km). For detonations above about 600 km altitude, debris ions may retain a significant fraction of their initial kinetic energy and constitute an implantation hazard to satellites. For detonations in the range from about 250 to 600 km, much of the initial debris ion kinetic energy will be expended in energization of air ions to energies as high as a few hundred keV and electrons to tens of keV. For detonations below about 250 km altitude, coupling between debris ions and the surrounding environment will convert initial debris kinetic energy to ionized, heated air (thermal particles), with the conversion efficiency increasing with decreasing burst altitude (increasing burst-point air density).

V.B.2 Induced Environments

Induced environments arise from interactions of direct weapon emissions at the time of detonation (gamma rays, X-rays, weapon debris) with the surrounding environment. Because mean free paths of direct weapon emissions are exceptionally long in the tenuous upper

---

[8] A magnetic bubble forms when a plasma of ionized species (debris and/or air) expand outwards from a burst point, carrying along the geomagnetic field outward and leaving a transient magnetic cavity (bubble) around the burst point.

atmosphere or in space, high-altitude nuclear detonations can profoundly alter the environment out to long distances from the burst point. Owing to the great energy and energy density available from a nuclear explosion, many different induced environments can result. Of these, some are of little consequence to physical integrity of satellites (but may inhibit functionality for seconds to hours) while others can materially alter the physical state of vital components. The latter category—direct material effects on satellites—includes electromagnetic pulse, energetic particles (ions and electrons), radiation belts, and induced photoemissions. Discussion of these follows below. The former category—inhibited functionality without physical damage—includes, for example, persistently ionized air that degrades radio signals (scintillation, absorption, etc.) and optical backgrounds that inhibit the operation of infrared and optical sensors (redout, optical clutter, etc.). Induced environments responsible for functional degradation without physical damage are beyond the scope of this paper.

V.B.2.a Electromagnetic Pulse

A nuclear detonation generates three varieties of electromagnetic pulse that, for historical reasons, have been arbitrarily designated E1, E2, and E3. E1 arises from the scattering of gamma rays by the atmosphere, principally at 20 to 40 km altitudes. Gamma ray scattering by atmospheric species generates Compton electrons that are emitted preferentially in the forward direction (same direction as gamma rays are traveling). Initial gyration of Compton electrons in the geomagnetic field generates a transverse electric current that radiates synchronously to produce a coherent electromagnetic pulse. Because the gamma pulse and electromagnetic pulse—each traveling at the speed of light—remain in phase, continuing Compton scattering strengthens the electromagnetic pulse as the gamma pulse weakens. Figure V.9 illustrates this process.

The E2 type of electromagnetic pulse arises from scattered gammas and from neutron-induced reactions in the air. Consequently, E2 follows E1 and has a lower frequency spectral content.

The E3 type of electromagnetic pulse (commonly called MHD-EMP) arises from two mechanisms that drive temporal variations in the geomagnetic field, thereby inducing very low frequency electric fields at ground level, as illustrated in Figure V.10. First, rapid expansion of ionized weapon debris forces the geomagnetic field outward from the burst point, creating a time-varying magnetic bubble that expands, then collapses over a period of a few seconds. Second, air heated by the detonation expands upward, carrying ionized air and weapon debris upward. Forceful upward motion of ions across the geomagnetic field also produces a time-varying magnetic field over an interval of tens of seconds to minutes. Time-varying magnetic signals generated by both mechanisms propagate from the burst region; upon reaching the ground, the associated inductive electric fields may couple to and induce electric currents in electric power transmission lines, pipelines, and other long-distance terrestrial systems.

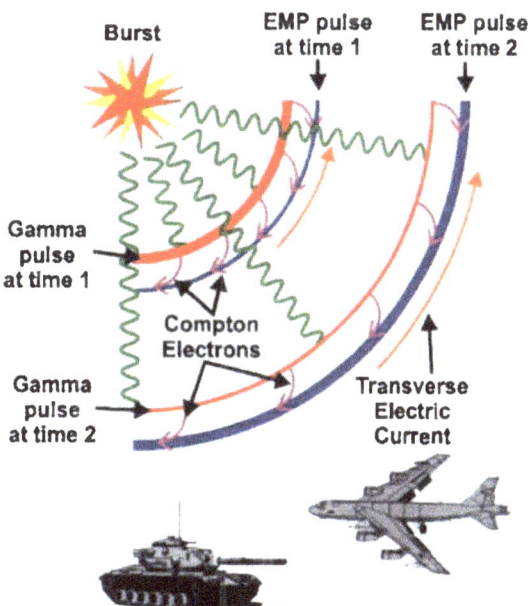

Figure V.9. E1 form of electromagnetic pulse is generated by scattering of gamma rays from air species, thereby producing Compton electrons that gyrate synchronously in the Earth's magnetic field to produce a transverse electric current that radiates a coherent electromagnetic signal. Both the gamma pulse and the electromagnetic pulse travel at the speed of light, so they remain in phase, and the electromagnetic pulse grows as the gamma pulse weakens.

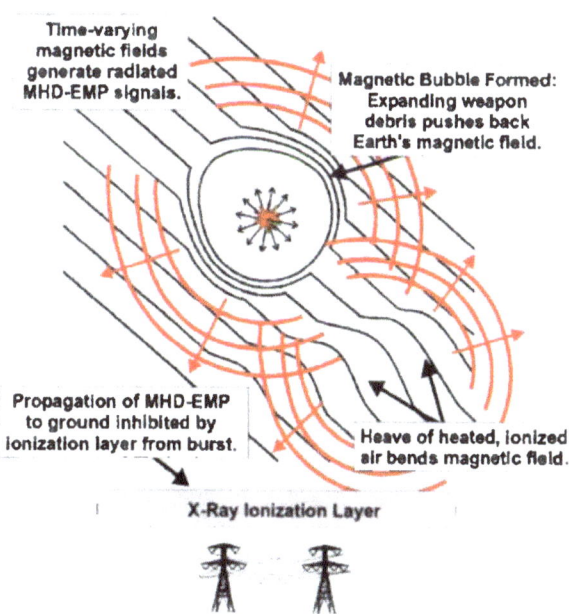

Figure V.10. MHD-EMP (a.k.a. E3) occurs when a high-altitude nuclear explosion creates time-varying magnetic signals that propagate to the ground and interact with large-scale electrical conductors such as electric power transmission lines and pipelines. Ionized weapon debris expanding from the burst point (along with ionized air that becomes entrained) push the geomagnetic field outward to form a time-varying magnetic bubble that lasts for a few seconds. Separately, upwelling air heated by the detonation drives ionized air and ionized weapon debris across the geomagnetic field, distorting it in a time-varying manner. Both of these processes produce the slowly varying, mHz range, magnetic signals responsible for E3 (MHD-EMP).

Each of the categories of EMP, E1, E2, and E3, has a distinctive time interval over which it is operative, and a corresponding spectral content. Figure V.11 illustrates these characteristics. The generation of EMP and its properties were reviewed by Longmire [1978].

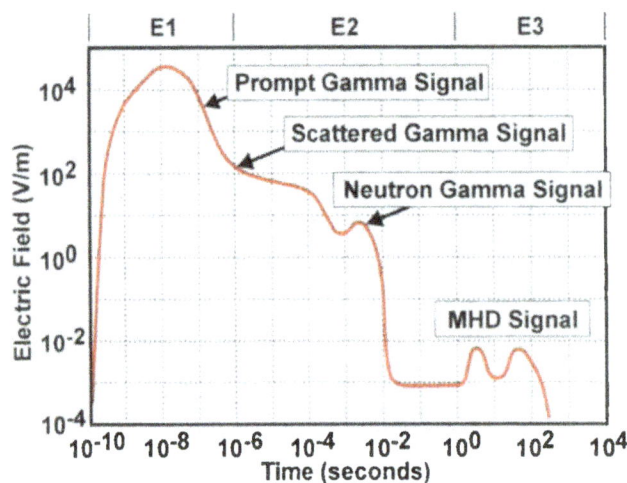

Figure V.11. Notional envelope of electric field (volts per meter) as a function time illustrates the three classes of electromagnetic pulse, E1, E2, and E3. (Graphic courtesy of J. Gilbert, Metatech Corp.)

V.B.2.b Energetic Particles

This category of Induced Environments includes energetic ions, electrons (including beta particles), and neutral (un-ionized) atoms that escape the immediate nuclear burst region (*i.e.*, blast wave region) with sufficient energy to produce multiple ionizing events upon impact with un-ionized species or materials. As defined, energetic particles have sufficient energy to alter materials with which they interact, and because they have escaped the immediate burst region, they may produce long-range effects. Detonations at altitudes from 50 km to above 1,500 km are considered.

V.B.2.b.i Sources of Energetic Heavy Ions

As noted in Table V.1, high-speed debris ions emanate from the exploding weapon at speeds that may exceed 2,000 km/s. Such ions have sufficient energy to implant themselves on satellite surfaces. For detonations above about 250 km altitude, the debris expansion proceeds in a largely collisionless manner, mediated primarily by the geomagnetic field and such surrounding air mass as exists in the zone of influence of the expanding debris. Figure V.12 shows a single photo of the high-Alfvén-Mach-number STARFISH PRIME debris expansion at 55 ms after detonation. The photo is replicated left and right, with the right frame annotated to describe features of the expansion process. Even without considering disassembly characteristics of a weapon (possibly mediated by an attached booster or other massive object), the spatial distribution of energetic debris ions departs strongly from spherical symmetry at distances beyond a maximum-magnetic-bubble radius owing to interactions between debris ions and the geomagnetic field.

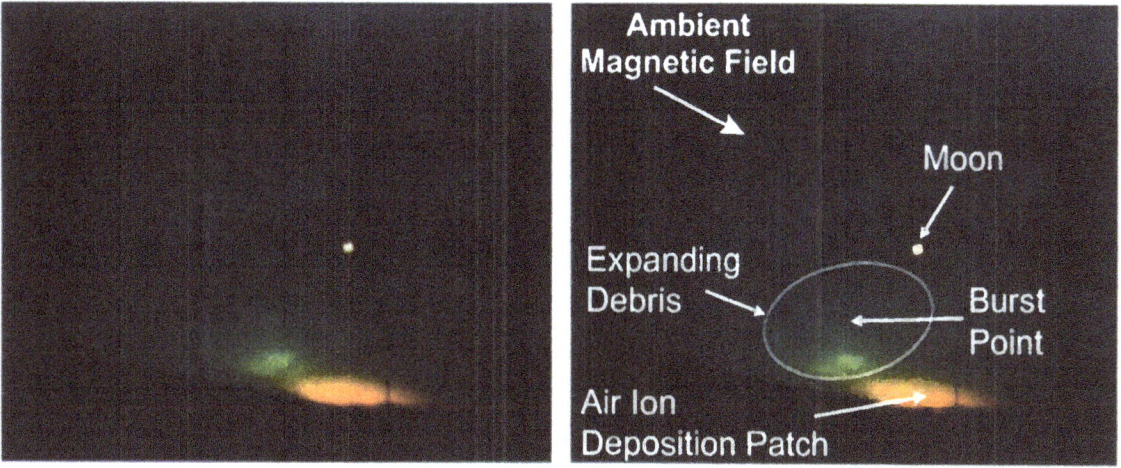

Distribution Statement C: Distribution authorized to U.S. government agencies and their contractors only.

Figure V.12. STARFISH PRIME detonation (1.4 Mt at 400 km altitude in vicinity of Johnston Island in mid Pacific) is shown at 55 ms as seen from Hawaii. Weapon debris initially expanding at speeds in excess of 2,000 km/s push the Earth's magnetic field away from the burst point to form a collisionless magnetohydrodynamic blast wave (ellipsoidal region in photo). At the periphery of the expanding blast wave, debris kinetic energy is transferred to air ions and electrons being over overrun. Energized air ions and electrons stream upward and downward along the geomagnetic field (direction of ambient field indicated in annotated photo). Downward-moving energetic air ions and electrons from the blast wave region encounter sufficiently dense air in the 100 to 200 km altitude range for collisions to stop them, the air there becoming heated and ionized sufficiently to produce the yellow air fluorescence seen in the photo. Upward-moving ions and electrons produce no readily visible air fluorescence because the air through which they are traveling is too tenuous. However, these air ions and hot electrons were observed to produce fluorescence in the atmosphere at the magnetic conjugate point in the Southern Hemisphere.

For detonations in the range from about 250 to 400–600 km, much of the initial debris ion kinetic energy will be expended in energization of air ions to energies as high a few hundred keV and electrons to tens of keV. A magnetically collimated flux of high-speed air ions, with some debris ions embedded, issues from a high-Alfvén-Mach-number detonation such as STARFISH PRIME in upward and downward directions along the direction of the geomagnetic field. These "beams" of high-speed ions can be tens to hundreds of kilometers wide (depending on yield). Fast air ions may undergo charge exchange reactions with cold neutral air species to produce energetic neutral species of like energies. For detonations below about 250 km altitude, coupling between debris ions and the surrounding environment can extract most of the initial debris kinetic energy and convert it to ionized, heated air (thermal particles). Thermal particles are of little consequence to satellites in terms of direct damage, save for possibly increased aerodynamic drag when heated air expands upward and increases by possibly several orders of magnitude the local air density for LEO orbits. For detonations above about 400 to 600 km altitude, detonations are in the low-Alfvén-Mach-number debris expansion regime. Debris ions may retain a significant fraction of their initial kinetic energy, expanding upward to very high altitudes (above 10,000 km for a 1 Mt detonation at mid latitude). As the URRACA test (~ 1 Mt above 1,000 km) planned as part of the 1962 Fishbowl series of Operation Dominic was cancelled by President Kennedy, there are little test data to guide theoretical studies or predictive modeling of low-Alfvén-Mach-number bursts, so this regime remains the most uncertain.

V.B.2.b.ii   Delayed Gamma Rays

Radioactive weapon debris—fission products and activated materials of the weapon and its carrier—emit delayed radiation, principally gamma rays and beta particles, well after the nuclear weapon has been detonated (hence the term "delayed") and at rates that decline with time after detonation. Energy spectra of the emissions soften (*i.e.*, shift to lower energies) with the passage of time as radionuclides cascade toward their ground states. Each radionuclide born in an explosion has its own specific decay properties [Parrington, *et al.*, 1996] with specific nuclear transitions (emission lines) evident in its gamma ray energy spectrum, but the aggregate delayed gamma ray spectrum from many different radionuclides and excitation states born in a detonation can be characterized as illustrated in Figure V.7. The spatial distribution of delayed gamma ray flux at 10 seconds after a 1 Mt detonation at 200 km altitude is illustrated in Figure V.13.

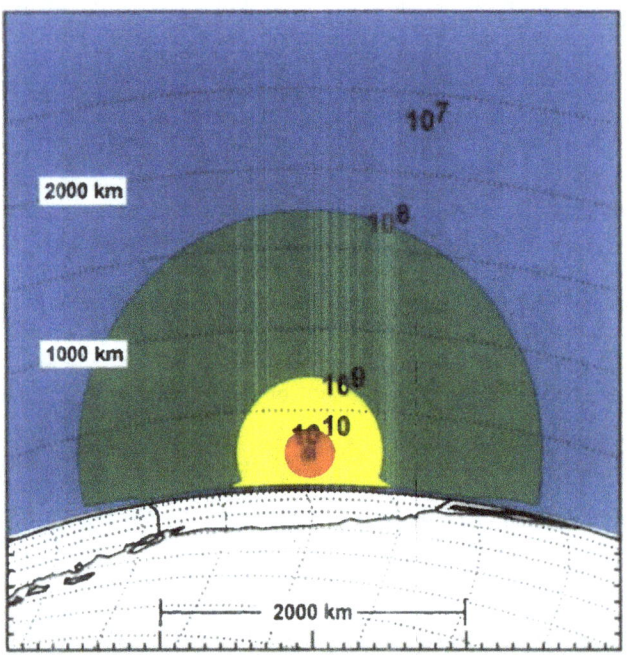

Figure V.13. Flux of delayed gamma rays (γ-cm^{-2}-s^{-1}) at 10 seconds after a 1 Mt nuclear detonation at 200 km altitude above the central United States. The view is from the west above the Pacific Ocean; the coasts of California, Oregon, Washington, and Canada are readily apparent. Departures from a purely spherical distribution in the downward direction result from multiple scattering and atmospheric attenuation.

V.B.2.b.iii   (Delayed) Beta Particles

Beta particles are energetic electrons emitted by beta-decay of radioactive weapon debris. Like delayed gamma rays, beta particles are emitted for the most part well after the nuclear weapon has detonated. Fission debris emits approximately six beta particles per fission event, so one kiloton of fission yield produces about 9×10^{23} beta particles. A nominal aggregate beta-particle energy spectrum (see Figure V.14) emitted by fission products includes electrons with energies from hundreds of keV to several MeV, with the spectrum extending above 7 MeV. The spectrum is most energetic immediately after the detonation and softens (shifts to lower energies) for betas emitted at later times. Details of the spectrum are dependent on the fissionable material used in the weapon and the energy spectrum of neutrons causing the fission reactions.

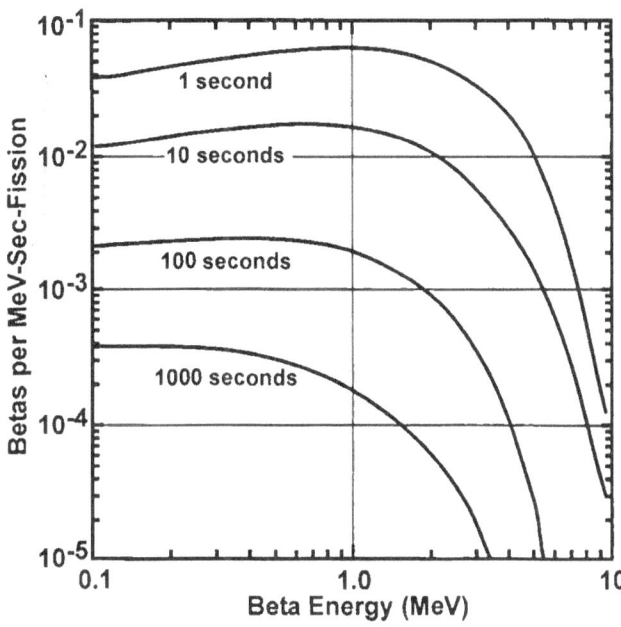

Figure V.14. Beta energy spectrum from fission of U^{235} by fast neutrons. The emission rate is noted to decrease slightly faster than the inverse of time in seconds after detonation and soften. Results are from the ORIGEN2 code [Croft, 1983].

In the absence of collisions with air atoms and molecules, beta particles are constrained by the Lorentz force[1] to move parallel and anti-parallel to magnetic field lines while gyrating around those field lines and (more slowly) drifting around the Earth. Beta particles with suitably small pitch angles emitted in the downward direction from above ~ 100 km travel to lower altitudes where collisions with air species extract their energy to produce ionized air and air fluorescence that constitute the beta tube (a.k.a. beta patch). Figure V.15 illustrates the beta tube produced by the KINGFISH detonation (1 November 1962). In this case, beta particles from radioactive weapon debris inside the fireball (white, overexposed region of photo) travel along (distorted) geomagnetic field lines to lower altitudes where collisions produce the violet-white beta tube in the photo. Bursts at lower altitudes (*e.g.*, TEAK at 77 km, 1 August 1958) will produce a visible upward-directed beta tube when air above the burst point is sufficiently dense that beta-air collisions produce visible fluorescence but not so dense as to absorb the beta particles close to the fireball.

Figure V.15. The KINGFISH high-altitude nuclear test above Johnston Island in the mid Pacific produced a brilliant visual display, including a prominent beta tube (violet-white region) below the fireball (white spheroidal region below the red cap of shock-excited atomic oxygen). Beta particles emitted by radioactive weapon debris inside the fireball traveled upward and downward along geomagnetic field lines that threaded the fireball. Those beta particles emitted downward encountered air sufficiently dense to produce visible air fluorescence, but (in this case) those emitted upward transited air too tenuous to produce a visible beta tube.

V.B.2.c Nuclear-Pumped Radiation Belts and Other Beta-Particle Effects

Just as naturally occurring energetic electrons are trapped in the Earth's magnetic field to form radiation belts, beta particles (energetic electrons) emitted by radioactive weapon debris can be magnetically trapped for extended periods. With approximately 9×10^{23} beta particles produced per kiloton of fission yield, even a low-yield nuclear weapon can be a copious source of energetic electrons. The trapped flux of beta particles realized after a detonation depends on the efficiency with which beta particles become trapped, the volume of space within which they are trapped, and the rate at which they are lost from the trapping region. We consider each of these points in turn.

Beta-particle trapping efficiency is at present not predictable with any degree of certainty owing to the number of physical variables that influence it, the difficulty of a comprehensive theoretical treatment, and limited availability of high-altitude nuclear test data. In near-Earth space, trapping occurs only on closed magnetic field lines[9] because only closed lines can support the mirroring process needed to maintain a trapped population of charged particles, and then only for particles with pitch angles sufficient to cause mirroring above the sensible atmosphere (~ 100 km for electrons). Beta particles can become trapped under several circumstances: (i) by

---

[9] Closed magnetic field lines are those that both originate and terminate in the Earth. This contrasts with open magnetic field lines that have one end in the Earth and the other dangling in space.

being born above ~ 100 km with a pitch angle sufficient for trapping, (ii) by being born above ~ 100 km with a pitch angle that does not support trapping, then being promptly scattered (by a collision or wave-particle interactions) to a pitch angle sufficient for trapping, or (iii) by being born below ~ 100 km, traveling upward to above ~ 100 km without being absorbed by the atmosphere, then being pitch-angle scattered as in (ii) when above ~ 100 km. Once trapped, a beta particle must avoid a pitch-angle scattering encounter with a random atom or wave-particle interaction that would place it in the loss cone (range of pitch angles for which electrons mirror below ~ 100 km and are likely to be absorbed by the atmosphere) from which it would be lost from the trapped population. The same scattering processes that cause trapped particle populations of natural origins to decay, as demonstrated by CRRES data in Figure V.4, also operate equally on beta particles (energetic electrons). (For further discussion of trapped electron lifetimes, see Abel and Thorne [1998].)

Circumstances (i) and (ii) require the detonation to take place above 100 km or at sufficiently high altitude that radioactive weapon debris will be transported to above 100 km within a few minutes after the detonation. The greater the mass of debris above 100 km, the greater the trapped population to be expected. Thus, the higher the burst altitude (within reason), the greater the expected trapped population of beta particles.

Circumstance (iii) applies to detonations with yields and burst-point altitudes such that debris is not transported above 100 km within a few minutes after burst. Collision cross sections of beta particles with air species are sufficiently small that beta particles originating from as low as 45 to 50 km altitude can reach 100 km altitude, largely unimpeded, provided their pitch angles are small (*i.e.*, their initial velocity is nearly parallel (anti-parallel) to the geomagnetic field). In such cases, circumstance (iii) can cause particle trapping.

While it is possible to enumerate circumstances for which beta particles can be trapped, it is far more difficult to compute trapping efficiencies that would be realized under realistic nuclear-burst conditions. The environment of the burst itself, involving complex debris transport processes and electromagnetic conditions, is beyond current capabilities to calculate with a degree of fidelity needed for viable trapping efficiency predictions. The problem is further exacerbated by electromagnetic variability of the natural space environment. As a practical matter, data from U.S. and Soviet high-altitude nuclear tests of 1958 and 1962 suggest trapping efficiencies in the range from about 10^{-7} to nearly 0.10 as inferred from [Walt, 1977]. We note, however, that these data apply to detonations within a narrow range of magnetic space (L shell parameter). Given known (and unknown) magnetic-field-line resonant phenomena in the magnetosphere, trapping efficiencies for bursts outside the range of L shells for which we have test data are considered to be highly uncertain.

The second factor controlling trapped particle flux from a high-altitude detonation is the volume of the trapping region. Even if latitude dependencies of initial trapping efficiencies are ignored, detonations of identical weapons at the same high altitude but at different magnetic latitudes should be expected to yield substantially different trapped fluxes. Both detonations would nominally produce the same inventory of beta particles, and in the absence of different trapping efficiencies, the higher-latitude detonation would yield a smaller trapped flux of beta particles. This point is readily understood by reference to Figure V.16.

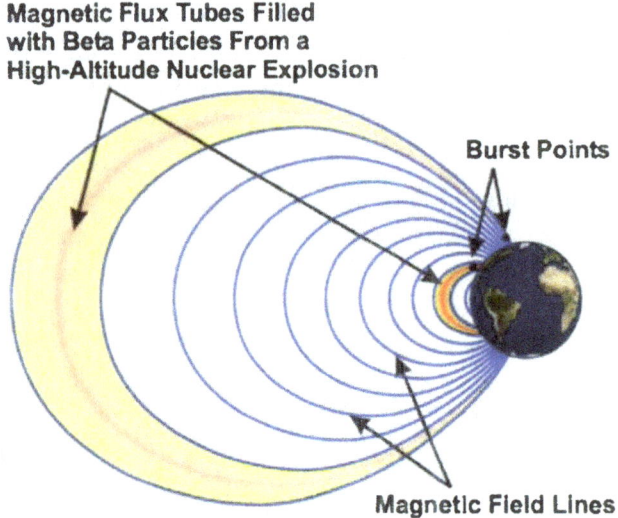

Figure V.16. The flux of trapped beta particles from a high-altitude nuclear explosion depends, in part, on the magnetic latitude of the detonation. On the basis of magnetic flux-tube volumes computed for a purely dipolar magnetic field and assuming equal trapping efficiencies, one expects a detonation at low latitude will produce considerably higher trapped flux compared to the same detonation at higher magnetic latitude. An inventory of beta particles injected into a small magnetic flux-tube volume will produce a greater particle flux than the same inventory injected into a large magnetic flux-tube volume.

One can readily quantify by analytic calculation the flux-tube volumes illustrated in Figure V.16 for a purely dipolar magnetic field. Because magnetic flux-tube volumes are three-dimensional, the figure must be interpreted as a two-dimensional representation of three-dimensional magnetic flux tubes that wrap around the Earth in longitude. Figure V.17 illustrates the ratio of circumferential differential magnetic flux-tube volumes for arbitrary magnetic L referenced to the circumferential differential flux-tube volume at L=6.6. This figure is based on flux-tube volumes above 100 km altitude with a differential extent of 100 km in magnetic latitude and a longitudinal extent of 2π. From Figure V.17 one sees that a low-latitude detonation such as STARFISH PRIME, if moved to sufficiently high latitude that the burst-point field line intersects geosynchronous orbit, would, on the basis of flux-tube volume arguments, produce peak trapped flux that is about $1/1000^{th}$ that observed in the actual STARFISH PRIME event. In the case of STARFISH PRIME scaled to such burst latitude, the expected geosynchronous trapped flux would be somewhat greater than measured natural fluxes of MeV-range electrons that rendered the AT&T Telstar 401 satellite permanently inoperable.[10]

---

[10] Conclusion is based on flux-tube volume scaling to geosynchronous orbit (L = 6.6) of Injun I data for trapped beta flux the day flowing the STARFISH PRIME detonation compared to GOES 8 and GOES 9 satellites data for geosynchronous particles fluxes immediately prior to the failure of the Telstar 401 satellite.

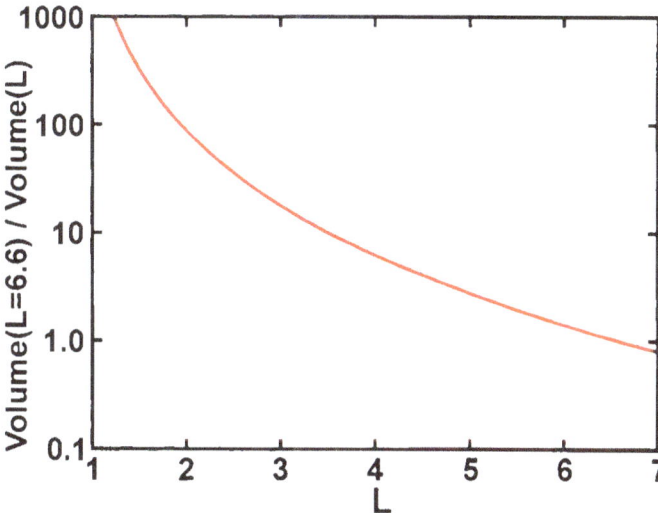

Figure V.17. Ratio of circumferential differential flux-tube volumes referenced to circumferential differential flux-tube volume for L=6.6. Circumferential differential flux-tube volume is the volume of a magnetic flux tube above 100 km altitude with latitudinal extent of 100 km at 100 km altitude and longitudinal extent of 2π.

The third factor controlling trapped beta-particle flux is the rate at which trapped beta particles are lost from the trapping region. It is important to recognize that a beta particle is an electron. Consequently, once a beta particle has been born by beta decay of a radionuclide, the behavior of the beta particle is governed by *identically* the same physics as any other electron. Loss mechanisms for electrons trapped in the natural radiation belts (discussed above) apply equally to trapped beta particles. In particular, the difficult-to-predict variabilities of the trapping environment and loss rates that one finds for the natural radiation belts apply equally to nuclear-pumped radiation belts, with the proviso that a high-altitude detonation may add a large, impulsive source of perturbations in atmospheric density profiles and electromagnetic environments that further complicate attempts to forecast radiation-belt environments.

Globally trapped beta particles are the most widespread and most persistent of radiation hazards for satellites, but they are not the most intense beta-particle hazards to LEO satellites. The transient magnetic bubble generated by a high-altitude detonation act, for tens of seconds after a detonation, as a magnetic container for both weapon debris and beta particles. The magnetic-bubble lifetime, short as it is, occurs during the period immediately after the detonation when debris is emitting its most energetic beta particles most rapidly. Consequently, beta flux inside the limited volume of a magnetic bubble can be many orders of magnitude greater than the persistent flux of trapped beta particles in a worldwide nuclear-pumped radiation belt, with orders of magnitude greater dose rate for satellites that might be exposed. While this might seem to be a serious hazard for satellites, it actually is not. Any satellite close enough to a detonation to be inside its magnetic bubble would already have been destroyed by combined effects of X-ray and gamma-ray fluences. For reference purposes, Figure V.18 illustrates the magnetic-bubble region of a 1 Mt detonation at 400 km at mid latitude.

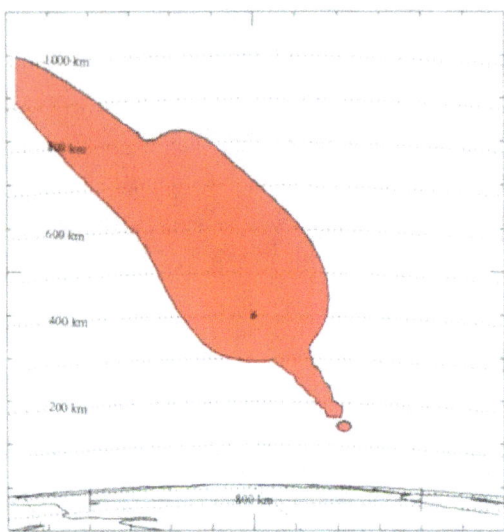

Figure V.18. Magnetic bubble region illustrated. The magnetic bubble generated by a high-altitude nuclear detonation will act as a magnetic bottle to contain very high-intensity beta particles fluxes for a period of seconds following the detonation. Result is from the DGBETS model.

V.B.2.d   Photoemissions Other Than X-rays and Gamma Rays

When a nuclear weapon is detonated in the atmosphere, the bulk of burst energy radiated in the infrared, visible, and ultraviolet portions of the spectrum comes not from the weapon itself, but from complex interactions between atmospheric species and X-rays, gamma rays, neutrons, and weapon debris expanding at high speed from the burst point. A detailed explanation is beyond the scope of this paper, but Figure V.19 provides illustrations of radiated power vs. time for a sequence of detonation altitudes. Note that at low altitudes the majority of radiated power (and energy) occurs at infrared and visible wavelengths. This is the origin of the "thermal pulse" from low or intermediate-altitude detonations. Thermal pulse may cause flash blindness and can be effective in starting widespread fires on the ground.

As burst altitude increases, the fraction of total power (and energy) radiated as UV dominates. One finds the debris-air blast wave can be an efficient radiator of UV photons, with as much as 80 percent of the kinetic yield of a weapon converted to UV photons. UV absorption cross sections in cold, un-ionized air are large, so UV photons emitted by the blast wave are strongly absorbed near the burst point to create a UV fireball. However, owing to decreasing air density above the burst, the majority of UV photons emitted in the upward direction may escape to space where they may impinge upon satellites and be a major contributor to surface degradation (see Chapter 6).

For detonations in the range from about 100 to 250 km altitude, burst-point air density is sufficient to support efficient conversion of debris kinetic energy to UV photons. At higher burst altitude, however, the air is too tenuous to support rapid conversion of debris kinetic energy to photons. The hot weapon case is another source of UV photons that form a low-energy tail on the emitted X-ray spectrum.

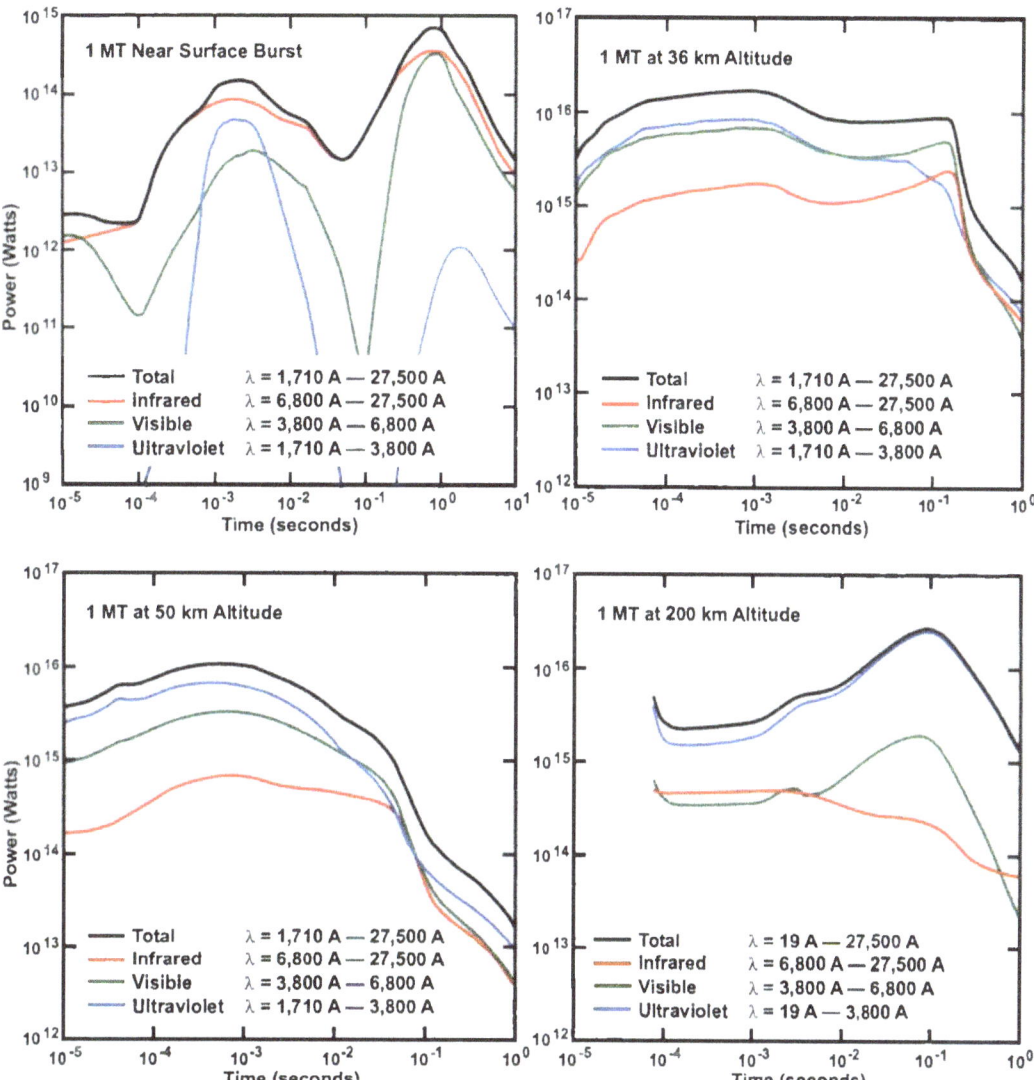

Figure V.19. Radiated optical power versus time for detonations near the ground and at 36, 50, and 200 km altitude. Note that for detonations below about 50 km, the majority of the radiated power is at infrared and visible wavelengths. At roughly 50 km burst altitude, predominant radiated power shifts from infrared and visible wavelengths to UV wavelengths. At higher altitudes, radiated power is primarily at UV wavelengths. Results generated by T.H. McCartor using the RADFLO and MODEL3 codes [Sappenfield, 1976].

CHAPTER VI
RADIATION EFFECTS ON SATELLITES

The ultimate failure of a satellite subject to radiation exposure will derive from an electrical, optical, mechanical, or thermal-control malfunction. The major satellite subsystems in jeopardy are:

- The power system:
    - Solar cells
    - Power management electronics
- Attitude control system electronics
- Communication systems
    - Antennas
    - Receiver/transmitters
- Surveillance systems
    - Passive optical components
    - Optical structural components
    - Spectral imaging
    - Focal plane detectors and processors
    - Information conditioners
- Information processing systems
    - Logic elements
    - Memories
- Thermal Control Systems
    - Radiator panels
    - Paints
    - Blankets
    - Louvers

Either temporary or permanent disruption of any of these subsystems may compromise a satellite's ability to perform satisfactorily. Electronic systems are controlled by semiconductor microcircuits that operate at low signal levels and have relatively low-energy damage thresholds. Microcircuit active element density has increased astronomically over the past several decades to support high processor speeds and memory densities. These improvements have been accompanied by dramatically decreased chip feature sizes and, in turn, increased sensitivity to small unwanted signals.

As described in Chapter V, nuclear detonations are prolific generators of energy. The manner in which energy is transferred to spacecraft components depends upon a satellite's geometry and constituent materials, and on the energy's carrier species. Electromagnetic photons in the ultraviolet, X-ray, and gamma ray regimes, and particle radiations such as electrons, ions, and neutrons have the capability to transfer this energy. The energy-transfer process may result in ionization, atomic displacement, molecular dissociation, and, on occasion, cross-linking of polymer chains. The behavior of electrons liberated by these processes produces macroscopic electrical effects. Table VI.1 [Northrop, 1996: Table 22.4] indicates the amount of coupled energy required to produce malfunction in generic satellite electronic components.

Concern for effects of nuclear radiation on electronic systems was first expressed in the early 1950s. Electronic circuits whose properties could be altered by constant exposure to neutrons and gamma rays were being used to control nuclear reactors. This stimulated engineering interest in radiation damage. In the mid 1950s the Air Force proposed to build a nuclear-powered aircraft. Every conceivable electronic piece-part underwent elaborate testing to determine its response to large neutron and gamma fluences. In the same time period, both the DoD and DOE laboratories started research programs to examine effects of nuclear weapon radiation doses to military electronic systems. In the late 1950s a group of experiments was performed in the Operation Plumbbob and Operation Hardtack nuclear test series in which the performance of active electronic components was actively monitored during a detonation. The dramatic experimental results catalyzed a new field of research called Transient Radiation Effects on Electronics (TREE) that eventually resulted in a new electronic engineering discipline. It is important to emphasize that the word "transient" refers to the radiation and not to the effects. The resulting effects can be transient or permanent depending on mechanisms of interaction. It is for this reason that the response of electronics is divided into "total-dose effects" and "dose rate effects."

Table VI.1. Upset and Burnout Thresholds for Satellite Electronic Components

MALFUNCTION MECHANISM/ COMPONENT	COUPLED ENERGY (μJ)
Upset	
Digital Logic	$10^{-3} - 10^{-2}$
Linear ICs	10^0
Low-Power Transistors	10^1
Bipolar ICs	10^1
Burnout	
Microwave Mixer	10^{-1}
Linear ICs	10^0
Low-Power Transistors	10^1
Bipolar ICs	10^1
Zeners, SCRs	10^3
High-Power Transistors	10^3
Thin-Film Resistors	10^3

Any penetrating radiation, such as high energy photons (X-rays and gammas), electrons, or other charged particles, produces tracks of ionization in materials; the liberated primary electrons may produce secondary electrons. Any of these electrons may participate in a conduction process before it is recaptured or thermalized. Photoelectrons ejected from metallic surfaces in an electronics package create an imbalance in surface electrical potentials such that currents will flow to overcome potential differences. These induced currents can override the functional currents of an electronic system. The severity of the effect is determined by piece-part and circuit designs, and by the type, energy, and intensity of the radiation.

VI.A Photon Effects

VI.A.1 Energy Distribution and Material Dependence

As discussed in Section V.B.1.a.i, a high altitude nuclear detonation typically releases 70 to 80 percent of its energy in the form of thermal X-rays, although devices may be specially designed to generate a much smaller proportion of their energy in this manner. Though not totally accurate, it is useful to assign a blackbody (BB) temperature to the X-ray spectral energy distribution function. In discussing the total photon output of the weapon and its carrier vehicle, the fluence of UV radiation can play a crucial role for some effects; we will return to this subject presently. It is customary in this technical field to express the BB radiating temperature in kilo-electron-volts (keV). (One keV equals 1.16×10^7 degrees Kelvin.) Photon X-ray energies that are absorbed primarily in the outer surfaces of the target are referred to as "cold" (~1-1.5 keV), whereas those that penetrate more deeply are called "warm" (~1.5-60 keV) or "hot" (>300 keV). Figure V.5 illustrates the radiant power of black bodies of different temperatures.

Note, from the top and bottom scales of Figure V.5, that there is an equivalence between energy, E, and wavelength, λ, or frequency, ν, expressed by the relationship $E = h\nu = hc/\lambda$, where h is Planck's constant (4.1354×10^{-21} MeV s) and c is the speed of light (2.998×10^8 m s^{-1}). Note also that the wavelength, λ_m, for which the BB curve for temperature T has maximum radiated power, satisfies $\lambda_m T = 2.8978 \times 10^{-3}$ m °K = 2.497 keV-Å.

The manner in which radiation interacts with matter determines how such energy will be absorbed. The probability of a photon traversing a given mass of material without any type of interaction is the product of the probabilities of its surviving various types of atomic interactions [Northrop, 1996]. For X-rays, the principal interaction mechanisms are the photoelectric effect (and subsequent fluorescence), Compton scattering, and pair production. In the photoelectric effect a photon is completely absorbed by an atom with the subsequent ejection of an electron; the atom may then fluoresce and emit a second newly created photon of lower energy than the original, or a second (Auger) electron may be emitted simultaneously with a third electron dropping into the vacant quantum state. In Compton scattering a photon rebounds inelastically off an electron and emerges from the collision in a different direction and with a lower energy. Pair production is a process in which a high-energy photon interacts with the Coulomb field of a nucleus and a positron-electron pair appears with total energy $h\nu$ equal to that of the impacting photon. Figure VI.1 [Evans, 1955] illustrates the relative importance of each of these processes as a function of target material atomic number, Z, for photon energies between 0.01 and 100 Mev. As shown in Figure VI.1, the photon energy threshold for pair production (> 1 McV) is greater than that commonly associated with X-rays, but the process becomes increasingly important with increasing photon energy. For materials and spectra for which the photoelectric cross-section dominates, dose (*i.e.* the amount of energy deposited per unit mass) may often be determined analytically. For instances where Compton scattering or fluorescence dominate, analyses require recourse to statistical algorithms and computers for solution.

A material's interaction cross section is a measure of the probability that it will react with a particular X-ray photon. It may be visualized as the cross sectional area of a sphere centered about the target particle. The probability that a reaction will take place is equal to the probability that the incident photon will pass within this cross section. The forces between the two particles determine the effective radius of this sphere. Normalized dose (cm^2/g) is the deposited energy (cal/g) per unit fluence (cal/cm^2). A plot of the normalized dose for gold, germanium and silicon as a function of X-ray photon energy is given as Figure VI.2 [see, for example, Biggs and Lighthill, 1988].

Figure VI.2 helps illustrate another feature of the photon absorption processes. The photo-electric absorption process dominates in the ultraviolet and low energy X-ray regimes. In the energy region around 1 MeV the Compton effect dominates, and all X-ray and gamma ray cross-sections are about the same, independent of the atomic number, Z. At energies several times its threshold the pair–production process dominates. A major effect of X-ray photon irradiation is the production of free electrons by the processes described above. These free electrons may dramatically influence the performance of the electronic components delineated in Table VI.1.

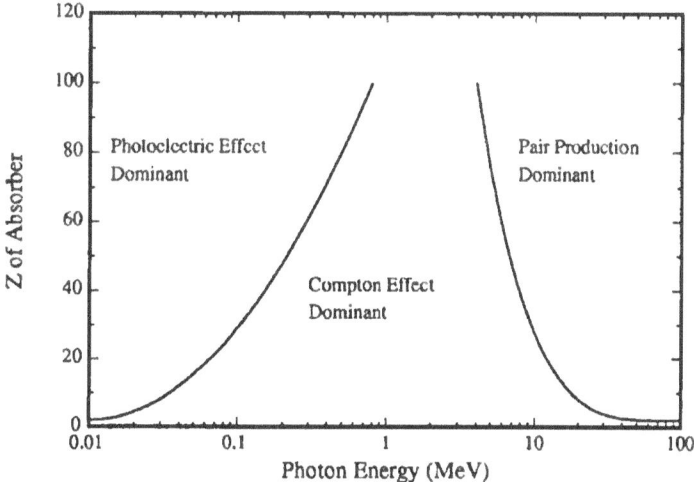

Figure VI.1 Relative importance of the major X-ray and γ-ray interactions. The lines indicate the values of Z and $h\nu$ for which the neighboring effects are equal. [Evans, 1955]

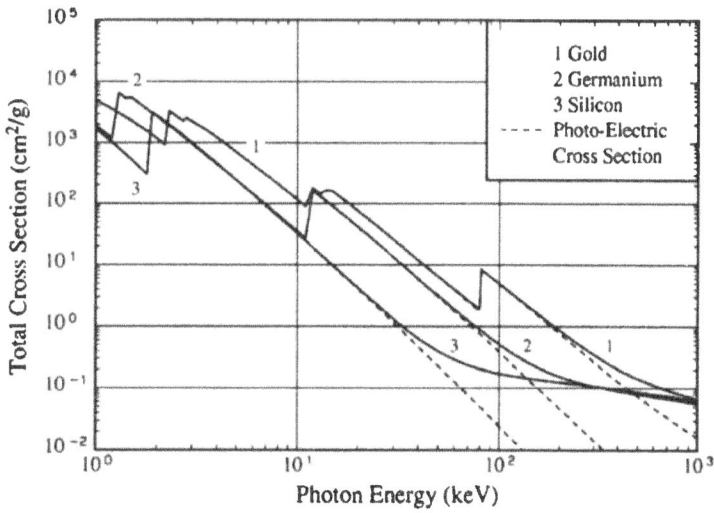

Figure VI.2. Total X-Ray Cross Sections (normalized dose) for Gold (Z = 79), Germanium (Z = 32) and Silicon (Z = 14) (solid lines) as a function of X-ray photon energy. The highest plotted photon energy is below the threshold for pair production.

Susceptibility of a piece part to nuclear radiation is dependent upon where it is located within the satellite and on energy of the radiation. Lower energy photons and electrons are absorbed close to the outer surface. At higher radiation energies the absorption coefficients decrease (Figure VI.2) and the radiation can penetrate further into the satellite. Therefore, optical components, solar cells, antennas and protective coatings are more susceptible to lower energy radiation. Internal components (processors, memories, transmitters and receivers) are typically affected or damaged by the higher energy radiation. The absorption cross-section for radiation increases with atomic number of the material (Figure VI.3). Some weapons can radiate X-rays of relatively high temperature (energy), which are more penetrating. Therefore, components fabricated with high-Z elements (*e.g.*, Au, Pb), regardless of their depth, can be placed at risk. Conversely, secondary radiation resulting from ionization of the weapons carrier vehicle may be a source of UV and cold X-ray photons so that satellite surface materials, even if low Z, may fail irrespective of the spectrum generated solely by the primary weapon.

Energy deposition as a function of depth (the so-called depth-dose profile) is illustrated in Figure VI.3. Figure VI.3 (a) illustrates the energy deposition for typical satellite surface materials when subjected to a unit fluence of 1 keV blackbody X-rays.

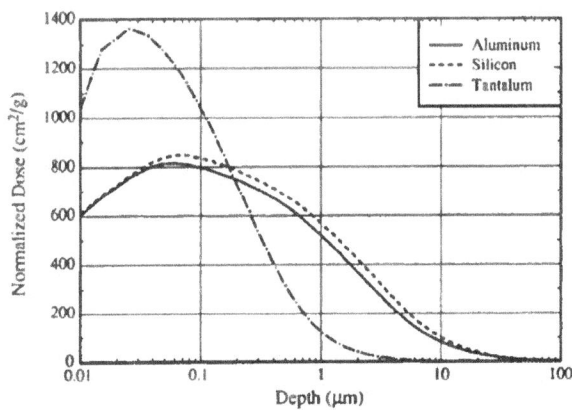

Figure VI.3(a). Normalized dose as a function of depth in Aluminum (Z=13), Silicon (Z=14) and Tantalum (Z=73) for a 1 keV blackbody.

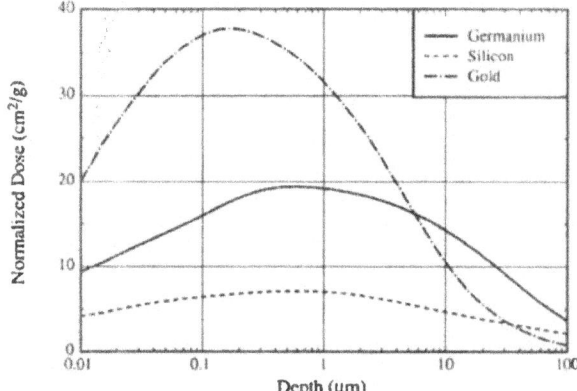

Figure VI.3(b) Normalized dose as a function of depth in Germanium (32), Silicon (14), and Gold (79) for a 10 keV blackbody.

Figure VI.3(b) shows energy deposition for typical satellite interior materials when subjected to unit fluence of a 10 keV blackbody X-rays. Silicon is likely to be found at both the surface and interiors of a satellite and affords an interesting comparison. Note that in both figures, peak dose does not occur on the material's front surface. Depending upon both material and spectrum, peak dose occurs at some depth within the target. This is due to photoionization followed by emission of secondary electrons in the interior of the absorbing material. The energy of secondary electrons is proportional to the blackbody photon temperature, and the range of those electrons is proportional to energy squared. Hence, the range of electrons generated by the 10 keV photon spectrum is 100 times that of the 1 keV spectrum. These emitted electrons are the source of System Generated Electromagnetic Pulses (SGEMP) in spacecraft.

VI.A.2 X-ray Effects

VI.A.2.a Dose and Dose Rate Effects

When a material is placed in a steady-state X-ray or gamma-ray environment, continuing ionization processes lead to a steady-state balance between the creation of free electrons and their recombination or de-excitation. Any existing electric fields then propel the free charge. Insulating materials, under irradiation, may allow charges (currents) to flow. Irradiation can also produce free radicals, break chemical bonds, or introduce trapping sites for charge carriers.

Both bipolar and field-effect transistors (FETs) can suffer a loss in gain. Today, the FET, and, preferably, the complimentary metal-oxide semiconductor (CMOS), are widely used in satellites because of their small architecture, speed and power economy. However, the introduction of traps (charge trapping defects) by ionizing radiation in gate oxides of these devices shifts their turn-on voltage and makes necessary special circuitry to circumvent the damage. Figures VI.4 and VI.5 indicate the total dose failure thresholds for Bipolar and MOS technologies.

Transient Radiation Effects on Electronics (TREE) are those that result from the exposure of electronic devices to transient radiation [Morrow-Jones, 2001]. The effects include those caused by X-ray deposition as well as Single Event Effects (SEE) caused by gamma rays. TREE effects may be permanent (latchup or burnout), or transient (*i.e.* upset which may be either transient or permanent). TREE upset thresholds may be exceeded in satellites exposed to X-ray fluence levels as low as 10^{-7} cal/cm^2, but the threshold is generally on the order of 10^{-6} cal/cm^2 for all but the coldest of blackbody irradiation The dose rate at a particular device scales linearly with fluence [Walters, 2003]. Figure VI.6 depicts dose rate as a function of blackbody temperature and fluence for silicon located within a satellite. Here it has been assumed that the X-rays traversed 0.120 inch of aluminum, and that the temporal source was a triangular pulse with rise time of 10 ns and full width at half maximum (FWHM) of 10 ns [Walters, 2003]. The reduction in dose at the cold end of the X-ray spectrum is a consequence of attenuation by the aluminum shield. Above 5 keV, however, the 0.120 inch aluminum is essentially transparent.

A transient burst of X-ray or gamma radiation causes ionization and associated electric fields in constituent materials of electronic piece-parts. Currents that arise from the ionization process can cause capacitors to be discharged. Cable insulation may become conducting as a result of free electrons generated within. Semiconductor junctions biased in the blocking direction can be turned on (Figure VI.7), causing binary logic to change state and memories to be erased. If the flow of electrical current exceeds power ratings of piece-parts, burnout can take place.

An event that produces an unwanted change of logic state in a digital electronic circuit is called *upset*. In some instances, the circuit is designed to restore the proper logic state by itself. In others, this can only be done by instructions from an operator. Figure VI.8 compares the upset thresholds for state-of-the-art integrated circuit technologies.

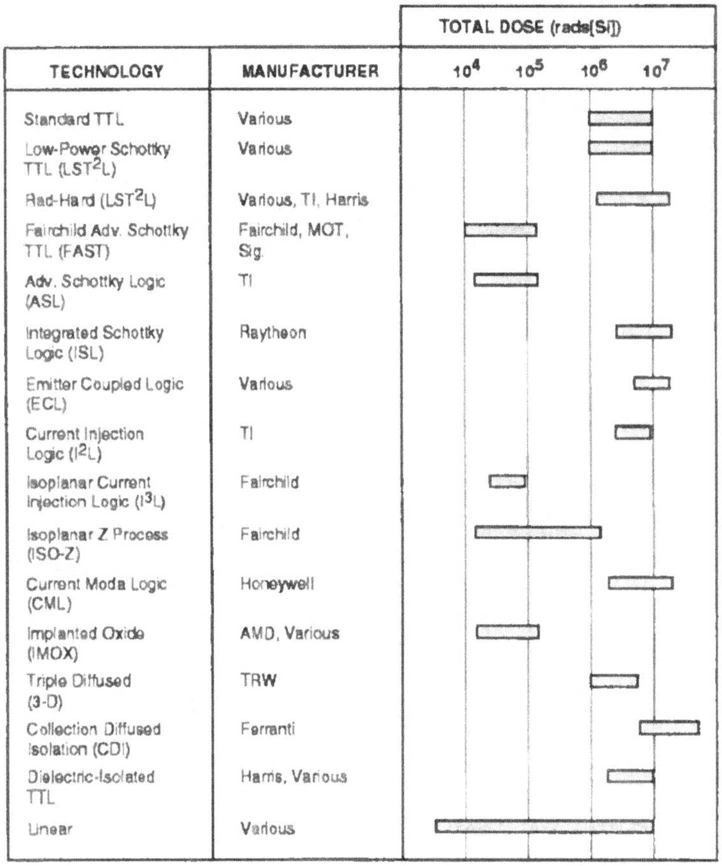

TECHNOLOGY	MANUFACTURER	TOTAL DOSE (rads(Si)) 10^4 – 10^7
Standard TTL	Various	
Low-Power Schottky TTL (LST^{2}L)	Various	
Rad-Hard (LST^{2}L)	Various, TI, Harris	
Fairchild Adv. Schottky TTL (FAST)	Fairchild, MOT, Sig.	
Adv. Schottky Logic (ASL)	TI	
Integrated Schottky Logic (ISL)	Raytheon	
Emitter Coupled Logic (ECL)	Various	
Current Injection Logic (I^{2}L)	TI	
Isoplanar Current Injection Logic (I^{3}L)	Fairchild	
Isoplanar Z Process (ISO-Z)	Fairchild	
Current Mode Logic (CML)	Honeywell	
Implanted Oxide (IMOX)	AMD, Various	
Triple Diffused (3-D)	TRW	
Collection Diffused Isolation (CDI)	Ferranti	
Dielectric-Isolated TTL	Harris, Various	
Linear	Various	

Figure VI.4. Total dose damage thresholds for bipolar IC technologies [Northrop, 1996: Table 22.18].

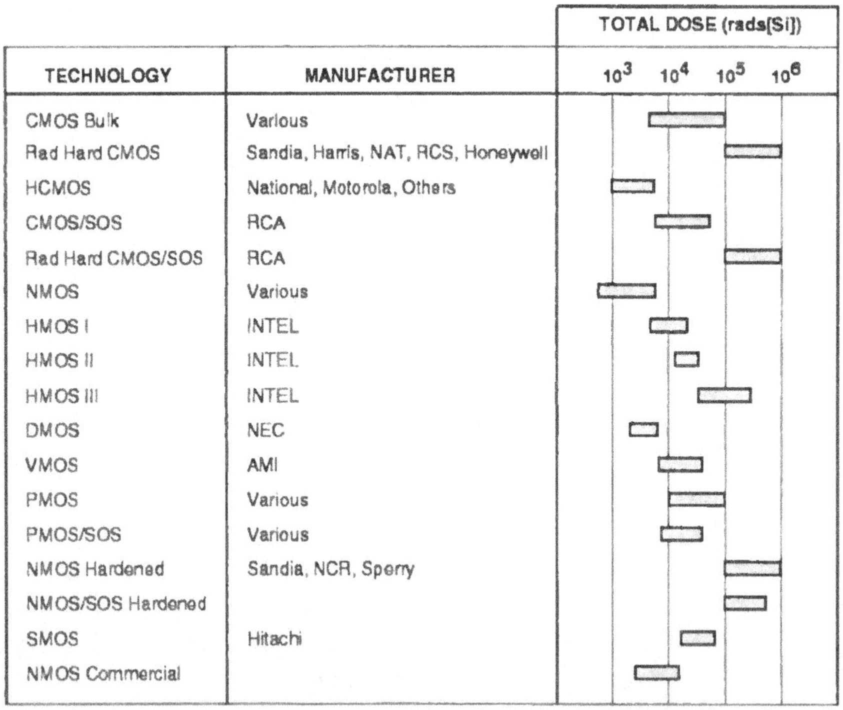

TECHNOLOGY	MANUFACTURER	TOTAL DOSE (rads(Si)) 10^3 – 10^6
CMOS Bulk	Various	
Rad Hard CMOS	Sandia, Harris, NAT, RCS, Honeywell	
HCMOS	National, Motorola, Others	
CMOS/SOS	RCA	
Rad Hard CMOS/SOS	RCA	
NMOS	Various	
HMOS I	INTEL	
HMOS II	INTEL	
HMOS III	INTEL	
DMOS	NEC	
VMOS	AMI	
PMOS	Various	
PMOS/SOS	Various	
NMOS Hardened	Sandia, NCR, Sperry	
NMOS/SOS Hardened		
SMOS	Hitachi	
NMOS Commercial		

Figure VI.5. Total dose damage thresholds for MOS technologies [Northrop, 1996: Table 22.19].

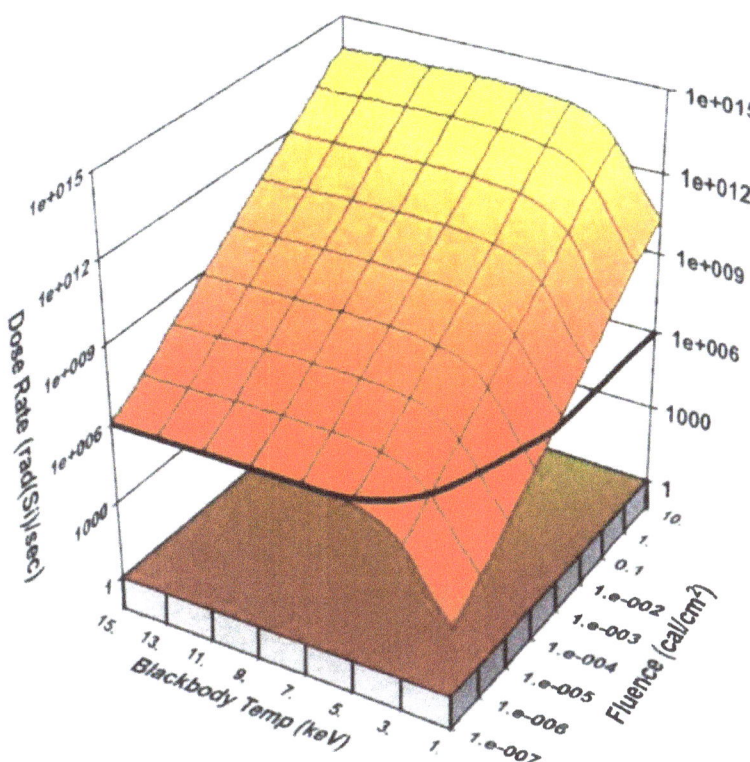

Figure VI.6. Dose rate vs. blackbody temperature and fluence in silicon shielded by 0.120 inch of aluminum.

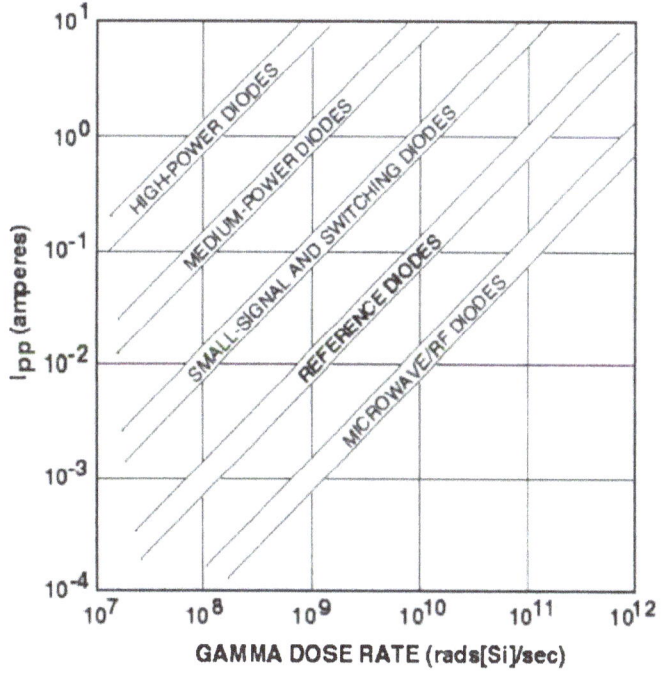

Figure VI.7. Typical diode photocurrents as a function of dose rate.

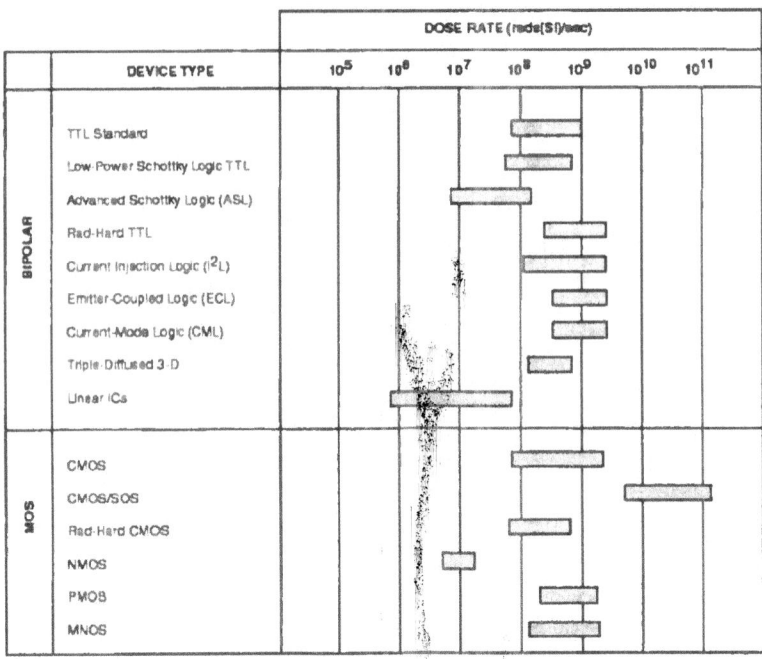

Figure VI.8. Comparison of upset thresholds for state-of-the-art integrated circuit technologies.

In some instances, the change in state can produce damage, such as burnout in transistor microcircuits or other components. An integrated circuit may be placed in a logic state that cannot be changed without the removal of electric power. If power is not removed, the circuit elements may experience burnout. This phenomenon is referred to as *latchup*. Figure VI.9 shows the thresholds for this effect.

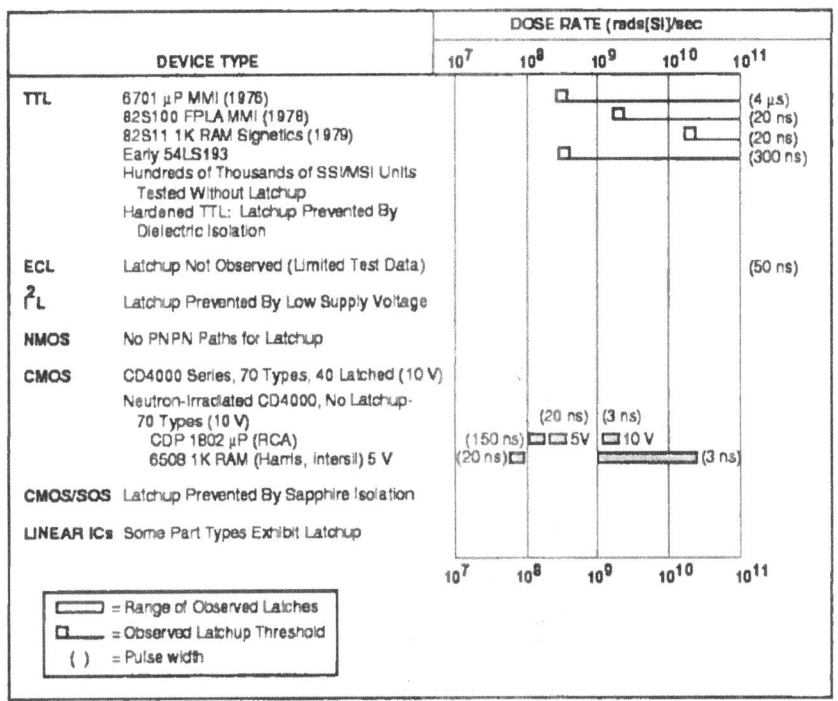

Figure VI.9. Integrated circuit latchup thresholds.

VI.A.2.b SGEMP[11]

The basic System Generated Electromagnetic Pulse (SGEMP) process is depicted in Figure VI.10. When X-rays (or gamma-rays) irradiate a system, photo-Compton (pC) electron currents are emitted from the various surfaces, and are driven throughout the various system materials. These electron currents induce electromagnetic fields within portions of the system, which in turn induce currents and voltages on various system components and cabling. Ultimately, these induced electromagnetic signals can couple to electronic devices where they have the potential to cause burnout or upset, and associated mission failure.

Another term that is often used instead of SGEMP is "internal EMP", or IEMP. The two terms are essentially synonymous (with the exception of external SGEMP).

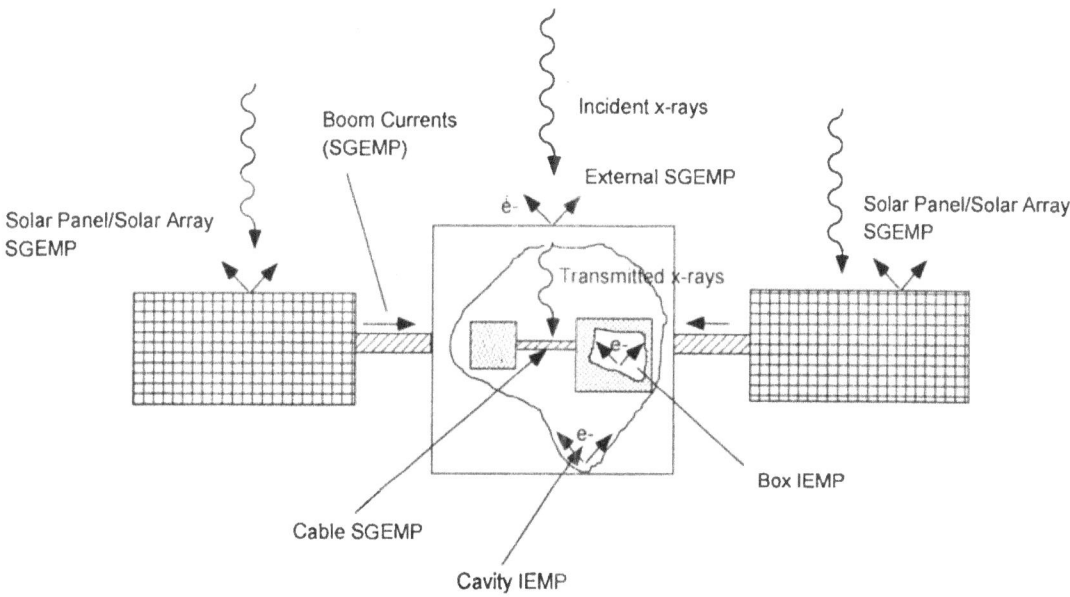

Figure VI.10. Basic SGEMP processes for a satellite.

SGEMP induced responses tend to occur in the same time regime as the prompt environments — typically the sub-microsecond time scale. However, SGEMP current can be lengthened relative to the X-ray pulse duration by transmission-line propagation effects. In some cases they can be shortened due to non-linear effects such as space charge limiting. In addition, as with any high frequency or fast transient electrical excitation, it is common in many cases for induced SGEMP signals to "ring." SGEMP is basically a time domain phenomenon. That is, the basic excitations tend to take the form of a pulse, typically roughly triangular in shape. Thus, "CW" (*i.e.* continuous wave) testing, so common in most fields of electronics hardening, is seldom relevant, and rarely used for SGEMP testing.

---

[11] The authors wish to acknowledge the contribution of Thomas A. Stringer and Charles Eklund, who allowed much of the introductory text in this section to be taken from their document, *A Guide to the Literature Treating the Subject of Systems Generated Electromagnetic Pulse*, (In Preparation).

Traditionally, for reasons that are evident from Figure VI.10, SGEMP is divided into External SGEMP, Cavity IEMP, Cable SGEMP, and Box IEMP. This is true for any type of platform (satellite, missile, RV, or interceptor). These categories are described briefly in Table VI.2.

Note that it is conventional to refer to SGEMP processes within cavities or boxes as Cavity IEMP and Box IEMP respectively. (The terms Cavity SGEMP and Box SGEMP would seem logical, but have rarely been used in the literature.) It is to be emphasized that the ultimate (and only) reason for being concerned with SGEMP/IEMP is the issue of how much energy couples into the electronics, and whether it is sufficient to cause burnout (a permanent electronics failure mechanism), or upset (which may be transient).

Both X-rays and gamma rays may induce these effects, although X-rays are usually the dominant concern. All types of SGEMP are also strongly affected by the presence of any ambient or enclosed gas. Gas ionization effects tend to neutralize surface charge, and reduce static electric fields. Because an ionized gas can neutralize space charge barriers, the pressure of air can dramatically increase replacement currents.

Table VI.2. A brief description of SGEMP categories.

Category	Brief Definition
External SGEMP	SGEMP occurring on the exterior surface of the platform, due to reverse pC electron emission from surface materials.
Cavity IEMP	SGEMP occurring within cavities of the platform, usually dominated by electron emission from the cavity walls.
Cable SGEMP	SGEMP occurring within system cabling harnesses, often dominated by electron emission from interior surface of the cable shield.
Box IEMP	SGEMP occurring within electronics boxes, often dominated by electron emission from the circuit board traces and connecting conductors.
Pin Level SGEMP	Net SGEMP signals appearing at the box connector pin interface, due to the combined effects of external SGEMP, cavity IEMP, and cable/connector SGEMP.

Historically, Cable SGEMP and Box IEMP stand out as posing the most severe threat to systems, as well as also representing the most difficult hardening challenge. The reason is that standard, good RF shielding practices can easily mitigate External SGEMP and Cavity IEMP. That is, electronics devices tend to be isolated from these effects by one or more levels of "Faraday cage" shielding. By contrast, Cable SGEMP and Box IEMP are driven by photon interactions within the RF shielding topology.

Cable SGEMP, depending on the incident X-ray fluence, can give rise to signals at the box pins of hundreds of amperes and voltages of kilovolts. The RF shield on a cable typically only affords a marginal degree of X-ray shielding. Potentially large Cable SGEMP signals can be handled by either placing terminal protection devices (TPDs) at the box pins, or by choosing low response cables (or by some combination of both).

Box IEMP is generally driven by radiation environments somewhat reduced from those external to the satellite. This is a consequence of X-ray shielding afforded by the box walls. In principle, the X-ray portion of Box IEMP could be entirely eliminated by sufficient X-ray shielding. In practice, such shielding generally causes an unacceptable weight penalty, but spot shielding on circuit boards is often employed. Nuclear weapons (and the natural environment) also contribute a gamma radiation component to Box IEMP signals. Box shielding to gamma rays is entirely impractical from both weight and space considerations. (Two inches of lead is typically required to reduce the gamma flux by one order of magnitude.) One hardening strategy is to reduce the X-ray environment to a level where the X-ray dose rate is at or below that of the gamma dose rate. Even in the absence of a gamma ray threat, it is usually necessary to have some degree of X-ray shielding on the box in order to harden against thermomechanical shock (TMS) and TREE effects. [Northrop, 1996].

To bound the order of magnitude of nuclear induced SGEMP and IEMP X-ray threats, we consider damage metrics for four generic situations [Walters, 2003]. For SGEMP upset the damage parameter is defined as voltage on a wire attached to a box pin by Cavity SGEMP. The nominal upset threshold is assumed to be 5 volts, but these values might be expected to be considerably lower for more recent digital electronic technologies. Figure 6.11 depicts SGEMP voltage as functions of blackbody temperature and fluence incident on the satellite. The calculation was done using the Testable Hardware Toolkit [Morrow-Jones *et al.*, 2001] and assumed a cylindrical body 1 meter radius × 1 meter length, with a 0.060 inch Aluminum wall and an empty cavity. The wire was taken to be bare (worst case) aluminum, 0.5 cm diameter and 100 cm length, and was located 1 cm above the wall/ground plane within the cavity [Walters, 2003].

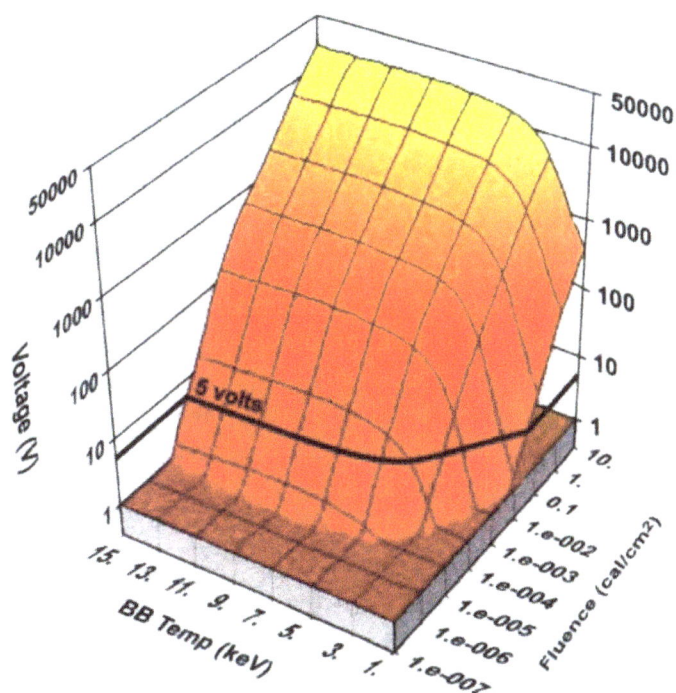

Figure VI.11. SGEMP Upset: Voltage as function of blackbody temperature and fluence.

SGEMP burnout for this geometry is assumed to occur at an absorbed energy of one microjoule. Figure VI.12 depicts absorbed energy as a function of blackbody temperature and fluence incident on the satellite.

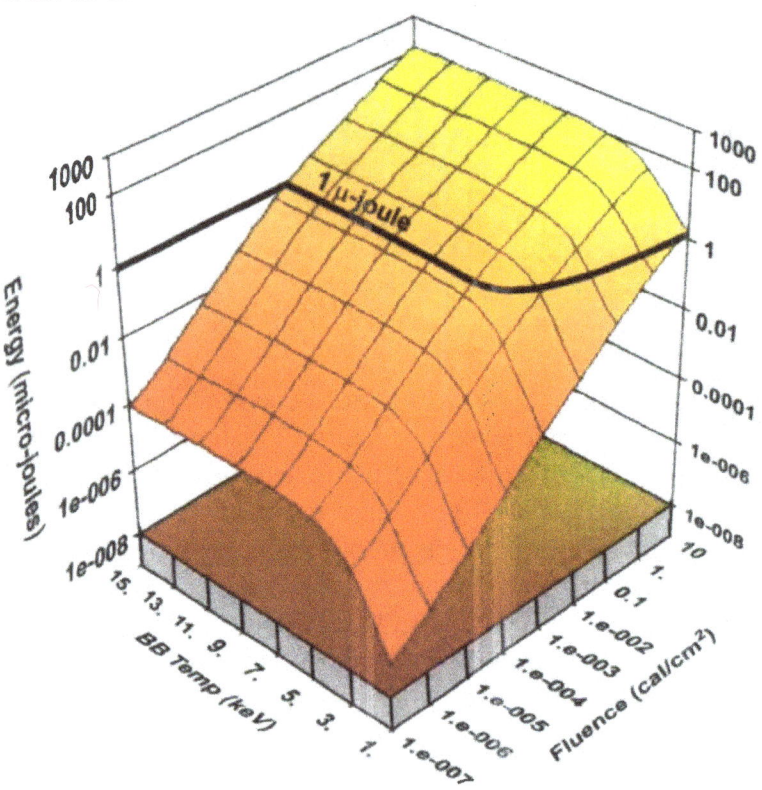

Figure VI.12. SGEMP Burnout: Energy as function of blackbody temperature and fluence.

We note that it requires approximately 3×10^{-4} cal/cm^2 for a 3 keV blackbody to trigger upset and 1×10^{-2} cal/cm^2 at 3 keV to cause burnout. One also sees evidence of non-linear response scaling with fluence, as the voltage in Figure VI.11 decreases much more rapidly than does the absorbed energy in Figure VI.12.

To estimate the severity of Box IEMP effects, we assume a 20 cm × 20 cm × 10 cm rectangular volume with uncoated 0.060 inch aluminum walls. Within the box we place a 0.032 inch FR4 circuit board with one copper bottom ground plane and locate the board 3 cm from the box wall. The board contains circuit traces which are 0.010 inches wide by 40 cm long, consisting of 0.0014 inch thick copper and 0.003 inch solder connections. We consider two hardness levels: one hardened board with a conformal coating of 0.003 inch of polyurethane, and one bare board with all metal exposed. We take upset and burnout damage metrics to be the same as those for SGEMP, *i.e.* voltage at device pin induced by circuit board land Box IEMP, and energy coupled to device pin induced by circuit board land for burnout [Walters,2003]. We assume the same damage levels for Box IEMP effects (5 volts for upset, 1 microjoule for burnout) but now assume that the X-ray photons must traverse 0.120 inch of aluminum, *i.e.*, 0.060 inch aluminum cavity plus 0.060 inch box walls.

Figure VI.13 depicts Box IEMP Upset results for a coated circuit board, and Figure VI.14 for its burnout.

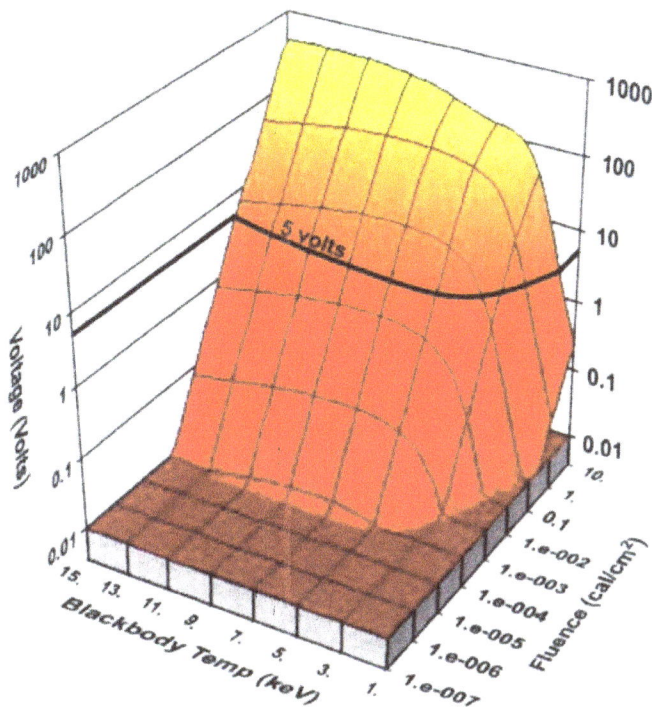

Figure VI.13 Box IEMP Upset (Coated Circuit Board): Voltage as function of blackbody temperature and fluence.

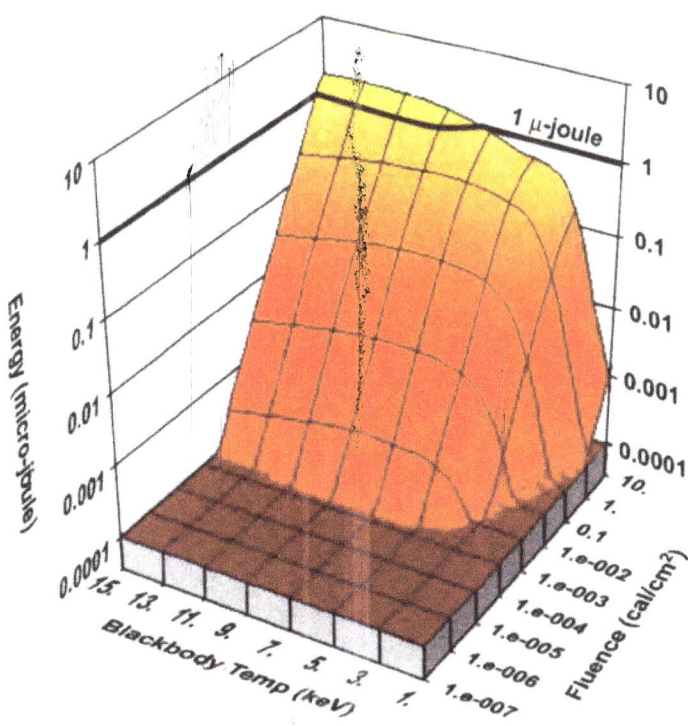

Figure VI.14. Box IEMP Burnout (Coated Circuit Board): Energy as function of blackbody temperature and fluence.

Upset takes place at a fluence of approximately 0.02 cal/cm² at 7 keV and 0.2 cal/cm² at 3 keV. Burnout occurs at about 10 cal/cm² at 7 keV increasing to as much as 100 cal/cm² at 3 keV.

For identical geometries and assumptions, equivalent uncoated circuit board upset and burnout plots are given in Figures VI.15 and VI.16. For this circuit board, upset would occur at a fluence of approximately 0.005 cal/cm² at 7 keV, a quarter of the fluence for the hardened configuration. At 3 keV upset occurs at 0.2 cal/cm², about the same as the coated configuration. Burnout however occurs at a fluence of about 0.2 cal/cm² at 7 keV, and 10.0 cal/cm² at 3 keV, roughly an order of magnitude less than the coated board.

External SGEMP consists of surface **E** and **B** fields with associated replacement currents. It is usually a primary concern for coupling into antenna apertures. (Occasionally there are other apertures through which the field can leak into the system interior.) The principal hardening technique involves designing the antenna so that fields and skin currents do not couple efficiently (*i.e.*, ensuring that the SGEMP is "out of band") to the antenna.

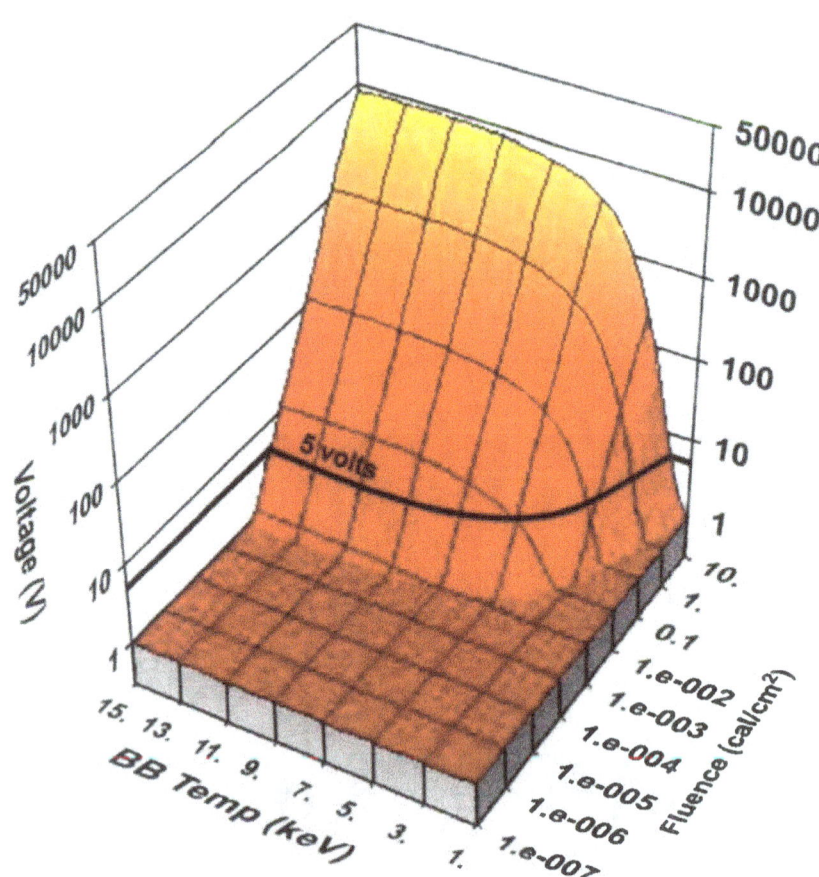

Figure VI.15. Box IEMP Upset (Uncoated Circuit Board): Voltage as function of blackbody temperature and fluence.

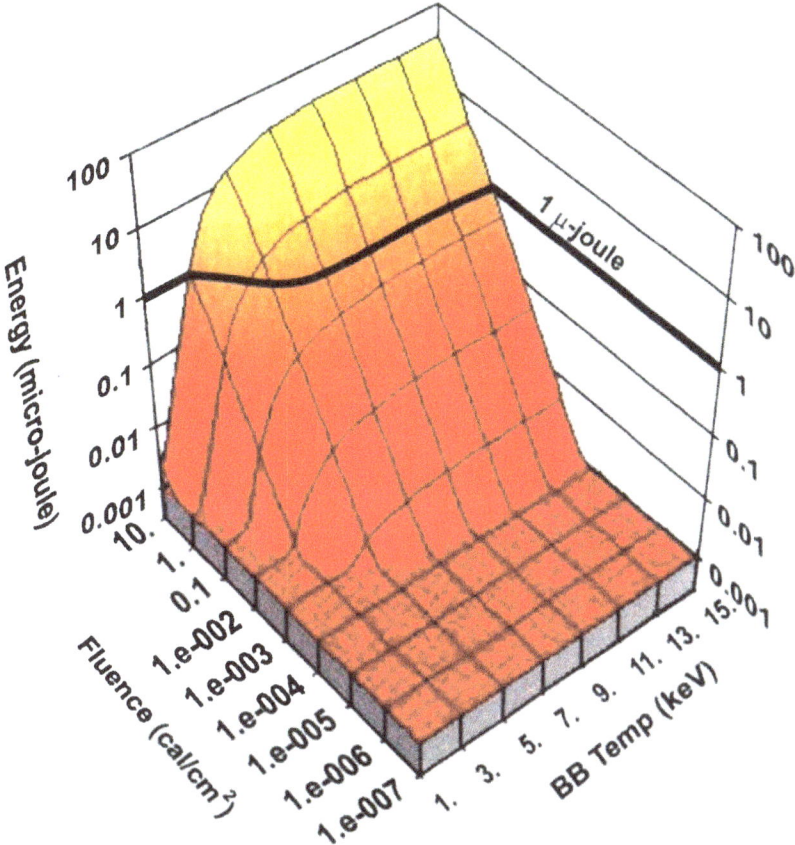

Figure VI.16. Box IEMP Burnout (Uncoated Circuit Board): Energy as function of blackbody temperature and fluence.

In the 1970s it was discovered that satellites orbiting the earth in the natural space plasma and charged particle environment are subject to differential charging. At some differential charging voltage threshold, an electrical discharge can occur between different portions of the satellite. This discharge creates an electromagnetic transient that can couple into satellite electronics.

This phenomenon is referred to as ECEMP, for "electron-charging EMP". However, it has sometimes gone by other names, such as DGEMP (discharge generated EMP), spacecraft charging, internal spacecraft charging, electronic discharge (ESD), or deep dielectric charging.

It is known that ECEMP can occur after a spacecraft dielectric is charged with more than a few times 10^{11} electrons/cm^2, which can happen following intense magnetospheric activity.

Such discharge transients were identified as being the possible cause of various operational problems observed in orbiting satellites. This led to various research efforts to understand how spacecraft charging occurred and what could be done to minimize the undesirable effects of discharges.

VI.A.2.c Photon-Induced Thermomechanical Effects

Ultraviolet radiation is not very penetrating and hence is generally not of concern to interior satellite components. It may however be a major influence on spacecraft surfaces. Ultraviolet radiation is capable of cross-linking polymeric materials, for example, and by so doing contributes to degradation of their structural integrity and/or insulating characteristics. Recent studies have analytically investigated effects of weapon-generated soft X-rays on spacecraft surfaces [Gurtman *et al.*, 2003]. The resulting analysis suggested that for materials that are known to have stress dominated failure modes, soft X-ray and UV radiation may be the principal factor limiting surface material survivability.

Typical L and M edge absorption cross-sections are 2 to 3 orders of magnitude greater than the K edge (Figure VI.2.). Surface doses and temperatures are, therefore, proportionally much higher for low energy photon fluxes.

Surfaces of spacecraft often consist of dielectrics (mirror and/or optical coatings), or carbonaceous materials (baffles, radiators). These materials are known to experience relatively little degradation in elastic moduli when heated. As a result, they generally fail due to stresses rather than melt or sublimation. Surface stresses are proportional to temperature, and while stresses can be predicted *a priori* given a material's thermomechanical properties, failure modes and levels cannot. The usual procedure of nuclear hardness prediction involves a radiation test. Failure data are acquired, a stress level determined by means of an analysis, and the failure mode and level are extrapolated to the environment of interest.

This approach becomes a matter of some concern, since the existing AGT/UGT data base for commonly used materials was generated on samples that had been shielded from the softest part of the X-ray weapon's spectrum. Actual failure levels may be substantially lower than those implied by the AGT/UGTs.

Consider the 1 keV blackbody spectrum depicted in Figure VI.17. Total fluence a sample would see when exposed to this environment is equivalent to the area under the curve, while the fluence due to photons below 1 keV photon energy is that due to the shaded area.

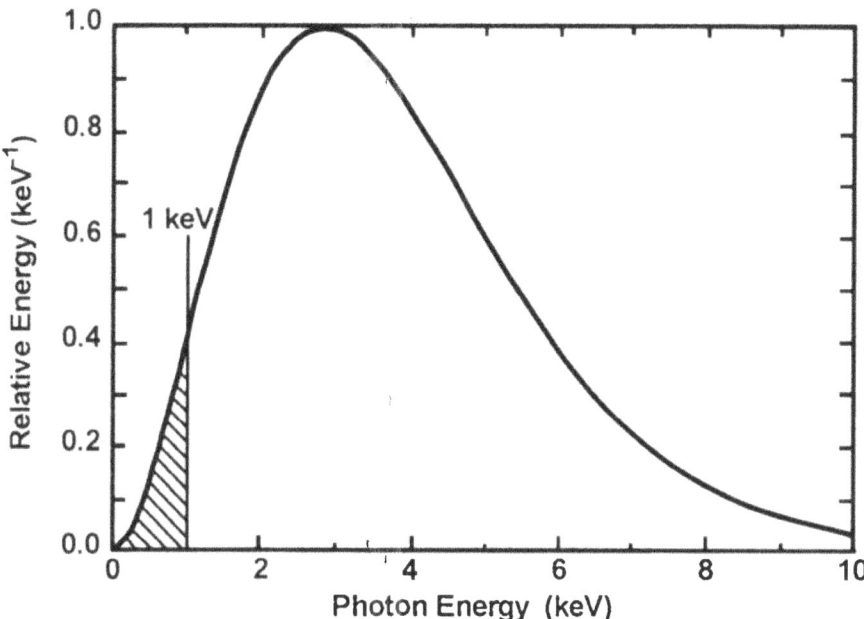

Figure VI.17. 1 keV blackbody energy density vs. photon energy.

When a 1 keV blackbody spectrum is applied to a dielectric coating enhanced IR reflecting mirror (5.5 × ZnSe/BaF$_2$ on Ni over Be), the resulting depth-dose profile is as shown in Figure VI.18. The depth-dose profile resulting from 1 keV source radiation on Poco Graphite is depicted in Figure VI.19.

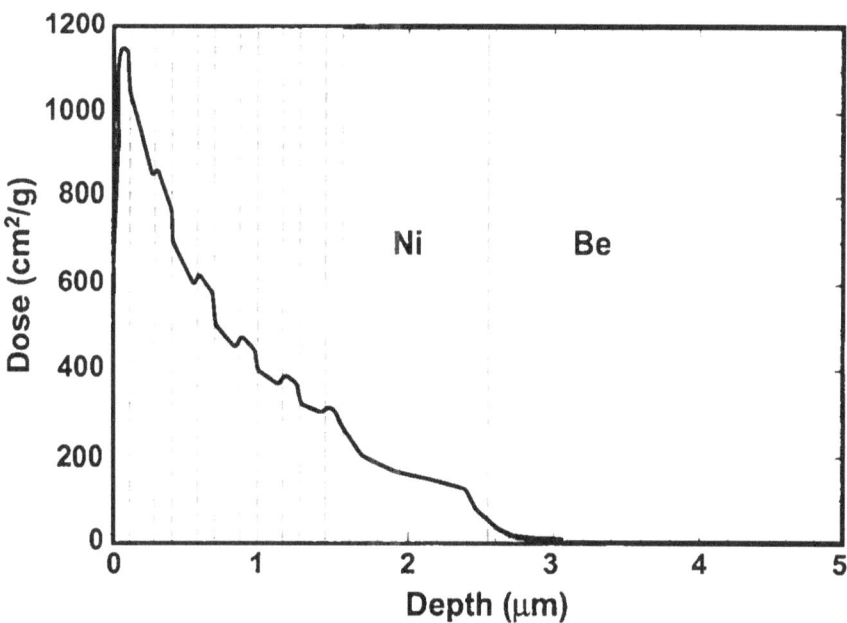

Figure VI.18. Normalized Depth-Dose; 1 keV blackbody source on IR mirror

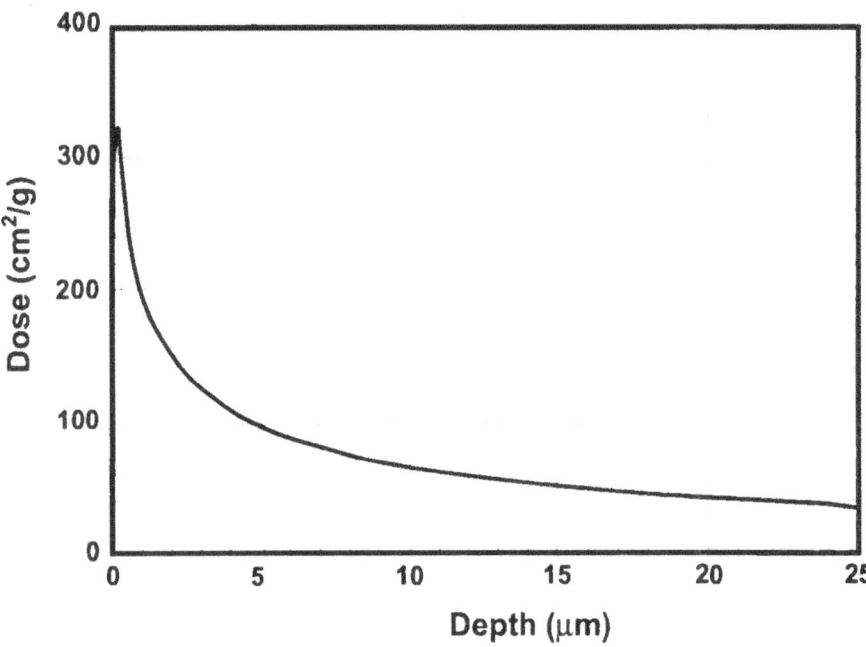

Figure VI.19. Normalized Depth-Dose; 1 keV blackbody source on Poco Graphite.

Fluence and in-plane compressive stress ratios for these two materials, as functions of blackbody temperature, are depicted in Figures VI.20 and VI.21. Solid lines illustrate the ratio of fluence below 1 keV photon energy to total incident fluence. The dotted line is the ratio of in-plane compressive stress below 1 keV photon energy to total stress caused by unit fluence of that particular blackbody.

We note that, for the mirror exposed to a 1 keV environment, approximately 18% of the peak stress but only 3.3% of the peak dose was due to low energy photons. In the case of Poco Graphite, some 40% of peak stress and 3.5% of peak dose were caused by photons at 1 keV and below.

As mentioned above, the AGT/UGT database for the vast majority of spacecraft surface materials was based upon passive experimental data (*i.e.* pre and post test examination of samples). In essentially all cases, samples were shielded from the radiation source, either by beryllium for most of the UGTs or kapton/kimfol in the AGTs. Further, the soft part of the actual radiation environments (*i.e.*, that below 1 keV photon energy) was rarely diagnosed.

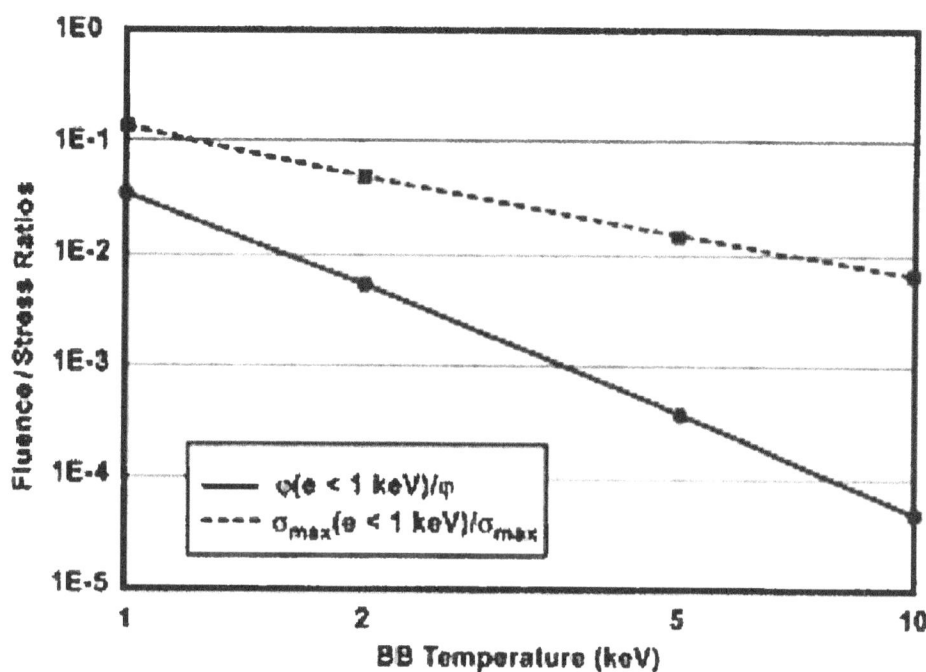

Figure VI.20. Stress and fluence ratios as functions of blackbody temperature for IR mirror.

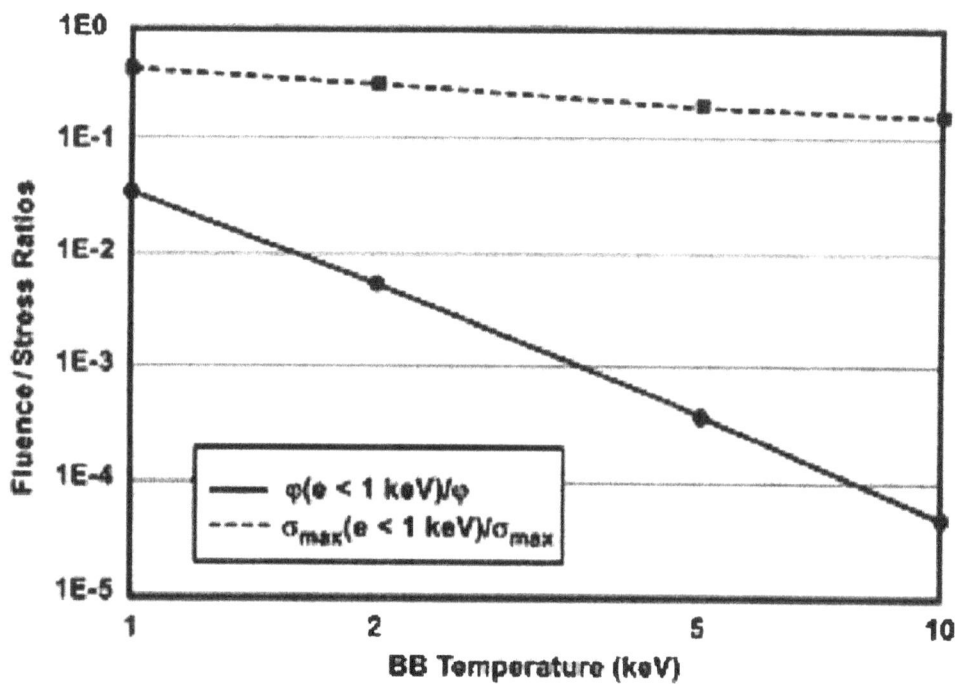

Figure VI.21. Stress and fluence ratios as functions of blackbody temperature for Poco Graphite.

Implications of this observation are potentially quite serious. While it is probably true that adversaries are not specifically targeting U.S. DoD satellites with nuclear weapons, such space assets are nevertheless expected to operate in an exo-atmospheric nuclear environment.

Nuclear weapons may be generating considerably more in the way of UV, VUV and sub-kilovolt X-rays than has hitherto been considered. Indeed, a current analytical study by the LLNL would appear to confirm this hypothesis [Thomson, 2002]. Such radiation may result from interactions between nuclear primaries and secondaries, interaction of the weapon with its transport vehicle, or detonations within the sensible atmosphere. These circumstances do not appear to have been considered by the RedBook community or the JCS exo-atmospheric threat documents used by Air Force SPOs.

We suggest that an experimental program be initiated to confirm or refute this soft photon vulnerability conjecture. Should the experiments verify the effect, the issue should be brought before those charged with specifying nuclear threats on U.S. exo-atmospheric assets.

As has been noted previously, interactions of X-rays with satellite components depend crucially upon photon energy. Figure VI.22 depicts peak dose results of X-ray deposition in aluminum-shielded silicon as a function of blackbody temperature. Here the fluence on the surface of the aluminum shield is taken as 1 cal/cm^2 while the peak dose is computed in an infinite half plane of silicon.

The resulting in-plane stresses in silicon are shown in Figure VI.23. In-plane refers to stresses in a direction perpendicular to that of the in-coming photons. Typically this dimension is large relative to the depth over which photons are absorbed, and hence the magnitude of the in-plane stresses are not strongly influenced by either the X-ray pulse width or stress wave propagation in the direction of X-ray deposition. In general, thermomechanical stress effects of concern to a satellite's performance occur when compressive stresses are on the order of 0.1 kilobars or above.

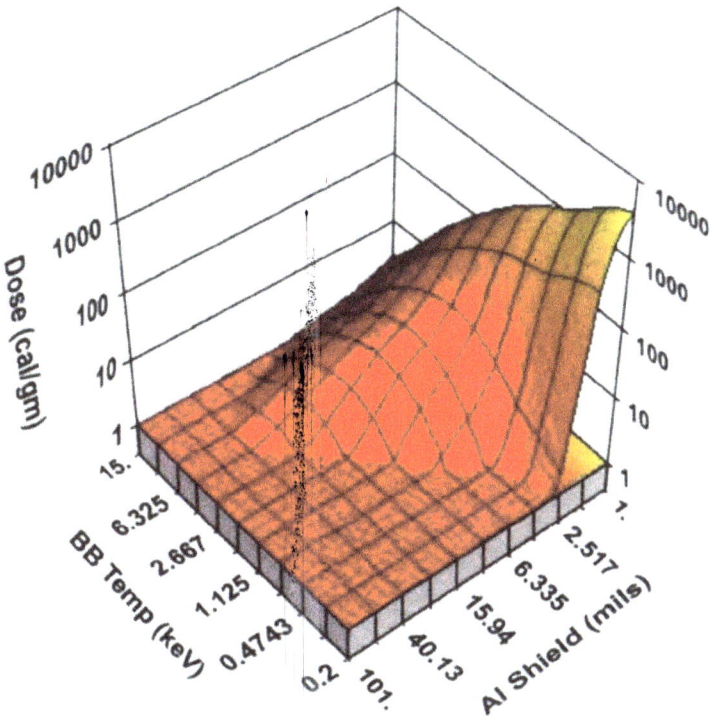

Figure VI.22. Peak dose in silicon as function of blackbody temperature and aluminum shield thickness. (Incident fluence on surface of the aluminum is 1 cal/cm^2)

In geometries such as those applicable to multi-layer thin films or circuit boards, longitudinal stresses (*i.e.* those in the direction parallel to photon deposition) are generally the dominant failure mechanism. In such cases, the magnitude of the lateral stress wave will depend strongly upon geometry, material properties and X-ray pulse shape, and hence has to be considered on a case by case basis. Frequently, failure will occur when the radiation-induced compressive stress wave interacts with either a second material or a free surface. The interaction may result in tensile stresses at the interface and cause delaminations or spall. For these tensile stresses, 0.1 kilobars becomes a reasonable rule of thumb as such levels are consistent with launch-generated g-loads.

For cold X-ray threats, or temporal pulse widths which are short with respect to wave transit time across an object's longitudinal dimension, in-plane stresses are generally more severe than longitudinal ones. For warm or hot X-rays, or for structures internal to the satellite, longitudinal stresses are frequently the cause of thermomechanical failure.

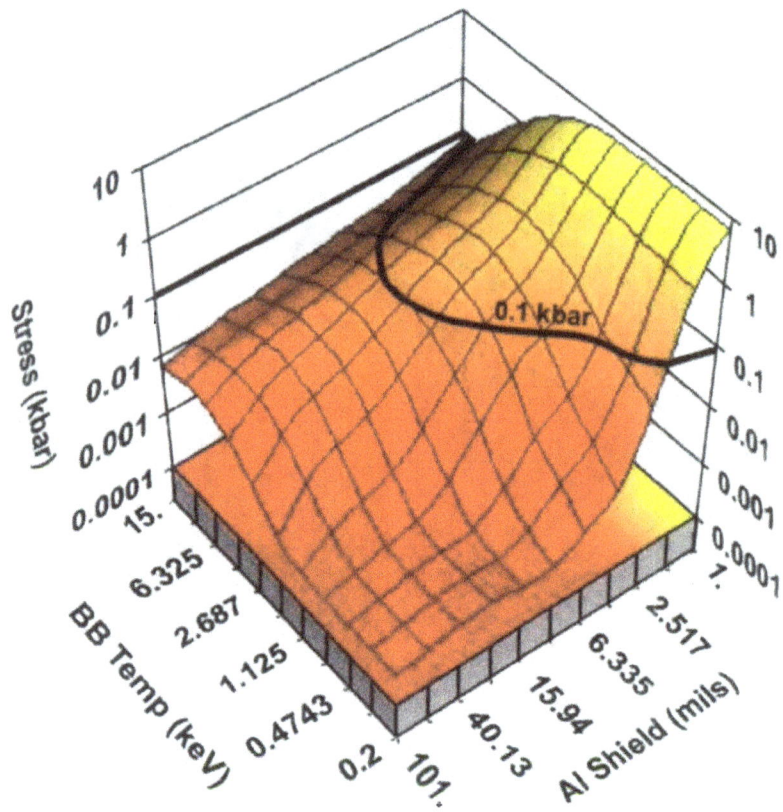

Figure VI.23. Peak in-plane compressive stress in silicon as function of blackbody temperature and aluminum shield thickness. (Incident fluence on surface of the aluminum is 1 cal/cm^2)

VI.B   Charged Particle Effects

VI.B.1   Electrons

Spacecraft encounter electron fluxes of varied energies and intensities, depending on the spacecraft's orbit and on the state of the environment. Figure VI.24 illustrates the wide spectrum of electron energies experienced by LEO spacecraft and the effects of those electrons on satellites. The electron spectrum incident on a spacecraft surface varies greatly in time and space. This figure shows the approximate average natural spectrum for a DMSP or NOAA orbit, together with the nuclear enhanced environment averaged over the first day after trial nuclear event 17. (See trial event descriptions in Section VII.) The plot shows the flux of electrons having energy above the value on the horizontal axis, so that the differential flux is proportional to the slope of the curve.

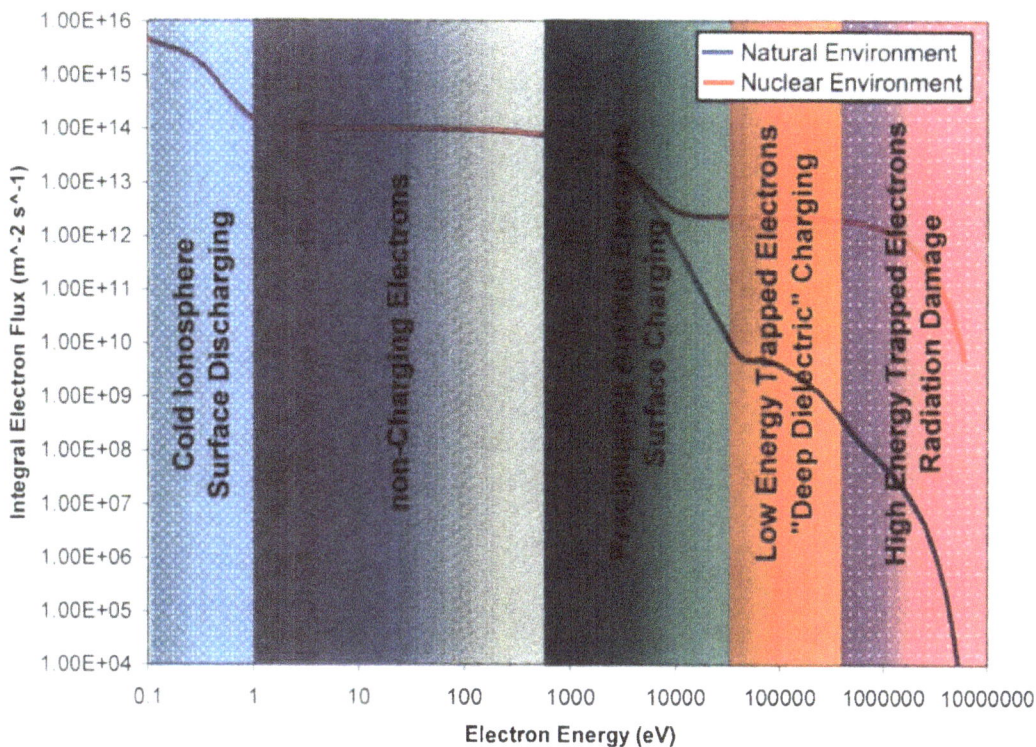

Figure VI.24. Effects of various energies of electrons on LEO spacecraft, together with the natural and nuclear-enhanced integral spectra.

LEO satellites are nearly always enveloped in "cold" plasma with electron and ion temperatures in the range of 0.1 to 0.3 eV. This plasma is responsible for many interesting effects, such as sheath formation, wake formation, and arcing of high voltage solar arrays. It keeps spacecraft surfaces at small negative potentials. The typical density of cold ionosphere plasma at the peak of the F layer is $\sim 10^{12}$ m^{-3} during daylight, and $< 10^{11}$ m^{-3} at night. This population is not present in GEO, so geosynchronous satellites can charge to several kilovolts negative when they encounter a swarm of high energy electrons. Numerous spacecraft anomalies, as well as a few well-documented failures, have been attributed to geosynchronous spacecraft charging [Fennell *et al.*, 2001].

During times of high geomagnetic activity spacecraft encounter electrons with energies in the 1 to 40 keV range. These electrons deposit charge in the outer few microns of spacecraft material, and cause "spacecraft charging" f the deposited charge is not neutralized by cold plasma or by photoelectrons. Geosynchronous spacecraft commonly experience charging in the midnight-to-dawn sector during magnetic reconnection at ~ 10 RE in the magnetotail, followed by rapid depolarization of reconnected field lines.

Polar-orbiting LEO spacecraft have been observed to charge during auroral passage due to energetic "precipitating electrons" ("inverted-V events") when such events occur at night and are accompanied by dropout (to density $< 10^{10}$ m^{-3}) of the cold plasma. Numerous such events have been recorded on DMSP satellites, with the largest negative charging potentials exceeding one kilovolt [Anderson, 2000].

Electrons with energies in the range 40 keV to 300 keV deposit charge at a depth of tens to a few hundreds of microns in spacecraft surface materials (*e.g.*, solar cell coverglasses, thermal blankets, and insulation of external cables), a phenomenon known as "deep dielectric charging." Such electrons are plentiful in the natural trapped population. Over time (typically a fraction of a day to a few days) internal electric fields may increase to discharge levels, *i.e.*, to levels exceeding a few times 10^6 Vm^{-1}. A particularly vulnerable configuration is an external cable near a cold surface. The fission beta-decay spectrum contains relatively few electrons in this energy range, so the hazard of deep dielectric charging is only moderately enhanced as a result of a nuclear detonation. However, because nuclear beta-decay electrons may appear in regions of space where natural radiation levels are benign, they have the potential of causing discharges on satellites not hardened against them.

Electrons with energies over 0.3 MeV pass through sensible thicknesses of spacecraft skin or shielding, and the transmitted electrons may then create electron-hole pairs in silicon, silicon dioxide, or other electronic materials. Such electrons are copiously produced by beta decay following a nuclear detonation and may be trapped for long times in Earth's magnetic field. Gradual accumulation of electron-hole pairs leads to performance degradation of solid state electronic components. The accumulation process is called "total induced dose" (TID), and the types of degraded performance include "gate oxide threshold voltage shift", "isolated transistor edge leakage", and "isolation oxide inversion." In DMSP/NOAA orbit, an unshielded part naturally accumulates dose at a rate of about 2.5×10^6 rads per year. A 0.040 inch aluminum shield reduces this to about 1.1×10^4 rads per year, and a 0.100 inch aluminum shield to about 500 rads per year. By contrast, the dose rate behind a 0.100 inch shield on the first day after a nuclear event is 10^5 to 10^7 rads per year. When a sufficient dose (see Figures VI.4 and VI.5) is reached the part effectively fails, with consequent reduction in spacecraft mission performance. Because nuclear-generated electrons may be trapped for months or years, the excess rate of degradation of electronic components on satellites in orbit during the burst, or even for replacement satellites, is a serious concern.

Shielding is the first defense against damage by energetic electrons and protons. For LEO satellites passing through the inner radiation belt, shielding is designed to defend against protons, which have energies extending to hundreds of MeV. Such a shield will be even more effective against lower energy electrons. A well-shielded satellite might have a 0.100 inch (2500 micron) shield, which blocks protons with energy below about 25 MeV, and electrons with energy below about 1.2 MeV. Proton damage is dominant behind such a shield, and additional shielding provides diminishing additional protection from protons. However, such a shield provides little protection against electrons originating from nuclear fission, which mostly have energies above 1 MeV. Figure VI.25 shows a comparison of the effectiveness of a 0.100 inch aluminum shield in natural and nuclear environments. The approximate effect of the shield is to move the spectrum 1.2 MeV to the left. In the mean natural environment, the vast bulk of electrons are blocked, leaving a relatively small flux of high energy electrons. Because the nuclear spectrum is much harder, the shield is much less effective.

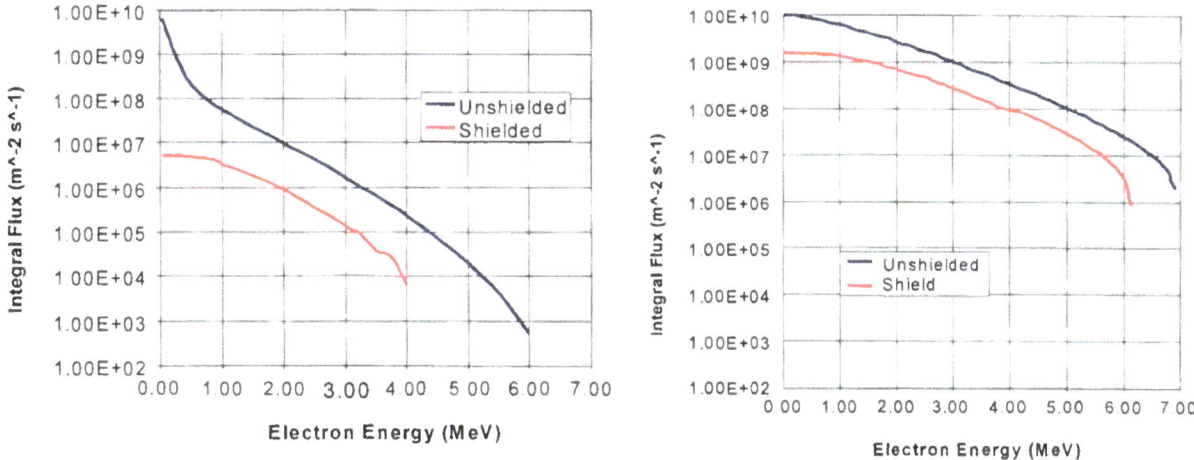

Figure VI.25. Effect of 0.100 inch Aluminum shield on the mean natural electron environment (left) and on the nuclear-induced trapped electron environment (right).

VI.B.2   Single Event Phenomena

A Single Event Upset (SEU) is a change of state of a device due to the ionization track of a single energetic charged particle. In the natural environment, SEUs are produced by energetic cosmic ray ions ranging from hydrogen to iron. These show up, for example, in satellite images as isolated white pixels. Single Event Latchup (SEL) is an irreversible change of state due to the same process.

Gamma rays, fission fragment and neutrons all contribute stresses but are generally not of primary concern relative to prompt effects with the possible exception of neutrons which are capable of SEU and damage [Walters, 2003]. We do not consider Single Event phenomena further in this report.

VI.C   Neutron Effects

Neutrons, absent a net charge, can penetrate deeply into a material and strike one of the constituent atoms in a process similar to a billiard ball collision. These atoms (called knock-ons) can be stripped of some of their electrons because of the kinetic energy they acquire, and are then capable of creating further ionization and other atomic displacements until they decelerate, recapture electrons, and come to rest at a site similar to their original location or in some interstitial position. In the latter case, the vacant site and the atoms displaced into an interstitial site within a crystal lattice form a pair known as a "Frenkel defect", [Bridgman, 2001]. Depending upon initial energy of the neutron, a first-generation displaced atom may have sufficient energy to displace still other atoms and may form a cascade of defects. These defects can act as trapping sites for a semiconductor material's electrical charge carriers. The defects, or traps, can decrease the carriers' mobility and/or free lifetime. The loss of carrier lifetime produces a decrease in gain of a transistor, with a resulting degradation in microcircuit performance. Figure VI.26 indicates the neutron fluence thresholds for degradations of different semiconductor technologies.

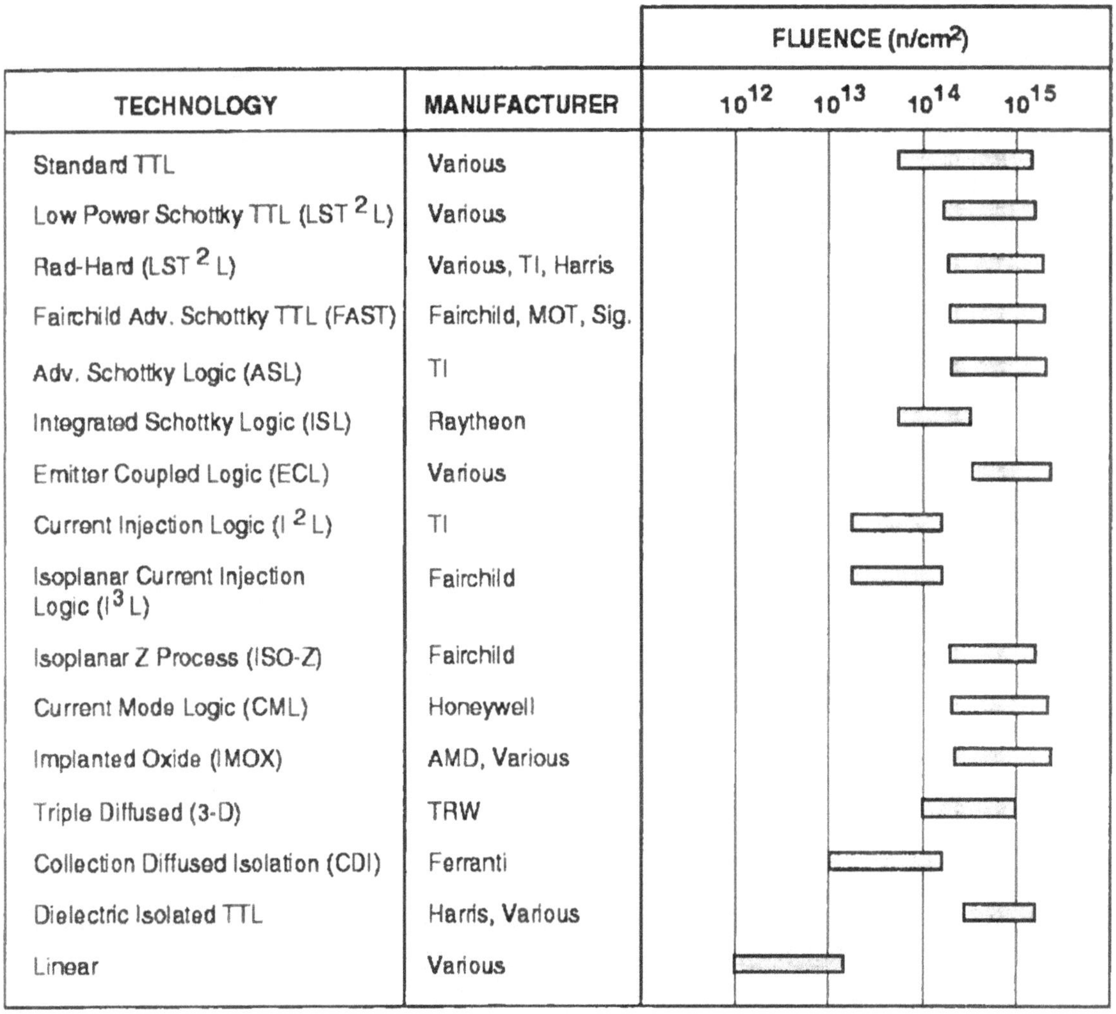

TECHNOLOGY	MANUFACTURER	FLUENCE (n/cm²) 10^{12} — 10^{15}
Standard TTL	Various	10^{14}–10^{15}
Low Power Schottky TTL (LST^{2}L)	Various	10^{14}–10^{15}
Rad-Hard (LST^{2}L)	Various, TI, Harris	10^{14}–10^{15}
Fairchild Adv. Schottky TTL (FAST)	Fairchild, MOT, Sig.	10^{14}–10^{15}
Adv. Schottky Logic (ASL)	TI	10^{14}–10^{15}
Integrated Schottky Logic (ISL)	Raytheon	~10^{14}
Emitter Coupled Logic (ECL)	Various	~10^{15}
Current Injection Logic (I^{2}L)	TI	~10^{13}–10^{14}
Isoplanar Current Injection Logic (I^{3}L)	Fairchild	~10^{13}–10^{14}
Isoplanar Z Process (ISO-Z)	Fairchild	10^{14}–10^{15}
Current Mode Logic (CML)	Honeywell	10^{14}–10^{15}
Implanted Oxide (IMOX)	AMD, Various	10^{14}–10^{15}
Triple Diffused (3-D)	TRW	~10^{14}
Collection Diffused Isolation (CDI)	Ferranti	~10^{13}–10^{14}
Dielectric Isolated TTL	Harris, Various	~10^{15}
Linear	Various	~10^{12}–10^{13}

Figure VI.26. Neutron damage thresholds for bipolar ICs. [Northrop, 1996]

CHAPTER VII
ANALYTICAL SCOPE

VII.A Representative Satellites

Because we believe low altitude satellites to be at greatest risk from the postulated threats, we elected to focus on three specific spacecraft in LEO for detailed analyses. These spacecraft constitute a reasonable surrogate for the U.S. space infrastructure. Representative MEO GPS satellites and geosynchronous communication satellites were given a relatively cursory investigation owing to their distance from detonations associated with either a direct terrestrial EMP attack or the nuclear events postulated below.

The LEO satellites were:

- International Space Station (ISS), because it is a major US and international investment and a symbol of technological achievement and human aspirations;

- TERRA, a civilian Earth observation satellite representative of many such geo-monitoring spacecraft;

- NOAA, an evolving constellation of government operated weather satellites. The Defense Meteorological Satellite Program (DMSP), a military Earth-observing satellite program, maintains similar assets in comparable orbits.

Approximate orbit parameters for these satellites are summarized in Table VII.1.

VII.B Nuclear Events

EMP can occur if a nuclear weapon is detonated anywhere on the surface of the Earth up to several hundred kilometers in altitude. A burst can quickly damage and disable satellites via energetic electromagnetic photon (ultraviolet, X-rays and gamma rays) and particle (electron and neutron) radiation. This prompt damage can be manifested as distortion of telescope and other structural members, destruction of optical components, damage to solar power panels, logic circuit upset, or burnout of sensitive microelectronics within the spacecraft. Additionally, energetic electrons trapped by Earth's magnetic field can cause spacecraft electronics to degrade over periods from days to years.

To address these issues we generated 21 trial nuclear events, as shown in Table VII.2, which we believe pose a plausible spectrum of threats to U.S. space assets. The disparate environments produced by these events were analytically imposed on the representative spacecraft to examine ancillary effects of an exo-atmospheric nuclear detonation. The timeframe of interest is the present out to the year 2015. Currently, threats that seem most credible are relatively low-yield (10-20 kt) detonations in regions of the world recognized as high-tension areas. We also postulated excursions in those regions where larger yield weapons could be used in the future.

Table II.1. Satellites Analyzed.

Satellite	Altitude (km)	Inclination (deg.)	Mission
NOAA DMSP	800 (LEO)	Polar	Weather, Military Situational Awareness, Search and Rescue
TERRA IKONOS	700 (LEO)	Polar	Moderate-High Resolution Imaging, Earth Resources & Earth Sciences
ISS	322 (LEO)	51.6	Space Science & Technology, Human outpost in space
GPS	20,200 (MEO)	55	Navigation
Generic GEO	36,000 (GEO)		Communications, NRO, Missile Launch detection, Military communications

Finally, high yield burst scenarios were chosen at latitudes to threaten either GPS or Geosynchronous satellites (events 18-21). These detonations must be at relatively high latitudes to allow high-energy electrons to migrate along those geomagnetic field lines that intersect very high altitudes where GPS and Geosynchronous satellites reside. Since these bursts must be detonated at relatively high latitudes, the primary motivation of the attacker in these cases would be to threaten these high attitude satellite assets. Terrestrial EMP in these scenarios is considered a secondary effect and was therefore not a primary focus of our analyses.

Table II.2. Trial nuclear events.

Trial Event	Location[12]	Yield, (kt)	HOB (km)	L-Value
1	33.0N	20	200	1.26
2	25.0N	100	175	1.09
3	25.0N	300	155	1.09
4	31.3N	10	300	1.19
5	31.0N	100	170	1.16
6	25.4N	800	368	1.27
7	28.6N	800	491	1.36
8	18.5N	4500	102	1.11
9	20.7N	4500	248	1.16
10	22.0N	30	500	1.23
11	22.0N	100	200	1.18
12	35.7N	20	150	1.24
13	36.0N	100	120	1.26

[12] In accordance with Commission policy of not explicitly specifying political contingencies, the location of the events will only be given in terms of latitude.

Trial Event	Location[12]	Yield, (kt)	HOB (km)	L-Value
14	36.0N	500	120	1.26
15	22.5N	100	200	1.03
16	22.5N	500	200	1.03
17	22.5N	5000	200	1.03
18	65N	1000	300	4.11
19	48.5N	10000	90	4.19
20	55N	1000	350	6.85
21	68N	10000	90	6.47

VII.C Computational Tools

VII.C.1 Prompt Radiation Effects

When a weapon is detonated at high altitude, the only satellites subject to direct prompt radiations will be those that lie within line of sight. Satellites shadowed by the Earth, as illustrated in Figure VII.1, will not be directly irradiated but will be subject to trapped electron radiation (pumped radiation belts) and, should the satellite transit the cloud of weapon debris and decay-products, direct exposure to beta-decay electrons and gammas from the debris. If there is intervening atmosphere between the detonation point and the satellite, direct radiations will be attenuated. Lacking this intervening shield, there is no absorption attenuation factor and the energy fluence, X, merely falls off as the inverse square of the distance, *i.e.*:

$$X = 6.4 \times 10^3 \, Y/R^2 \quad (cal/cm^2)$$

Similarly, for neutrons and gamma rays respectively,

$$N = 1.6 \times 10^{15} \, Y/R^2 \quad (n/cm^2)$$

$$G = 2.5 \times 10^5 \, Y/R^2 \quad (rads(Si))$$

for a typical nuclear device, where R is the distance (in kilometers) from a yield Y (in megatons) [Northrop, 1996]. The consequence is that under these conditions energy can propagate for great distances without change in its spectral content. It is for this reason, along with the large material absorption coefficients, that assets in space such as launch rockets, boost vehicles, reentry vehicles and satellites are so susceptible to direct exposure to weapon-produced photon radiation.

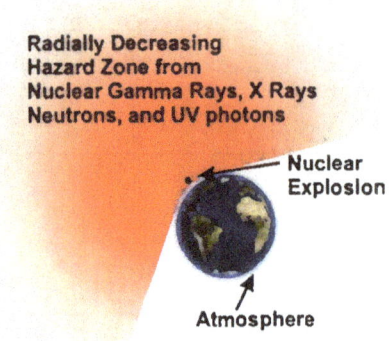

Figure II.1. Where not shadowed by the Earth or shielded by atmospheric attenuation, X-rays, γ-rays, neutrons, and ultraviolet (UV) photons travel great distances from a high-altitude nuclear detonation where they may inflict damage to satellites.

VII.C.2 Line-of Sight Photon Threat

Hypothetical fluences for NOAA/DMSP, TERRA and ISS satellites were calculated using the Satellite Tool Kit (STK) [Analytical Graphics, 1997], which accounted for absorption in those instances in which Earth's atmosphere occluded the line of sight between satellite and nuclear burst. Atmospheric absorption turned out to be a factor only for events 8, 19, and 21, none of which were sufficiently severe to cause thermomechanical damage to any of the three satellites (see Chapter VI). The worst case, (*i.e.,* minimum range) fluences incident upon each satellite for the 21 events, are depicted in Figures VII.2, VII.3, and VII.4.

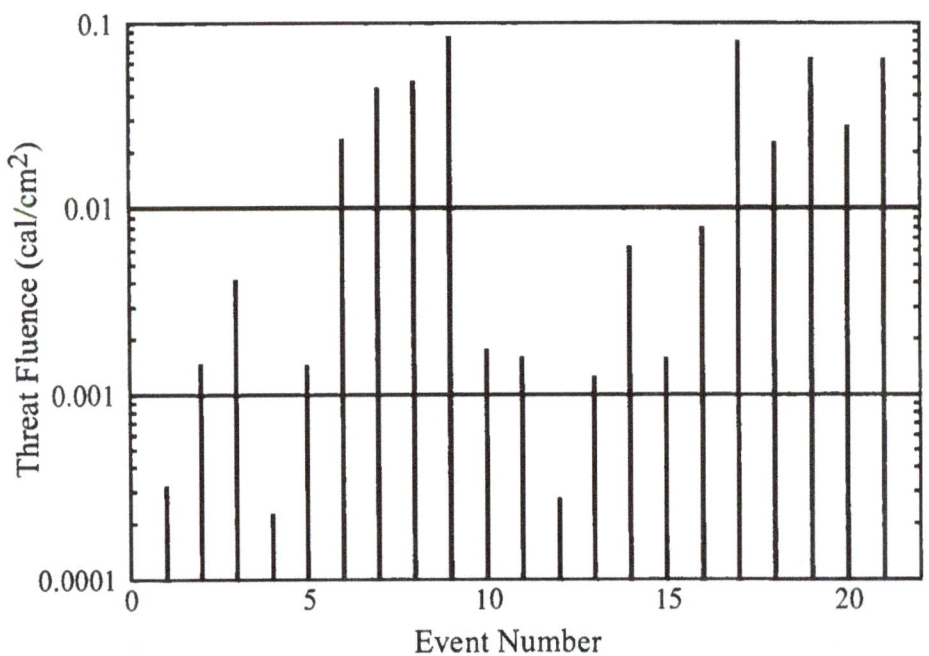

Figure II.2. Worst case threat fluences for the DMSP/NOAA satellite.

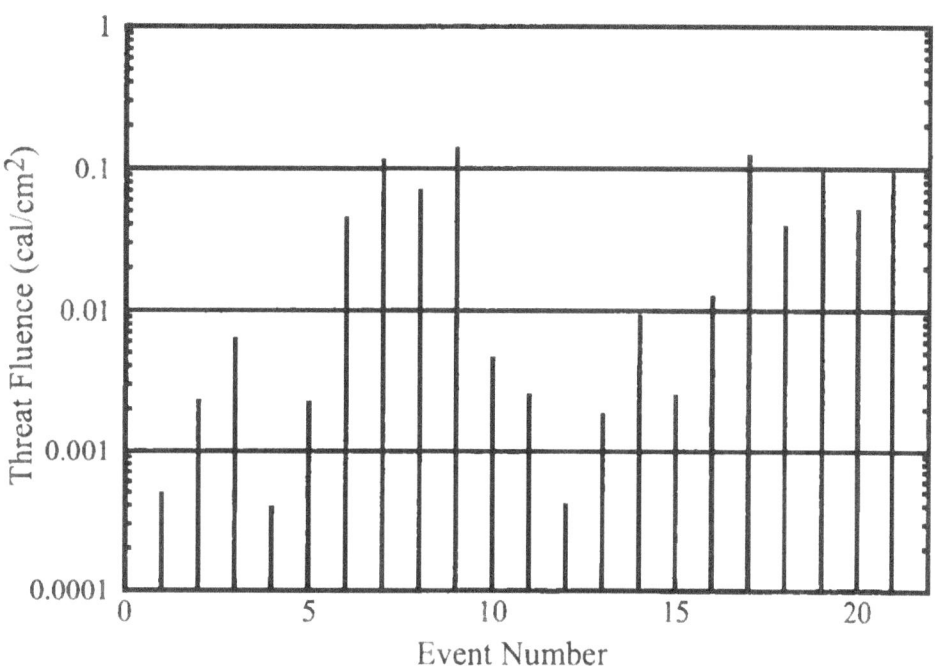

Figure II.3. Worst case threat fluences for the TERRA satellite.

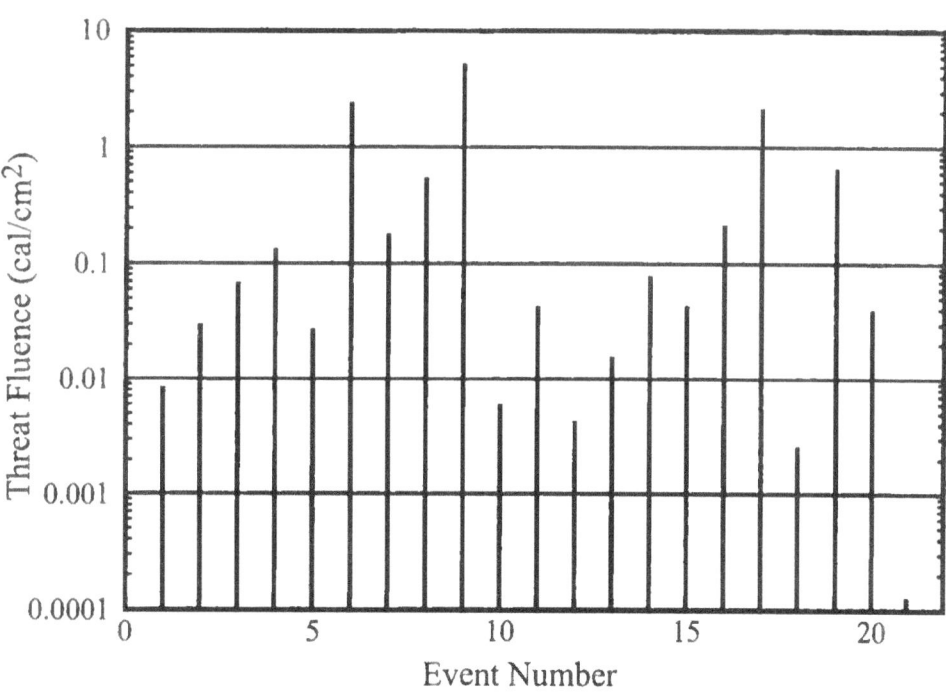

Figure II.4. Worst case threat fluences for the ISS satellite at an altitude of 322 km.

VII.C.3 Line-of Sight X-Ray Probability Methodology

The methodology used for calculating the probability of a satellite encountering a particular prompt X-ray or ultraviolet fluence requires several steps. The Satellite Tool Kit allows one to conveniently determine the geometry between a specific high altitude nuclear burst and the satellite. For a high altitude nuclear burst, the relevant geometric relationship is the distance between detonation point and satellite, absent shielding by the Earth or attenuation by relatively dense atmosphere. Fluence incident upon the target is then inversely proportional to the square of the range. We consider the time of detonation to be arbitrary in our 21 nuclear events. As a computational expedient, a number of trial runs in STK were performed to arrive at a statistically valid probability that a satellite will be at a given range from the burst. Elevation angle between Earth's center and satellite, as measured from the burst point, is also a factor if the Earth's atmosphere occludes the line of sight. In that case, preferential spectral absorption and fluence reduction in addition to that due to inverse square scaling will occur. STK calculations were iterated a sufficient number of times to determine the probability that the satellite will be at a particular range from the burst. In general, for low-Earth orbiting satellites, the likelihood that a satellite will be in view of a burst altitude of a few hundred kilometers is usually small — on the order of 5-20 percent. This may increase significantly if the satellite and/or the burst are at higher altitudes (see Figure VII.1). For our 21 scenarios, the probabilities of any of the LEO satellites being in the line of sight are quite low, typically 5 percent or less.

VII.C.4 Radiation-Belt Effects

The Air Force SNRTACS (Satellite Nuclear Radiation Threat Assessment Code System, [Jakes *et al.*, 1993]) and Defense Threat Reduction Agency DGBETS (Debris Gamma and Beta Threat Environments for Satellites) computer codes were available to model nuclear radiation-belt environments. For this report, SNRTACS was used for estimates of trapped fluxes and predicted satellite lifetimes.

The SNRTACS code consists of three modules, two of which are utilized to calculate the radiation environments that LEO satellites encounter. The Satellite Protection and Environment Codes for Trapped Electron Radiation (SPECTER) module models the initial high-altitude distribution of radioactive bomb debris, generation of high energy electrons from beta-decay of debris radionuclides, temporal and spatial distribution of these high energy electrons in a "pumped belt", and eventual loss of these electrons via various diffusion processes.

SPECTER is a semi-empirical code meaning that approximates debris and electron motion in the geomagnetic field, the model being tuned to empirical data obtained from radiation monitors on satellites in orbit at the time of high-altitude nuclear tests in the late 50's-early 60's. For simulated bursts with parameters close to the empirical database, uncertainties are estimated to be a factor of four to ten [Jakes *et al.*, 1993; Greaves, 1994]. This estimate is based on limited comparisons with the radiation database. Bursts whose parameters differ significantly from those for which data exist (*i.e.*, higher latitudes, higher altitudes, higher or lower yields, different device characteristics) have higher uncertainties, but to what degree is difficult to quantify. The Air Force Research Laboratory is currently taking steps to try to minimize, or at least quantify, areas of uncertainty in trapped radiation. In February 2003, a meeting was held at AFRL to attempt to define particular sources of uncertainty and develop strategies to mitigate these issues. Some of the proposed efforts included a reexamination of old satellite and sounding rocket radiation data taken during the high altitude tests. In addition, a proposal was made to look at old engineering data from spacecraft on orbit at the time of the nuclear events to glean additional information on the radiation environment. New computer codes are also being developed that will model the natural space radiation environment in much higher fidelity. In combination with best-available contemporary models for debris dispersal following a high-altitude detonation, better predictions of the temporal and spatial evolution of pumped belts should result. Other phenomena, such as shock acceleration of ambient electrons and wave-particle interactions, need to be investigated.

The second module in SNRTACS that applies to LEO satellites is called Satellite Assessment for Exoatmospheric Radiation (SAFER). This module essentially "flies" the satellite through the model of an enhanced radiation belt and accumulates dose behind a specified shielding kernel. Unlike SPECTER, which has many uncertainties, the SAFER code is on much firmer ground since the calculations involve well understood orbital mechanics and radiation transport principles.

VII.C.5 Satellite Tool Kit Software

Satellite Tool Kit software (STK) was utilized in the prompt radiation probability analysis (Section VIII.a.2). This powerful pc software was developed by Analytical Graphics Inc., King of Prussia, PA. It models complex geometries between ground and airborne targets and orbiting satellites. The code is widely used within the aerospace community for:

- Planning, design, and analysis of complex aerospace systems
- Real-time space operations
- 3-D situational awareness and decision support

The software was an essential part of the analysis conducted in Section VIII.a.2 to calculate the probability that a satellite would encounter a particular X-ray fluence as a result of a high altitude nuclear detonation at a random time.

CHAPTER VIII
RESULTS OF ANALYSES

In Chapters V and VII we defined the parameter space within which we would perform quantitative analyses, *i.e.* the space environment, the threat events, and a target set we believe to be representative of U.S space assets in LEO. Herein we present the results of those analyses. In Chapter VI we defined nuclear-induced satellite damage as being either temporary or permanent, and further defined permanent damage as being either prompt or cumulative. In the latter instance (cumulative damage), we assume each of our representative satellites will cease useful operation when it has received the equivalent of twice the total ionizing dose of natural radiation for which it was nominally designed.

VIII.A Prompt Line of Sight Damage

VIII.A.1 Probability Analysis of Prompt Line-of-Sight Damage

As noted, the worst-case situation generally occurs when the range between satellite and burst is a minimum and the UV and X-ray fluences incident upon the satellite are maximized. Full assessment for situations other than worst case requires a statistical description, but for events and satellites similar to those considered, the likelihood that a LEO satellite will be in view of a burst is typically 5 to 20 percent. Even then, damage may on occasion be mitigated by intervening atmosphere.

As described in Chapter VII, fluences on the DMSP/NOAA, TERRA and ISS satellites were calculated using the Satellite Tool Kit which accounted for absorption when Earth's atmosphere occluded the line of sight between satellite and nuclear burst. Atmospheric absorption turned out to be a significant factor only for events 6, 9, and 11, none of which were sufficiently severe to cause thermomechanical damage to any of the three satellites. Worst-case (*i.e.*, minimum range) fluences incident upon each satellite for the 21 events are depicted in Figures VII.2, VII.3, and VII.4.

STK calculations described above yield the probability that a satellite will be exposed to a given X-ray fluence. With this information one can estimate the probability of satellite damage based upon damage thresholds for spacecraft materials. Damage thresholds used here are at or near those generally accepted by the spacecraft community (see Chapter VI.). Results appear in Table VIII.1. Here thermomechanical damage refers to removal or degradation of coatings on solar cell surfaces. Depending upon nuclear weapon output spectra, thermomechanical damage is frequently a satellite's most sensitive (*i.e.* minimum fluence) damage mode, an observation that applies for the events and satellites analyzed for this study. SGEMP burnout and/or latch-up/burnout may also result in unacceptable damage.

Calculations of X-ray exposure probabilities were performed for events 9, 13, 17 and 18. Uncertainties associated with device UV output make quantitative analyses of their effects problematic, but the X-ray results may be scaled for UV radiation as elucidated in Chapter VI.

Figure VIII.1, Figure VIII.2, and Figure VIII.3 depict exposure probability vs. X-ray fluence for the three satellites on which we have focused. Dotted vertical lines bound bands of generally accepted fluence values at which particular damage modes are likely to occur. The reader is referred to Chapters V and VI for caveats associated with weapon spectrum and shielding thickness used in the construction of these damage metrics.

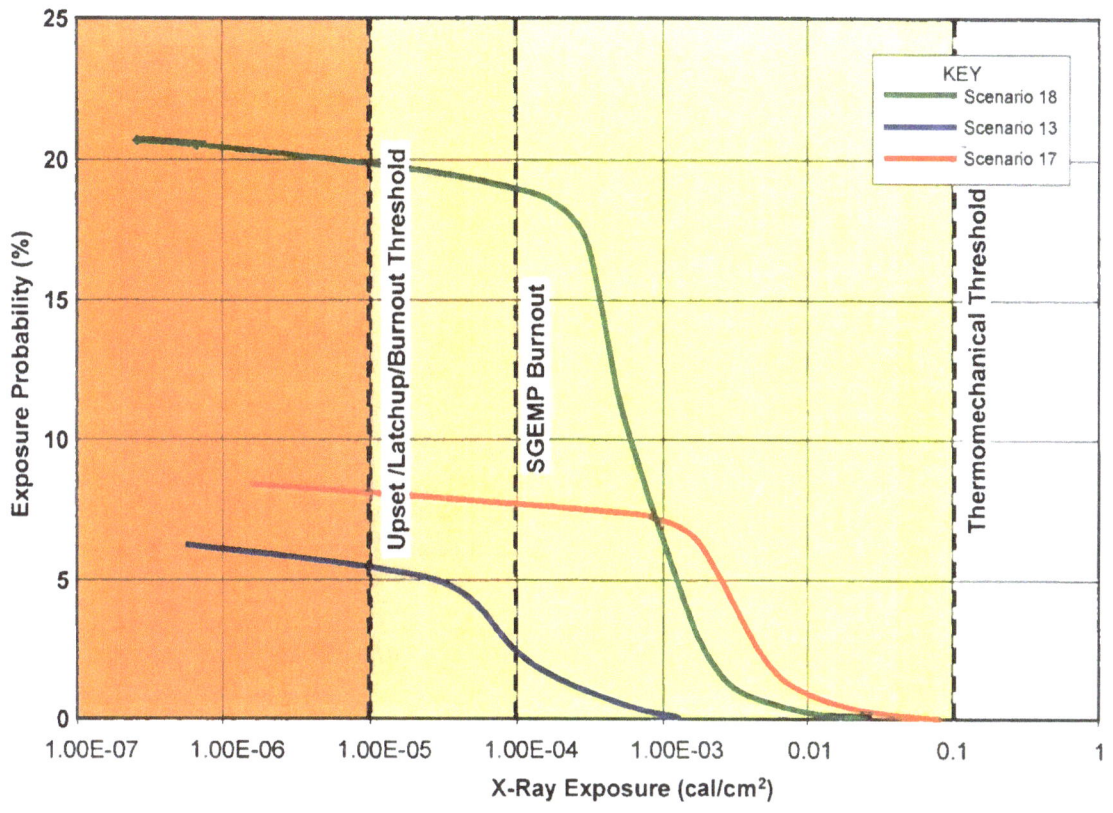

Figure III.1. NOAA X-ray events.

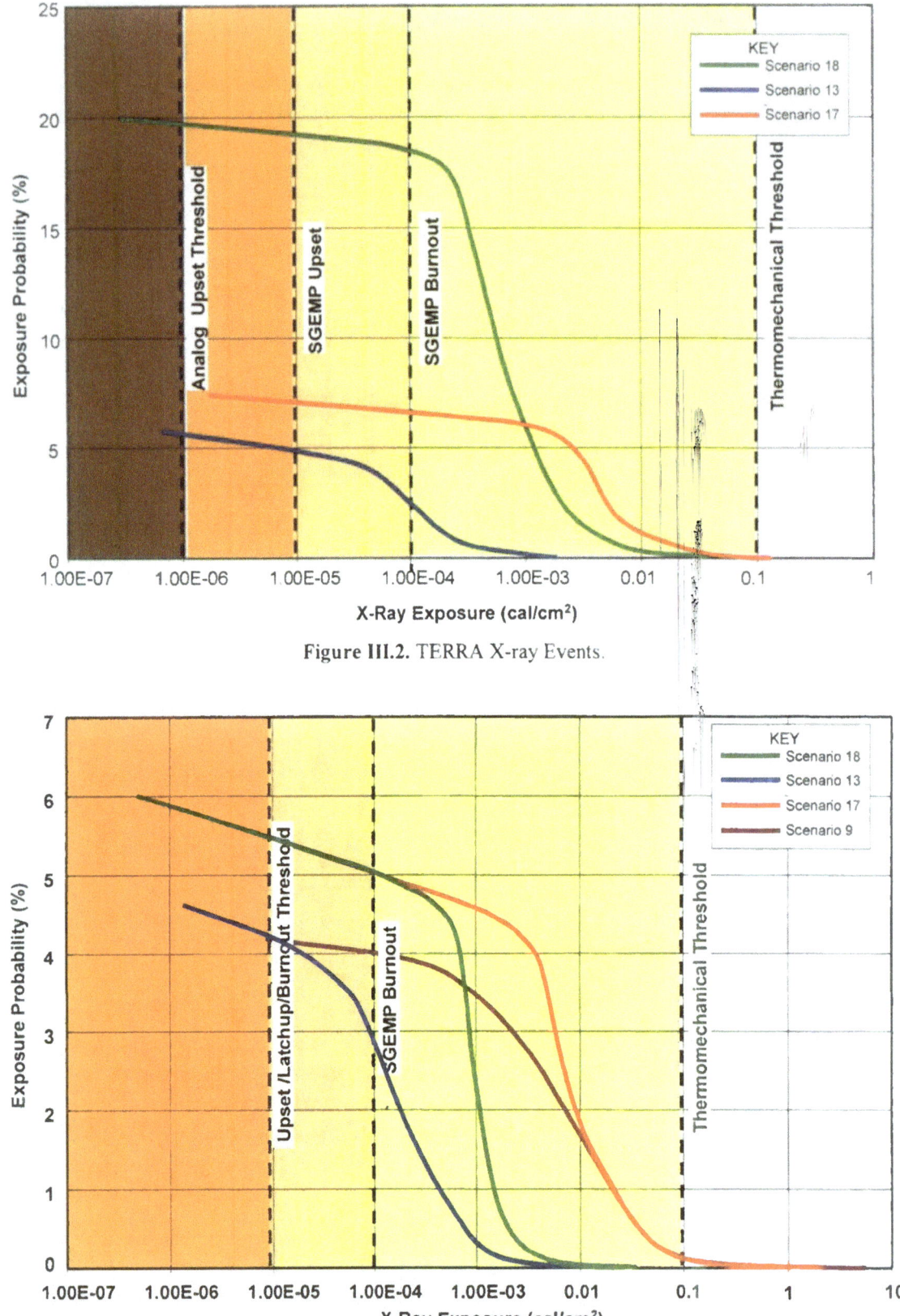

Figure III.2. TERRA X-ray Events.

Figure III.3. ISS X-ray Events.

Table III.1. Probability of the satellites' suffering damage from prompt X-radiation.

Satellite	Event	Thermomechanical ~0.01 cal/cm^2 (%)	SGEMP/Burn-out ~10^{-4} cal/cm^2 (%)	Latch up/ Burnout ~10^{-5} cal/cm^2 (%)	Worst Case cal/cm$^2 \times 10^{-3}$
ISS	9	1.9	4	4.2	5300
	18	No Issue	5	5	3
	13	No Issue	3	4	10
	17	2.0	5	5	2200
NOAA	18	No Issue	19	20	24
	13	No Issue	3	5	1
	17	1.4	7	8	81
TERRA	18	No Issue	18	18	40
	13	No Issue	2	5	2
	17	1.2	7	7	128

VIII.A.2 Photon Effects

VIII.A.2.a Spectrum Issues

As discussed in Chapter VI, X-ray spectra resulting from nuclear detonations are broad. Consequently, photons are absorbed at different depths within a spacecraft depending upon photon energy, photons of low energy being absorbed nearer the surface and those of high energy penetrating deeper. In the discussion that follows, we have chosen to stress effects of low energy photons (UV and X-rays). Further, we note common hardening techniques such as spot shielding are not applicable to surface mounted assemblies as solar cells, radiators and optical components. Analogously, below we have focused on the low energy, surface-charging electrons for much the same reasons.

VIII.A.2.b Photon Induced Thermomechanical Damage

The three LEO satellites analyzed for thermomechanically induced surface damage all utilize silicon solar cells with coverglass made of CMX, a ceria-doped borosilicate whose coefficient of thermal expansion is designed to match that of its accompanying solar cell. The ISS coverglass is coated with 17 layers of SiO_2 /Ta_2O_5 designed to minimize reflectivity in the visible, and to maximize it in the UV and IR regions of the solar spectrum. TERRA utilizes a CMX coverglass coated with a single layer of MgF_2 to minimize reflection in the visible. We have not been able to determine definitively which, if either, of these coatings is used on DMSP and/or NOAA, and consequently both were considered. The three exemplar satellites were selected on the basis of their orbits, not their configurations.

We chose to analyze coverglass coatings in detail [Gurtman, 2003], as past experience has generally shown them to be ubiquitous satellite components, and among those most vulnerable to nuclear radiation induced thermomechanical damage. Both coatings are dielectrics and have been extensively probed in X-ray environments in above- and below-ground tests. Consequently there exists a well-populated database upon which to make damage estimates. Lastly, the two coatings are representative of those used with solar arrays on most U.S. satellites in terms of performance and X-ray hardness and become, therefore, good surrogates for all U.S. satellites.

Our analyses consider the possibility of compressive stress failure on both coatings for the 21 events listed in Table VII.1. The identical X-ray spectrum is used for all the calculations. This spectrum, and associated pulse width, were generated by LLNL [Thompson, 2003] for a representative threat, and will be referred to as the 'baseline' spectrum. Fluences on target were scaled from the LLNL calculation on the basis of yield, but no adjustments were made to pulse shape. Parametric calculations of damage show pulse width to have a noticeable effect on coating hardness (perhaps as much as ± 15%), but this effect was thought small with respect to other uncertainties in analyses of nuclear induced damage.

The single-layer anti-reflective (SLAR) coating consisted of a 103.62 nm thick layer of MgF_2 on CMX. The multilayer (MLAR) coating consisted of 9 layers of Ta_2O_5 which varied in thickness from 96 nm to 285 nm, and 8 layers of SiO_2 with thickness between 265 and 336 nm.

VIII.A.2.b.i Single Layer Anti-Reflection (SLAR) Coating

Calculations were performed using SAIC's XRT X-ray deposition code. Normalized dose (*i.e.* dose per unit fluence in units of cal/gm/cal/cm^2) as a function of depth for the SLAR coating is plotted in Figure VIII.4.

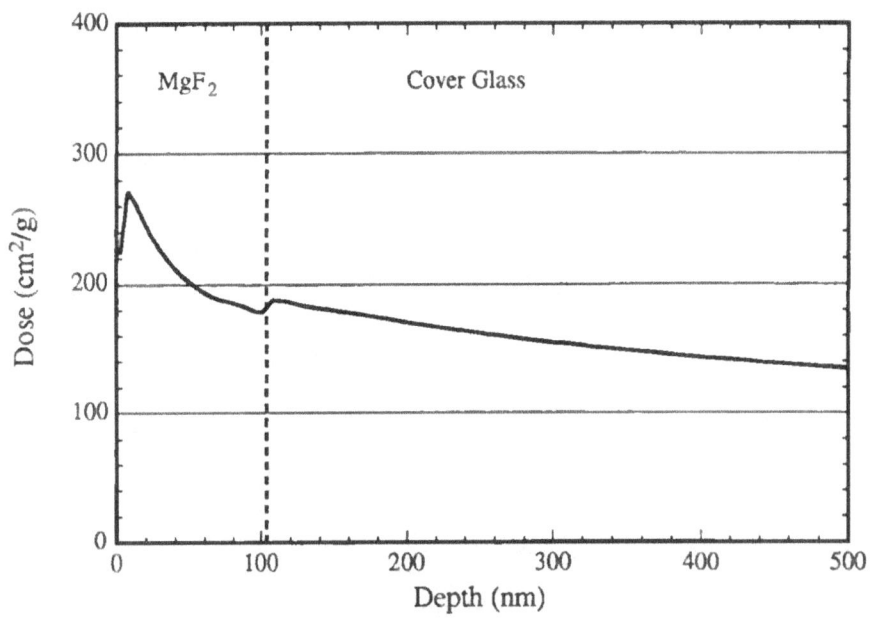

Figure III.4. Normalized dose for the SLAR configuration. Photo-electron migration has been taken into account, but not heat conduction.

A plot of peak temperature as a function of depth, taking into account heat conduction during the postulated X-ray deposition time (800 ns) is shown in Figure VIII.5.

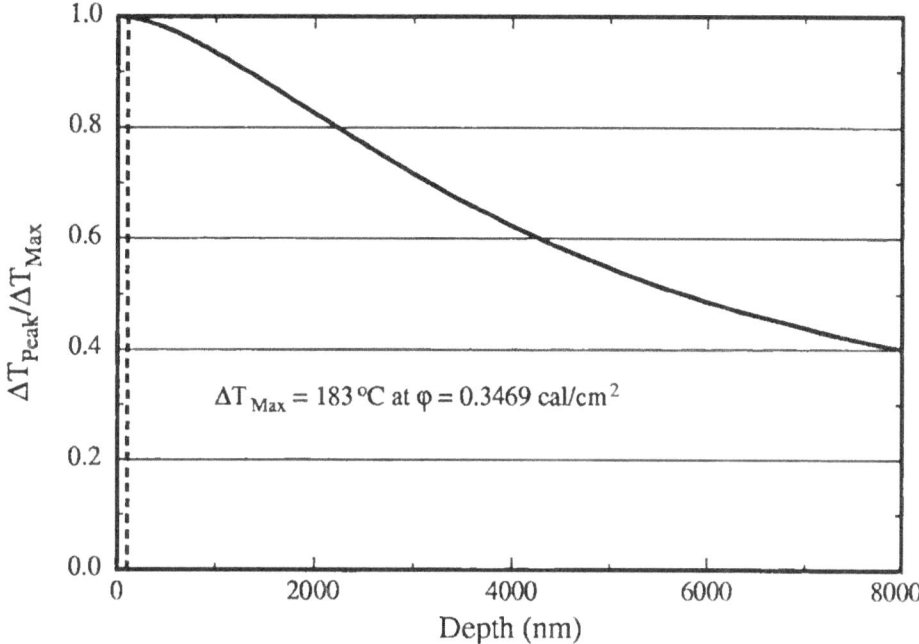

Figure III.5. Ratio of peak temperature at a given depth to the maximum temperature achieved by the SLAR coating. Thermal conduction is taken into account over the deposition pulse time of 800 ns.

The ratio of the peak *in-plane* compressive stress as a function of depth to the maximum compressive stress is shown in Figure VIII.6.

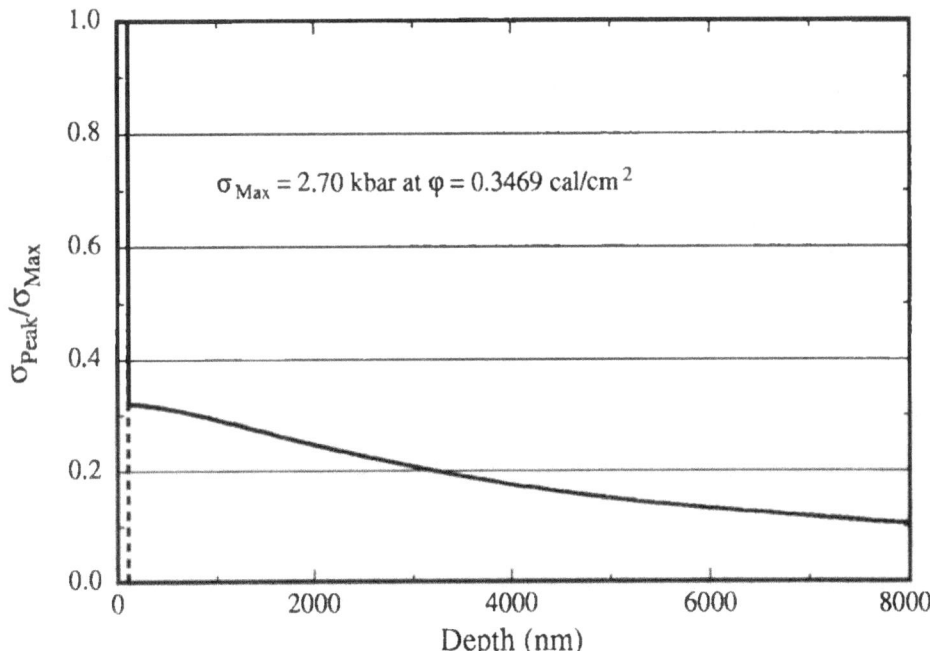

Figure III.6. Ratio of the peak in-plane compressive stress to the maximum compressive stress for the SLAR coating.

The coating failure criterion used here is based upon the magnitude of the maximum *in-plane* compressive stress, as discussed below. In a coordinate system where the *x*-axis is perpendicular to the surface of the coverglass, and with the assumption of plane strain in the coating, an increment of the *in-plane* compressive stress $\sigma_{yy,zz}$ is given in terms of a temperature increment dT by

$$d\sigma_{yy,zz} = -\frac{\alpha E}{1-\nu} dT, \qquad (1)$$

where α is the linear thermal expansion coefficient, E the elastic (Young's) modulus and ν the Poisson's ratio. The plane strain ε_{ii}, assumption also assumes zero lateral expansion, *i.e.*,

$$\varepsilon_{yy} = \varepsilon_{zz} = 0, \qquad (2)$$

and zero stress perpendicular to the surface,

$$\sigma_{xx} = 0. \qquad (3)$$

Tables of (temperature dependent) numerical values for these physical properties as used in the XRT calculations, most of which were taken from Childs [1981], are summarized in Appendix C of Gurtman, *et al* [2003].

Plots of maximum in-plane compressive stress for the three satellites where they all are assumed to be carrying a MLAR coating are shown in Figure VIII.7, Figure VIII.8, and Figure

VIII.9. Failure threshold for MgF$_2$ (based upon the X-ray damage database for this material) was assumed to be between 2 and 3 kbars.

We note that only ISS is likely to experience failures for the 21 nuclear threats, and then only for events 6, 8, 9, 17, and 19. Probability analyses as described above indicate that for these particular events, the ISS is only within the range at which damage occurs less than 0.5 % of the time. In those instances however, loss of solar power is likely to be instantaneous and catastrophic.

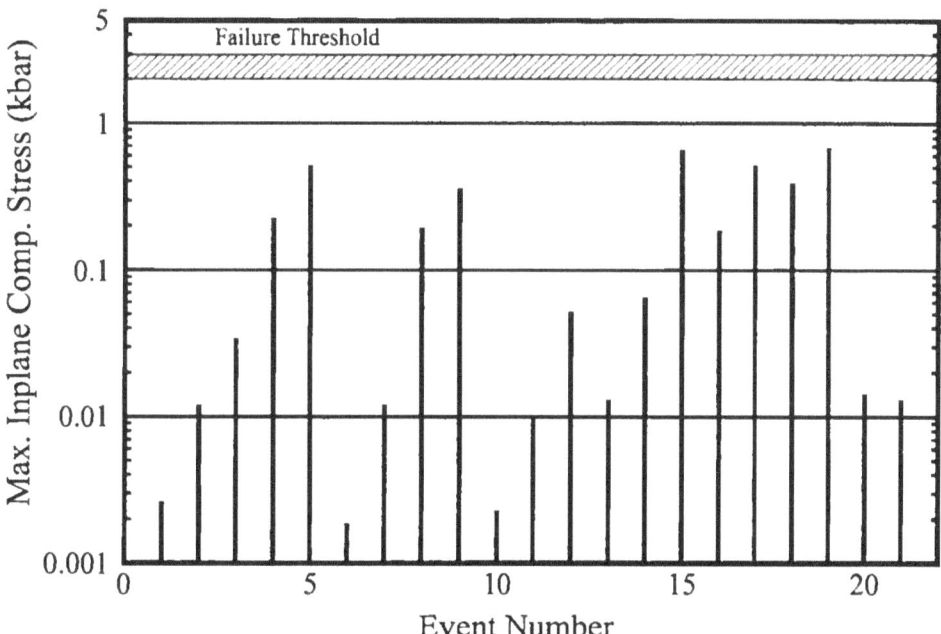

Figure III.7. Maximum in-plane compressive stress in a SLAR coating on DMSP/NOAA subjected to the threat events.

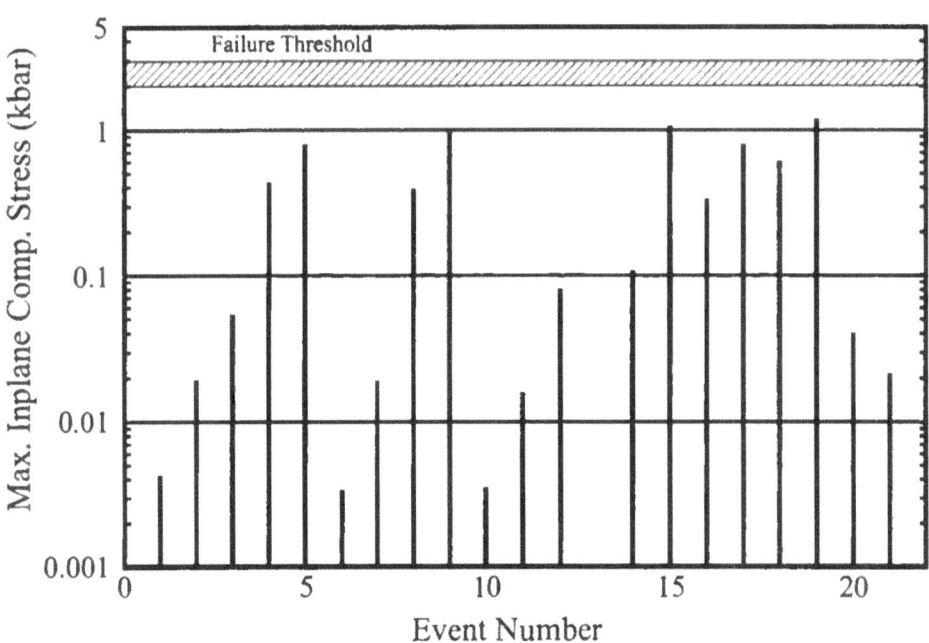

Figure III.8. Maximum in-plane compressive stress in a SLAR coating on TERRA subjected to the threat events. Note: Event 13 falls below the minimum value for this chart.

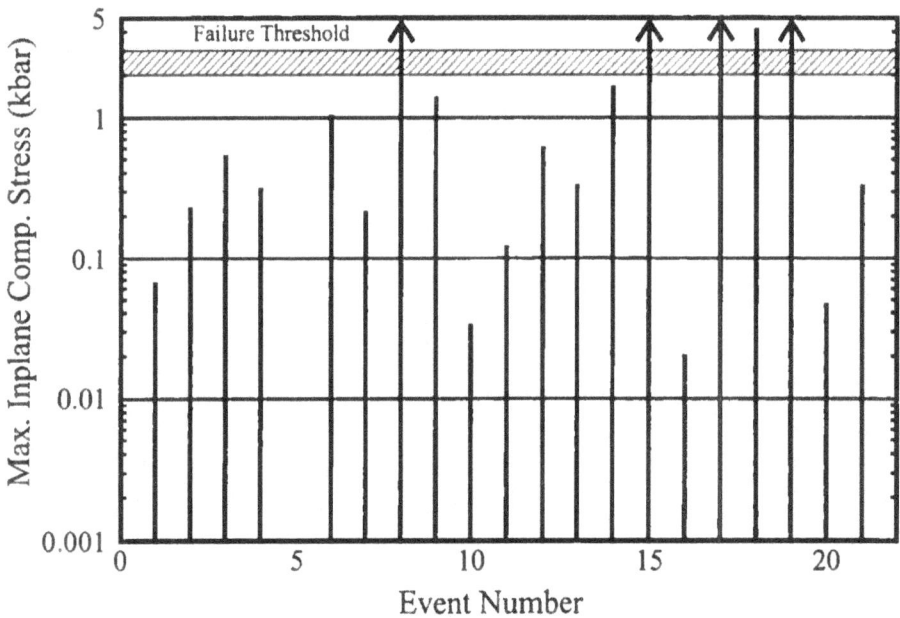

Figure III.9. Maximum in-plane compressive stress in a SLAR coating on ISS (322 km altitude) subjected to the threat events. Note: Event 5 falls below the minimum value for this chart.

VIII.A.2.b.ii Multi-Layer Anti-Reflection (MLAR) Coating

Normalized dose as a function of depth for this coating is plotted in Figure VIII.10.

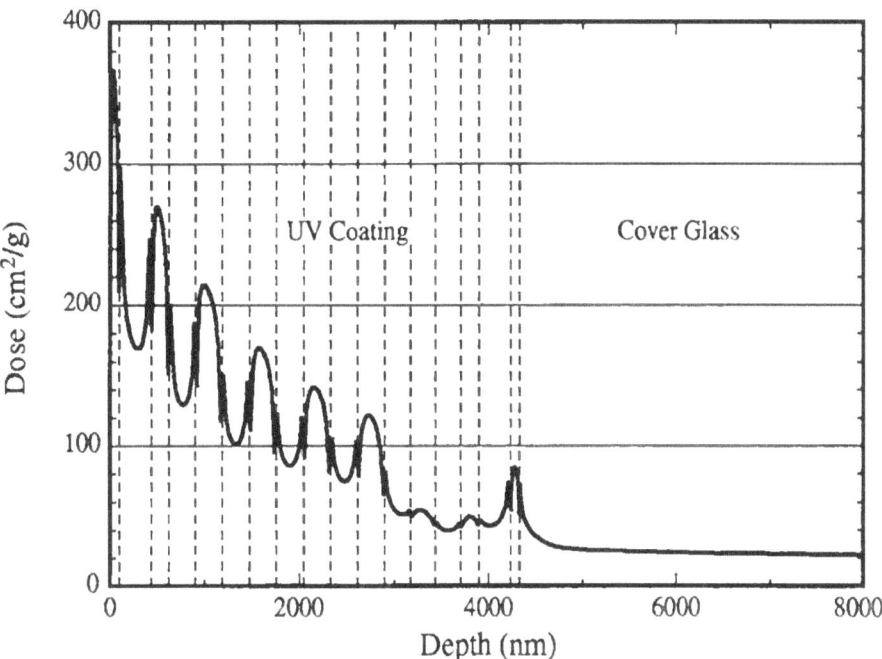

Figure III.10. Normalized dose for the MLAR configuration. Photo-electron migration has been taken into account, but not heat conduction.

Peak temperature as a function of depth is shown in Figure VIII.11.

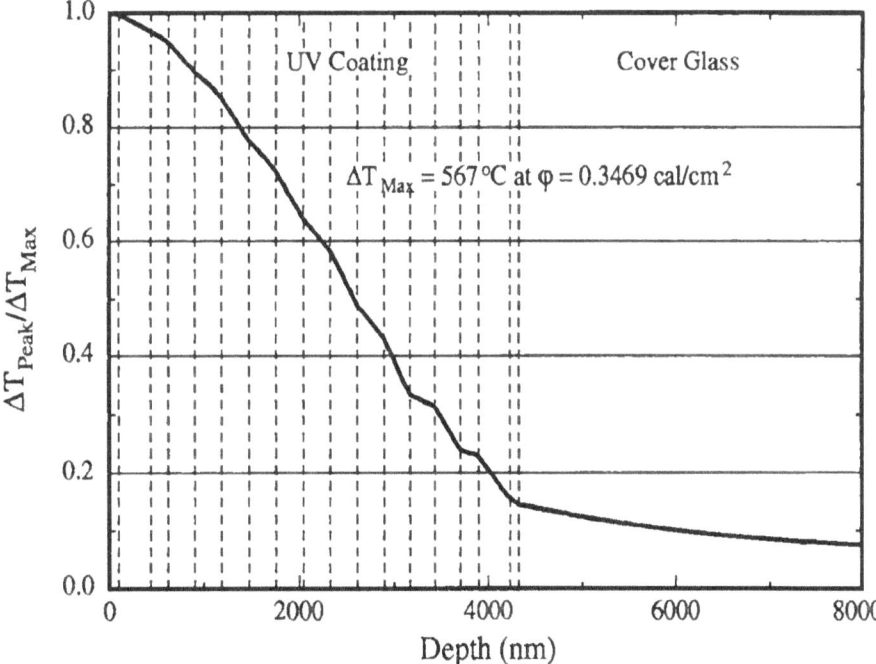

Figure III.11. Ratio of peak temperature at a given depth to the maximum temperature achieved by a MLAR coating. Thermal conduction is taken into account over the deposition pulse time of 800 ns.

An example of the ratio of peak compressive in-plane stress to the maximum stress for this coating is given in Figure VIII.12.

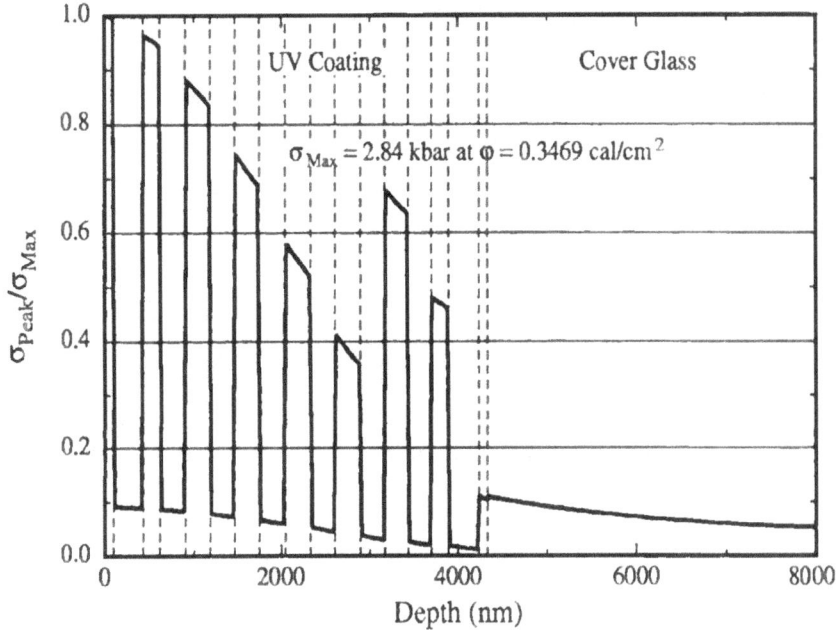

Figure III.12. Ratio of the peak in-plane compressive stress to the maximum compressive stress for the MLAR coating

Plots of maximum in-plane compressive stress for the three satellites, where they all are assumed to be carrying a MLAR coating, are given in Figure VIII.13, Figure VIII.14 and Figure VIII.15. Failure threshold for this particular MLAR (based upon the X-ray damage database) is, as was the case for the SLAR, somewhere in the range of 2 and 3 kbars.

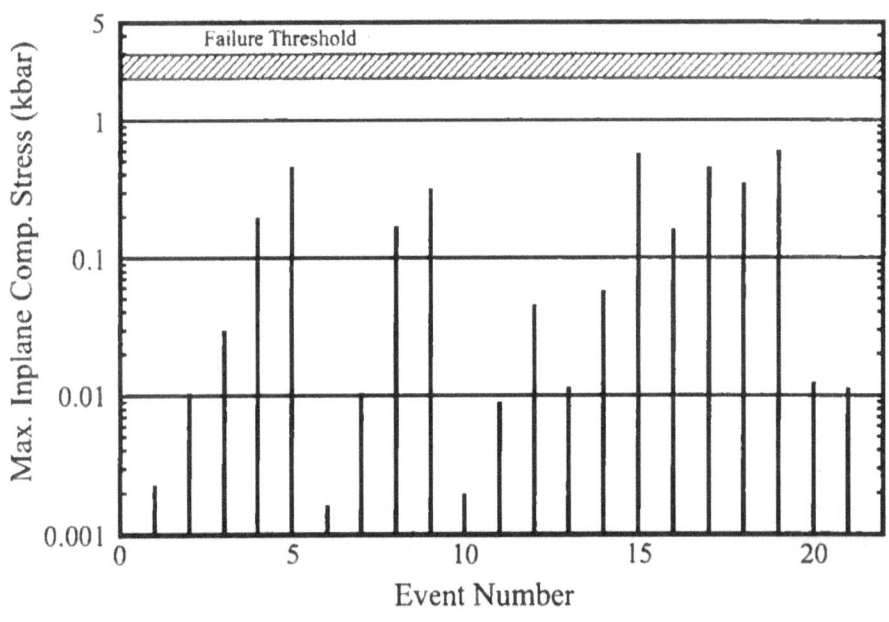

Figure III.13. Maximum in-plane compressive stress in a MLAR coating on DMSP/NOAA subjected to the threat events.

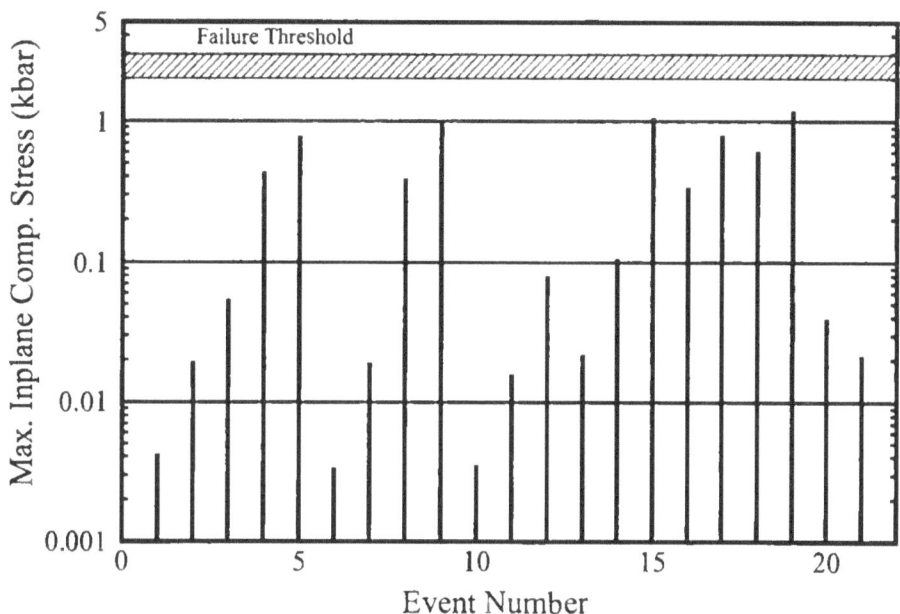

Figure III.14. Maximum in-plane compressive stress in a MLAR coating on TERRA subjected to the threat events.

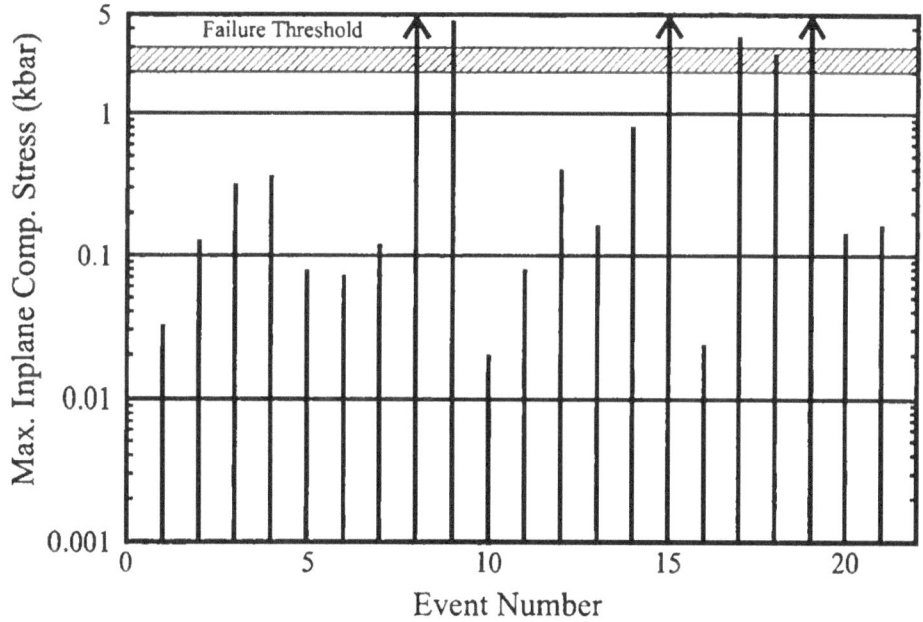

Figure III.15. Maximum in-plane compressive stress in a MLAR coating on ISS (322 km altitude) subjected to the threat events.

As was the case with the SLAR, assuming all three LEO satellites utilized MLAR's, only ISS is likely to experience failures for the 21 nuclear threats, and then only for events 6, 7, 8, 9, 17 and 19. Since the probability analysis used takes no account of satellite structural details and both the MLAR and SLAR coatings fail at essentially the same fluence, this eventuality will again occur less than 0.5 % of the time.

VIII.A.3 Surveillance Satellite Subsystems

LEO satellites are frequently used to perform generic earth surveillance functions, and such missions generally require photonic imagers of some sort. Such is true of each of the three satellites chosen in this study. The detectors used in imagers and their related components comprise a satellite subsystem that poses unique problems when forced to operate in a radiation intensive environment. The most significant difficulty for surveillance systems that are required to operate through and after a nuclear event is reduced sensitivity due to an increase in ionization-induced noise. [Northrop, 1996].

Tables VIII.2 [Bell, 1990] and VIII.3 [Pickel, 2003] discuss degradation thresholds for various photonic materials. Here, degradation threshold is defined as that fluence at which the sensitivity of the detector is degraded by a factor of 2.

Table III.2. Generalized elements, malfunctions and susceptibilities of surveillance sensors.

Susceptible Elements	Potential Malfunction Items	Performance Parameter	Susceptibility Threshold
Detector array and multiplexer	High rates of false targets; saturation of buffer due to dose rate interference	S/N ratio; false alarm	10^{-3} rads/sec without noise suppression 1 to 5 rads/sec with time-delay integration Up to 10^3 rads/sec with pulse-biased thin-film technology
Detector array/MUX/analog processor, digital processor, and data processor	Saturation of detector and MUX; momentary upset of processor	Allowable outage time	1 to 10 rads prompt (higher for P_bS)
Optical surface damage	Loss of resolution; loss of function	False alarm rate Link margin Resolution	0.1 to 1 cal/cm^2
Red-out	Loss of target and/or increase in false alarm rate	S/N ratio; false alarm rate	TBD
Detector/coolant	Heating of low-temperature detectors	S/N ratio (temperature)	$\approx \times 10^{-3}$ cal/g (detector) (several degrees)

Table III.3. Degradation Thresholds of Various Detector Materials [Pickel, 2003].

Detector Type	Radiation Environment	Irradiation Temperature (°K)	Displacement Damage Threshold
LWIR HgCdTe	Fission Neutrons	78	~3×10^{14} n/cm^2
	14-MeV Neutrons	78	~1×10^{14} n/cm^2
	2-MeV Electrons	78	~6×10^{11} e/cm^2
	Co^{60} Gammas	78	~4×10^{7} Rad(HgCdTe)
Photoconductive InSb	14-Mev Neutrons	78	~5×10^{12} n/cm^2
Photovoltaic InSb (n/p)	14-Mev Neutrons	78	~3×10^{11} n/cm^2
Photoconductive PbS	Thermal Neutrons	300	~5×10^{15} n/cm^2
	14-MeV Neutrons	300	~2×10^{13} n/cm^2
	7.5-MeV Protons	300	~2×10^{12} p/cm^2
	12-MeV Protons	300	~7×10^{12} p/cm^2
	133-MeV Protons	300	~1×10^{13} p/cm^2
	450-MeV Protons	300	~2×10^{13} p/cm^2
SiAs	Fission Neutrons	10	~1×10^{11} n/cm^2

For our 21 events and line-of-sight probability analyses, it appears unlikely that the three selected LEO satellites will experience complete failure of any of their surveillance sensor systems.

On the other hand, for those satellites specifically designed to monitor nuclear detonations and/or perform missile launch and tracking, it is likely that threshold values in Table VIII.3 will be met with resulting loss of sensor performance. Optical surface damage may only occur on ISS and be limited to events 6, 8, 9, 17 and 19, but all the other susceptibilities are to be expected for each of the three satellites when in line of sight of a detonation. The probability of being in line of sight is quite small for a satellite whose primary mission is the tracking of missiles or monitoring of nuclear events.

Performance parameters of Table VIII.3 are seen to depend primarily upon decreased signal to noise ratios (S/N), and while permanent degradation is an important aspect of the radiation response of photonic and particularly infrared detectors, ionization-induced transients are often the critical issue in actual applications. To detect optical photons (as in missile plumes), infrared detectors are likely in their bare state to be very sensitive ionization detectors. They must be capable of detecting low energy IR photons, and this requires a low noise baseline. As a result, they are also extremely effective detectors of ionization, and hence IR sensors are often based on the same physical principles and rely on the same materials as do nuclear detectors [Pickel, 2003].

Gamma flux exposure is generally the cause of greatest concern for sensors designed to observe transient phenomena and operate in a nuclear enhanced space environment. These gamma pulse effects are, however, frequently not the result of the primary nuclear detonation. Instead they arise from nuclear gammas (and neutron generated gammas) interacting with materials surrounding the detector — via Compton scattering, the photoelectric effect, and pair production — to generate energetic primary electrons. These primaries in turn create many secondary electrons [Bridgman, 2001]. It is the secondary electrons that create charge within the detector and degrade its performance by decreasing S/N ratios.

The rate of charge buildup induced in a detector will be proportional to the gamma pulse rise time, the so-called γ-dot. The higher γ-dot, the greater the time rate of change of sensor charge [Bridgman, 2001].

VIII.B Cumulative Damage Resulting from Radiation Belt Exposure

VIII.B.1 SNRTACS results for low L-shell events

For each of our 21 trial events, and for each of our three representative spacecraft, we received SNRTACS output giving fluence of electrons as a function of time out to five years. Integral flux (i.e., fluence per unit time, integrated over energies above a specified threshold) was provided for electrons with energies > 0.04 MeV and for electrons with energies > 0.25 MeV. This enabled us to separate 40 keV to 250 keV electrons responsible for surface effects such as "deep dielectric charging" from more energetic electrons responsible for cumulative radiation damage to electronics. Note that SNRTACS results do not include electrons resulting from neutron decay or other non-fission sources. These non-fission sources may contribute significantly to the fluences in the 40 keV to 250 keV range, though perhaps less significantly to the total fluence. Table VIII.4 shows an example of results received from SNRTACS.

Fluences received from SNRTACS can be differenced in time to obtain approximate fluxes, and fit to functional forms to obtain decay rates. Figure VIII.16 shows typical decay rates as a function of time. For all low L-shell bursts considered, flux first decays rapidly with a time scale of about ten days at the ISS orbit and about 20 days at the NOAA orbit. The decay rate gradually slows during a six-month period following the burst, after which the decay time constant steadies at about 300 days. The interpretation of this result is that most electrons incident on our selected satellites during the first few days are encountered in regions of B-L space where electron lifetimes are short. Later on, the spacecraft encounter electron radiation only when passing through regions of B-L space with long electron lifetimes.

Table III.4. Example of information received from a SNRTACS run.

EVENT-ORBIT SURVEY		
EVENT: HAWAII SCEN. 7: 4500KT, 28.6N, 156.8W, 491KM		
ORBIT: APOGEE 700.0 KM, PERIGEE 700.0 KM, INCL 98.0 DEG, 14.6 REV/DAY		
FLUENCE ABOVE THRESHOLD ENERGY (ELECTRONS/SQ CM)		
Time (days)	Fluence > 0.04 Mev	Fluence > 0.25 MeV
1.0000E+00	9.6645E+12	9.4769E+12
2.0000E+00	1.6359E+13	1.6038E+13
1.4000E+01	5.5066E+13	5.3947E+13
3.0000E+01	7.8557E+13	7.6934E+13
9.0000E+01	1.1553E+14	1.1308E+14
1.8000E+02	1.3734E+14	1.3440E+14
3.6500E+02	1.5780E+14	1.5437E+14
7.3000E+02	1.7314E+14	1.6937E+14
1.0960E+03	1.7796E+14	1.7409E+14
1.8260E+03	1.8002E+14	1.7611E+14

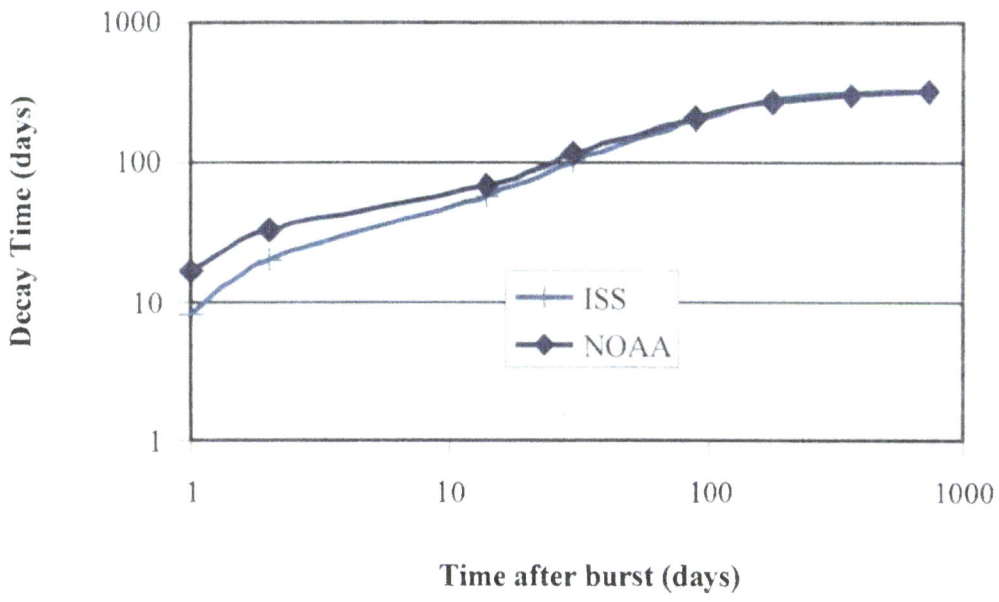

Figure III.16. Decay time vs. time after burst for trapped electron flux to spacecraft for trial 9. All low L-shell bursts exhibit similar behavior.

The SNRTACS-calculated first-day average fluxes incident on the representative spacecraft can be fit as a function of yield and L-shell. The fits we have derived are:

Flux of electrons E > 250 keV:

ISS: $\dot{\Phi}(Y, L) = 8.1 \times 10^{10} Y(1+0.2\log_{10}Y)(0.96L-0.117)$

TERRA: $\dot{\Phi}(Y, L) = 2.07 \times 10^{11} Y(1+0.34\log_{10}Y)(1.84-0.73L)$

DMSP: $\dot{\Phi}(Y, L) = 3.04 \times 10^{11} Y(1+0.35\log_{10}Y)(2.29-1.1L)$

Flux of electrons 40 keV < E < 250 keV:

ISS: $\dot{\Phi}(Y, L) = 1.9 \times 10^{9} Y(1+0.25\log_{10}Y)(1.5L-0.73)$

TERRA: $\dot{\Phi}(Y, L) = 4.86 \times 10^{9} Y(1+0.3\log_{10}Y)(2.32-1.13L)$

DMSP: $\dot{\Phi}(Y, L) = 7.15 \times 10^{9} Y(1+0.305\log_{10}Y)(2.74-1.5L)$

where $\dot{\Phi}(Y,L)$ is the flux in ($m^{-2} s^{-1}$), Y is the yield in Mt, and L is the L-shell of the burst. It is worth noting that the fluxes at ISS increase with L, while the fluxes at the higher altitude spacecraft decrease with L. First-day fluxes increase faster than linearly with yield.

Figure VIII.17 shows a comparison of $\dot{\Phi}(Y, L)$, SNRTACS-calculated first-day average fluxes, and corresponding natural fluxes. Note that low yield events (< 100 kt) are underestimated by the fit. Also, note that only the most powerful bursts produce low energy electrons in excess of those naturally present, while nearly all the bursts produce a higher-than-ambient flux of energetic electrons.

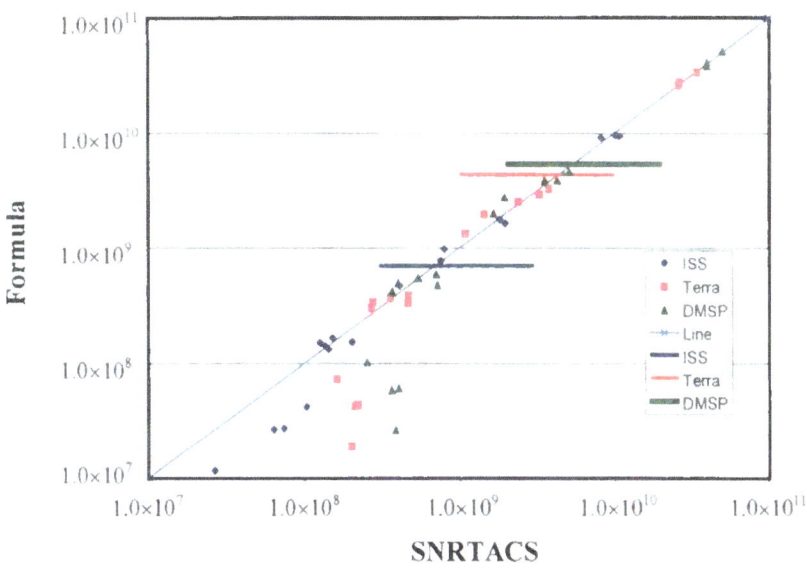

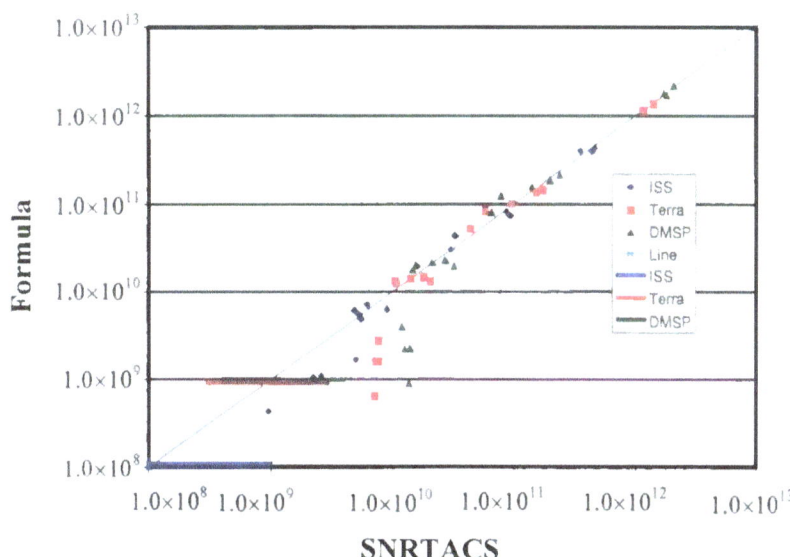

Figure III.17. Comparison of fluxes ($m^{-2} s^{-1}$) from fitting formula vs. SNRTACS data for electrons with energy 40 keV < E < 250 keV (upper plot) and E > 250 keV (lower plot). The four events (twelve points) below the line near the low end are for the ten kiloton, two twenty kiloton, and thirty kiloton events. Horizontal lines indicate the corresponding mean natural fluxes.

VIII.B.2 SNRTACS results for high L-shell events

Table VIII.5 shows the first-day fluxes for high L-shell events 18-21 (intended as direct attacks on GPS and GEO satellites) along with the corresponding average natural fluxes. Note that, at these L-shells, it is not unusual for fluxes to rise an order of magnitude above average due to natural activity. By this standard, only high-energy (E > 250 keV) electrons from the 10 Mt bursts exceed levels that should have been anticipated in the spacecraft design, and even then only by about a factor of two. Note also that the flux increases less than linearly with yield from 1 to 10 Mt. This is in sharp contrast with the low L-shell burst fluxes on LEO satellites, which increased faster than linearly with yield. The low energy fluxes remain below the mean natural levels for all events.

Decay of the fluxes occurs far more rapidly than for the LEO events. The decay is due to both pitch angle diffusion and radial diffusion. The decay time (e-folding time) is shown in Figure VIII.18. For the GPS attack, decay time starts at one week and increases to nearly two weeks after one month, with negligible flux remaining after 90 days. For the GEO attack, decay is more rapid, beginning at 2.5 days and increasing to about 8 days after two weeks. Negligible flux remains after thirty days. While electron fluxes are nonlinear with yield, their decay, as modeled by SNRTACS, shows no yield dependence.

Table III.5. First day average fluxes ($m^{-2} s^{-1}$) of low energy (40 keV < E < 250 keV) and high energy (E > 250 keV) electrons from high L-shell bursts.

Event	Low Energy	High Energy
18. GPS 1 Mt	3×10^{10}	7×10^{11}
19. GPS 10 Mt	2×10^{11}	3×10^{12}
---GPS Natural	3×10^{11}	1×10^{11}
20. GEO 1 Mt	2×10^{10}	4×10^{11}
21. GEO 10 Mt	1×10^{11}	2×10^{12}
---GEO Natural	3×10^{11}	8×10^{10}

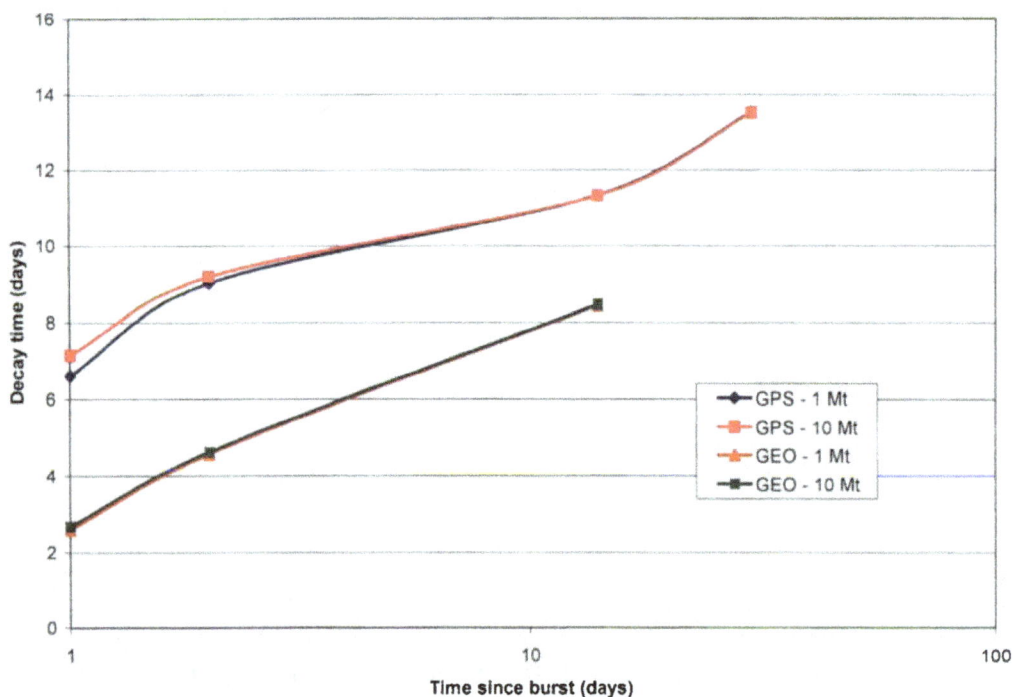

Figure III.18. Decay time vs. time since burst for GPS and GEO events.

We believe SNRTACS computed the decay of trapped fluxes under the assumption of low solar activity. Radial diffusion of trapped electrons increases markedly with solar activity. We have calculated how flux evolves according to the radial diffusion equation using parameters corresponding to high solar activity. From these results we infer a decay rate of peak flux of about 3.5 days near GPS orbit, and about 0.5 days at GEO. These results suggest that a spacecraft might encounter flux well in excess of the daily average for a short time during day one.

Figure VIII.19 depicts the ratio of high-energy to low-energy electrons for these events. In both cases, the ratio has an initial value of about 20, gradually increasing to approximately 80. The increase is as expected, since high energy electrons have considerably longer lifetimes than do low energy electrons at these L-shells. Corresponding lifetime ratios in the natural environment are about 0.5 near GPS and about 0.3 near GEO. The nuclear environment is much harder spectrally than the natural environment, even immediately after a burst.

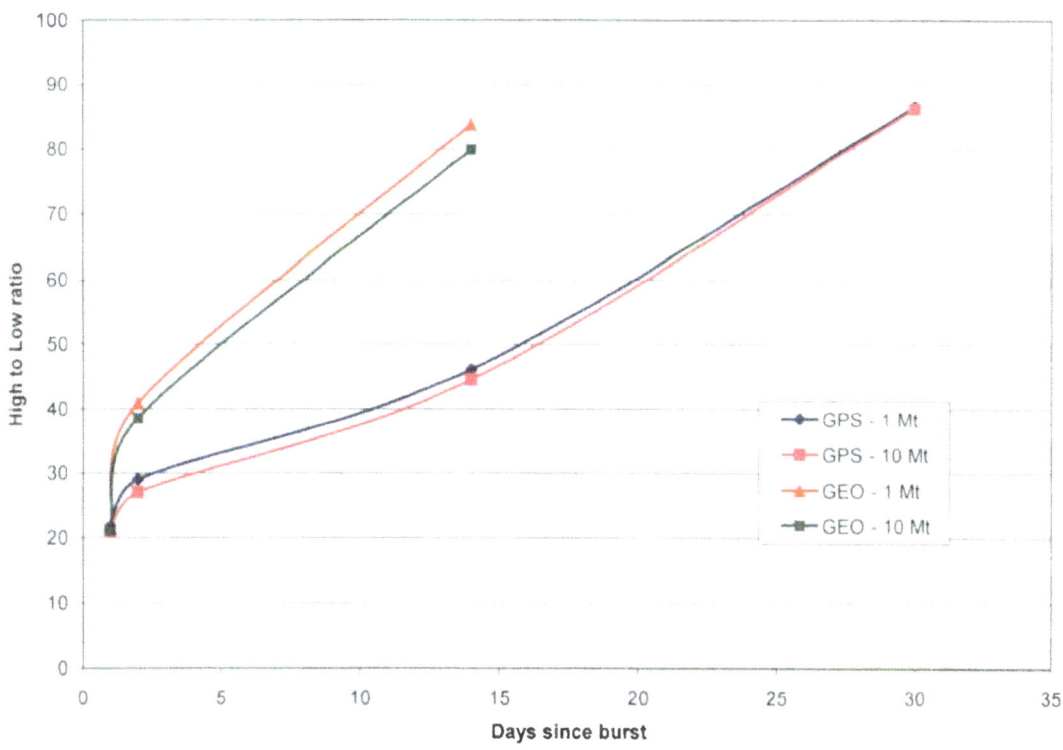

Figure III.19. Ratio of high-energy to low-energy electrons for the high L-shell events.

VIII.B.3 Predictions of Electric Stress

Calculations in this section are based on models from the SEE Interactive Spacecraft Charging Handbook [Katz et al., 2000] developed for the NASA Spacecraft Environmental Effects Program. This interactive handbook includes a model [Frederickson and Bell, 1995] for the accumulation of charge in insulating materials on the exterior of spacecraft (*e.g.*, solar cell covers, thermal blankets, circuit boards, and cable insulation) due to electrons with energies ranging from 40 keV to several MeV. Electric fields form within the material due to this charge deposition. If the electric field exceeds about 10^7 Vm^{-1}, discharges are possible; if the electric field exceeds about 10^8 Vm^{-1} discharges are likely.

For this project, a custom code was built, based on the Java classes in the SEE Handbook, that computes charge deposition and resulting electric field. To these classes an interface was added for input of the nuclear trapped electron spectrum and appropriate material parameters.

An important consideration in determining an appropriate environment is the time to equilibrium. The timescale (RC time constant) is the dielectric constant divided by the conductivity. Table VIII.6 gives the timescale for insulators of different conductivities assuming a dielectric constant of 5 for the insulator. For an insulator with a conductivity of 10^{-16} (Ω-cm)$^{-1}$, the time to reach the equilibrium charge deposition is of the order of one orbit. Therefore, for conductivity values of 10^{-16} (Ω-cm)$^{-1}$ and lower, orbit-averaged fluxes should be used to determine the steady-state electric field. For higher conductivities the maximum flux (probably three to ten times the average) may be more appropriate. Thermal control insulators (*e.g.* Teflon® and Kapton®) tend to fall into the high-resistance, long-timescale category. Modern doped coverglasses tend to have conductivities of order 10^{-15} (Ω-cm)$^{-1}$ (depending on temperature) and thus fall into the short-timescale category.

Table III.6. Timescale for charge deposition in insulator.

Conductivity (Ω-cm)$^{-1}$	Timescale (sec)	Timescale (hours)
10^{-14}	44	0.012
10^{-15}	440	0.12
10^{-16}	4400	1.2
10^{-17}	44,000	12

Parameters used in the calculation are the average atomic number, average atomic weight, thickness, density, conductivity, and dose-enhanced conductivity coefficient for the dielectric. For coverglass, appropriate values of these parameters are given in Table VIII.7; for thermal blankets (Kapton®, Teflon®, or Mylar®), parameters are shown in Table VIII.8.

Table III.7. Coverglass parameter ranges.

Parameter	Value
Atomic number	10
Average atomic weight	20
Thickness	4 to 20 mil (the higher values in high radiation orbits)
Density	2.2 to 2.6 gm/cm^3
Conductivity	10^{-14} to 10^{-18} (Ω-cm)$^{-1}$
Dose-rate-enhanced conductivity coefficient	10^{-18} s (Ω-cm rad)$^{-1}$

Table III.8. Thermal blanket parameter ranges.

Parameter	Value
Atomic number	between 6 and 8; use 7
Average atomic weight	between 12 and 16; use 14
Thickness	2 to 10 mil
Density	1.4 to 2.1 gm/cm^3
Conductivity	10^{-16} to $10^{-18} (\Omega\text{-cm})^{-1}$
Dose-rate-enhanced conductivity coefficient	10^{-18} s $(\Omega\text{-cm rad})^{-1}$

We next seek to determine an appropriate electron flux spectrum. Here we use the two spectral shapes shown in Figure VIII.20. The lower curve is a "fission spectrum" whose differential flux between one and seven MeV is given by

$$Y(E) = 3.88 \exp[-0.575E - 0.055E^2]$$

with E in MeV. See Gurtman *et al.* [2003] for details of the actual flux used. The upper curve includes neutron decay electrons comprising ten percent of the fission flux. These neutron-decay electrons are not accounted for by SNRTACS. To put this in context, the flux of neutron decay electrons from STARFISH PRIME has been estimated [Hoerlin, 1976] at 10^6 to 10^7 electrons cm^{-2} s^{-1}. The upper limit of this estimate is comparable to about ten percent of the first-day averaged flux of fission electrons per megaton seen by DMSP/NOAA and TERRA in our events.

Of the various events provided, the ones with highest fluxes between 40 keV and 250 keV are those in Table VIII.9. All are 4.5 to 5 Mt explosions. For fixed spectral distribution, the highest fluence case will cause the most damage.

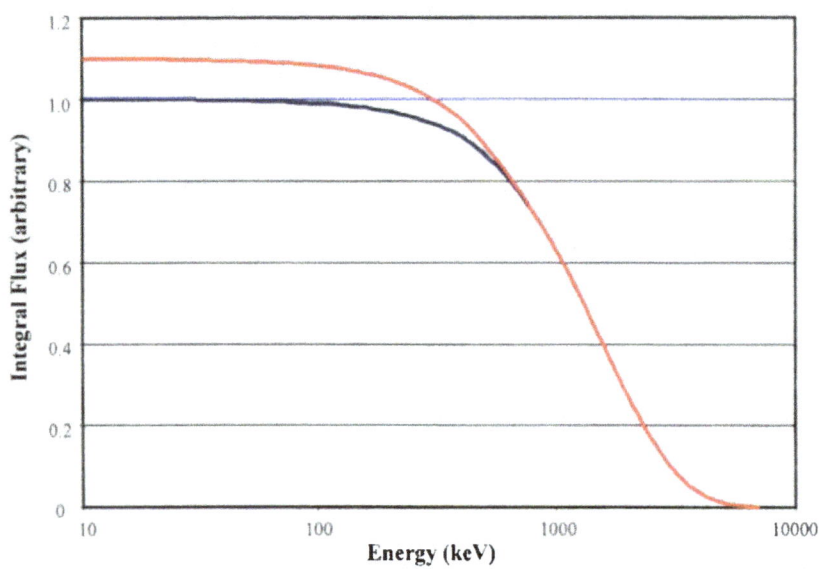

Figure III.20. Integral fission electron spectrum (lower curve), and the fission spectrum augmented by ten percent with neutron decay electrons (upper curve).

Table III.9. Fluence for various high-yield events.

Spacecraft	Event	First day fluence (electrons cm^{-2})		
		Above 40 keV	Above 250 keV	Between 40 keV and 250 keV
ISS	Event 9	0.41×10^{13}	0.40×10^{13}	0.87×10^{11}
TERRA	Event 17	1.24×10^{13}	1.22×10^{13}	2.97×10^{11}
NOAA/ DMSP	Event 17	1.83×10^{13}	1.78×10^{13}	4.37×10^{11}

Electron fluxes used in the calculations described below are spectral distributions shown in Figure VIII.20 multiplied by the "Above 250 keV" value shown in Table VIII.10, and divided by 0.9577 (the 250 keV value for the integrated fission spectrum) and again by 8.64 s m^2 day^{-1} cm^{-2} (a net division by 8.27). We restrict consideration to the NOAA/DMSP event in Table VIII.10 with total fission flux of 2.1×10^8 cm^{-2}s^{-1} (2.3×10^8 including neutron decay electrons) as that is the worst case.

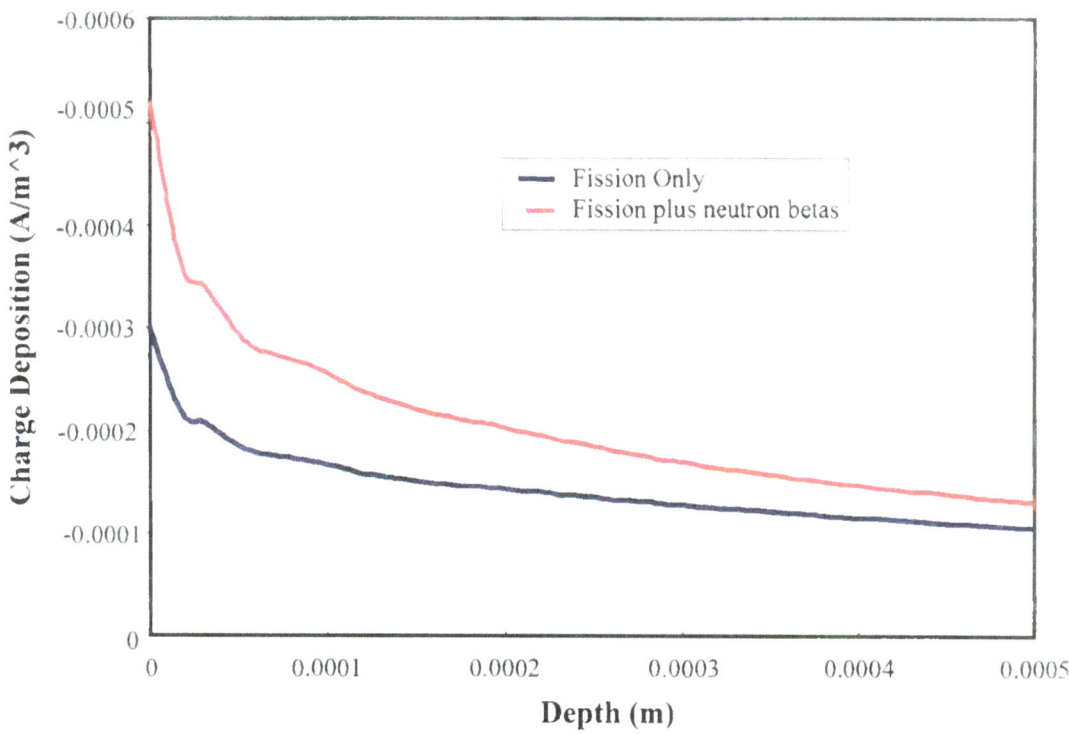

Figure III.21. Charge deposition rate in insulator (coverglass) for the two spectra.

Figure VIII.21 shows the rate of electron deposition in an insulator (coverglass). Note that most of the deposition occurs near the front face, and nearly half the deposition is due to neutron decay electrons, which make up only ten percent of the total spectrum. Typical coverglass thickness is 0.003 to 0.006 inch (75 to 150 microns), though coverglasses are commercially available with up to 0.020 inch (500 micron) thickness. (Presumably the thicker coverglasses are used for radiation protection.) Thermal control materials, such as Kapton® and Teflon®, are commonly used in thicknesses from 0.0005 inch (12 microns) up to 0.010 inch (250 microns).

The cold (0.1 to 0.3 eV) plasma thermal flux at LEO altitudes is generally high enough to ground all exterior surfaces, including the exposed faces of coverglasses and thermal coatings. Thus, the exposed face should normally be treated as grounded. The rear face of a coverglass is grounded to the spacecraft structure, at least capacitively if not conductively. However, one might imagine that an exterior surface faces the spacecraft wake and/or is in a region of extremely low plasma density, so that the exterior surface is floating. In that case, the boundary condition at the front face is that the electric field is zero (so that no conductive current flows), and the maximum field occurs at the rear face. If both front and rear surfaces are grounded, the boundary condition is that the mean electric field is zero, and the maximum field occurs at the front face. The two cases are illustrated in Figure VIII.22.

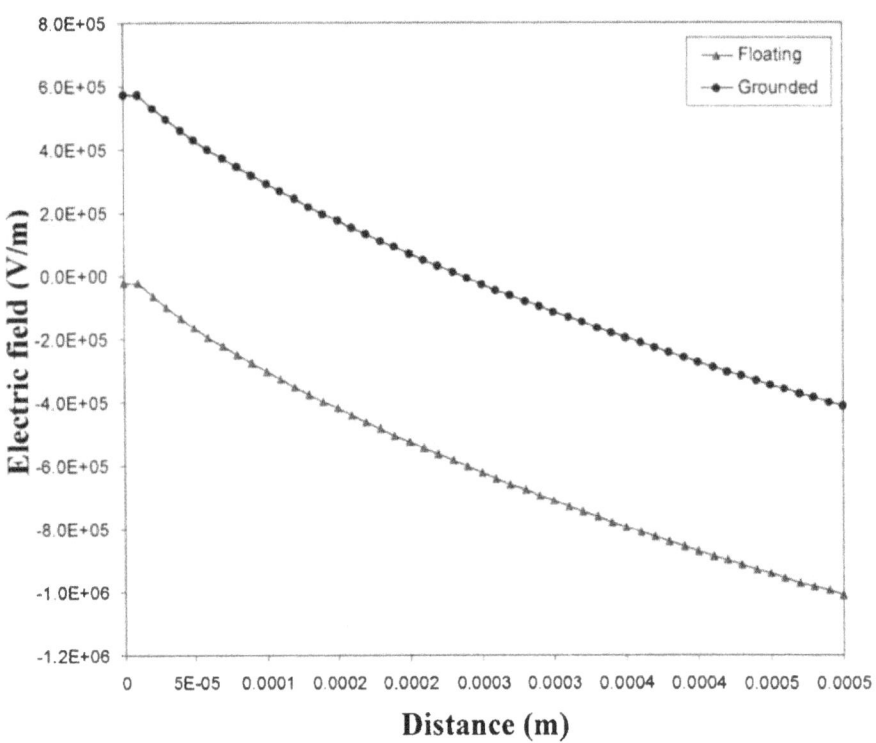

Figure III.22. Electric fields in an insulator for the front face grounded (upper curve) and floating (lower curve).

Table VIII.10 shows results for coverglass in the NOAA/DMSP orbit subject to the electron fluxes of event 17. There are a number of observations that can be made from this set of results. An 18% change in coverglass density gives a 15% change in peak electric field. A factor of 5 change in thickness gives a factor of 3 change in peak electric field. Grounding the front surface decreases the peak electric field by a factor of 1.8 to 2.5. The nominal conductivity for doped borosilicate (CMX) coverglass is 10^{-15} $(\Omega\text{-cm})^{-1}$, but it can easily drop an order of magnitude when cold. We see from the table that while coverglasses appear safe under nominal conditions, a thick, cold coverglass is close to the danger zone. A non-conductive coverglass (represented by conductivity of 10^{-18} $(\Omega\text{-cm})^{-1}$) is definitely in the danger zone. Note that for such low values of intrinsic conductivity, radiation-induced conductivity is dominant.

Table III.10. Results table for coverglass in NOAA/DMSP orbit, event 17.

Thickness (microns)	Density (gm/cm^3)	Conductivity $(\Omega\text{-cm})^{-1}$	Max field (V/m)	
			Floating	Grounded
100	2.2	10^{-15}	2.74×10^5	1.48×10^5
100	2.6	10^{-15}	3.13×10^5	1.69×10^5
500	2.6	10^{-15}	1.01×10^6	5.72×10^5
500	2.6	10^{-18}	8.87×10^7	3.49×10^7
500	2.6	10^{-14}	1.02×10^5	5.80×10^4
500	2.6	10^{-16}	9.25×10^6	5.02×10^6

Another external insulating material into which charge may be deposited is thermal blankets. The most common exterior surfaces of thermal blankets are Kapton® and Mylar®. Black (carbon impregnated) Kapton and Teflon® are also commonly used. We ignore Black Kapton here as it is conductive enough that internal electric fields do not become significant. The range of values of parameters for these materials is shown in Table VIII.10. Results of calculations for a grounded exterior surface are shown in Table VIII.11. Electric field levels are within the safe range except for the case of a 0.010 inch blanket. These calculations assume that the back surface of the blanket exterior layer is well grounded. If the ground tabs are broken or there are not enough ground tabs (such as may occur if a thin layer of semi-conducting Germanium is used) a much larger field could develop.

Table III.11. Table of results for exterior layer of thermal blankets with grounded front surface.

Thickness (microns)	Density (gm cm^{-3})	Conductivity (Ω-cm)$^{-1}$	Max field (V m^{-1})
100	1.4	1×10^{-18}	6.05×10^6
100	2.1	1×10^{-18}	8.39×10^6
100	2.1	1×10^{-16}	1.21×10^6
254	2.1	1×10^{-18}	1.78×10^7

VIII.B.4 Effect on solar arrays

We now consider the effect of trapped electrons on the lifetime of solar arrays. Solar arrays are exposed to the radiation environment and cannot be substantially shielded. While there is some variation among different types of solar cells, roughly speaking, solar cells begin to show radiation effects at a fluence (of 1 MeV electrons) of 10^{13} electrons-cm^{-2}, show noticeable degradation at 10^{14} electrons-cm^{-2}, and reach end of life at about 10^{15} electrons-cm^{-2}. Taking the SNRI ACS fluence of electrons with energy greater than 0.25 MeV as equivalent to a fluence of 1 MeV electrons (as the median energy in the spectrum of Figure VIII.20 is only slightly above 1 MeV), our various events lead to one-year fluences shown in Table VIII.12. (Except for events 18-21, five-year fluences are about fifty percent higher.)

Table III.12. One-year fluences of electrons (cm^{-2}) with energy over 0.25 MeV. Color coding indicates severity of damage to solar cells. (See text.)

Event	ISS	TERRA	NOAA/DMSP	GPS/GEO
1	9.34×10^{11}	4.80×10^{12}	8.31×10^{12}	
2	1.58×10^{12}	7.51×10^{12}	1.26×10^{13}	
3	4.75×10^{12}	2.27×10^{13}	3.82×10^{13}	
4	2.72×10^{11}	4.81×10^{12}	1.27×10^{13}	
5	9.57×10^{11}	3.52×10^{12}	5.43×10^{12}	
6	1.31×10^{13}	4.18×10^{13}	6.13×10^{13}	
7	8.51×10^{12}	2.53×10^{13}	3.61×10^{13}	
8	9.72×10^{13}	6.09×10^{14}	9.87×10^{14}	
9	1.13×10^{14}	5.03×10^{14}	8.50×10^{14}	
10	1.13×10^{12}	2.51×10^{12}	4.28×10^{12}	
11	1.88×10^{12}	7.81×10^{12}	1.29×10^{13}	
12	7.97×10^{11}	5.24×10^{12}	9.91×10^{12}	
13	7.43×10^{11}	2.28×10^{12}	3.32×10^{12}	
14	3.96×10^{12}	1.21×10^{13}	1.75×10^{13}	
15	3.19×10^{12}	1.90×10^{13}	3.07×10^{13}	
16	1.29×10^{13}	8.02×10^{13}	1.31×10^{14}	
17	1.32×10^{14}	6.62×10^{14}	1.08×10^{15}	
18				4.56×10^{13}
19				2.43×10^{14}
20				8.60×10^{12}
21				4.78×10^{13}

Most of the cells in Table VIII.12 are coded green (fluence < 3×10^{13}) indicating little or no radiation effect. Those in yellow (3×10^{13} < fluence < 1×10^{14}) experience minor degradation, while those in ORANGE (1×10^{14} < fluence < 3×10^{14}) experience noticeable degradation. The cells in red (fluence > 3×10^{14}) experience substantial loss of life due to trapped electron radiation. The DMSP/NOAA/TERRA orbital regime, which contains most of our valuable weather and imaging satellites, is strongly affected by the more powerful bursts of our event set. ISS at 322 km sees only a modest effect from the most powerful bursts. ISS solar arrays are planned for fifteen year lifetime, so even a moderate unexpected degradation of the solar arrays might hamper operations for a significant time, assuming that ISS continues to function after a nuclear event.

VIII.B.5 Reduction in lifetime of electronics

VIII.B.5.a Effects on LEO satellites

Nuclear enhanced electron belts provide a slowly decaying, damaging electron environment. Tables VIII.13, VIII.14, and VIII.15 display reduced lifetimes of satellites resulting from 17 of the 21 events. Results of events 18-21 will be discussed in the text.

Reduction in lifetimes of LEO satellites is based on total dose from higher energy electrons to internal electronics. Electronics were assumed to be shielded by a 0.100 inch "semi-infinite" slab of aluminum. This conservative shielding configuration assumes that the electronics are mounted on an internal wall of the spacecraft and essentially no radiation comes from the opposite direction (*i.e.*, no radiation impacts the side of the electronic device that is facing away from the wall). In some cases sensitive electronics may be lightly shielded and/or exposed to radiation from all directions, for example, a sensor at the end of a boom. In this case, an electronic device may encounter a factor of three or greater radiation level. For assessments of risk to astronauts aboard ISS, 0.220 inches is more representative of shielding. Satellites are assumed to be hardened to twice the natural radiation environment that they would encounter during a normal mission lifetime. In addition, satellites are assumed to start with zero rads at the time of the nuclear burst. In other words a satellite possesses its full 2-times-natural radiation budget at the time of the nuclear event. This is ann optimistic assumption since, in reality, satellites will have some level of natural dose accumulation due to their time on orbit. As with photons, damage to spacecraft thermal, optical, and other surface coatings is caused by exposure to electrons of relatively low energy.

Table III.13. Middle East Events.

Event	Location	Yield (kt)	HOB (km)	Time to Failure (days)		
				NOAA	TERRA	ISS
1	33N	20	200	30	70	100
2	25N	100	175	15	30	50
3	25N	300	155	4	7	9
4	31.3N	10	300	20	60	5000
5	31N	100	170	30	70	100

Except for the International Space Station (ISS) in event 4, smaller yields in our event set are capable of imposing a much-reduced lifetime on the satellites. As shown in Table VIII.14, the large weapon utilized in event 17 inflicts severe damage on the ISS. More significantly, this exposure would cause radiation sickness to the astronauts within approximately one hour and a 90% probability of death within 2-3 hours.

The large yields are from foreign weapons that are assumed salvage-fuzed when intercepted by a missile defense system. Again, large yields and geographic location result in severe damage to all exemplar three satellites.

Table III.14. Far Eastern Events.

Event	Location	Yield (kt)	HOB (km)	Time to failure (days)		
				NOAA	TERRA	ISS
12	35.7N	20	150	25	60	200
13	36N	100	120	60	200	200
14	36N	500	120	4	6	3
15	22.5N	100	200	10	20	30
16	22.5N	500	200	1	3	4
17	22.5N	5000	200	0.1	0.1	0.1

The previous analysis on LEO satellites assumed that the satellites started with their full 2-times-natural radiation budget. In reality, satellites on-orbit have various radiation margins remaining due to cummulative time on orbit. For example, a satellite launched 10 years ago will most likely fail more quickly than a comparable satellite launched only a year ago. Figure VIII.23 illustrates this effect using the TERRA satellite orbit. One can see that in this particular case the spacecraft lifetime will be longer if the burst occurs closer to the beginning of satellite life.

Table III.15. Hawaiian Events.

Event	Location	Yield (kt)	HOB (km)	Time to Failure (days)		
				NOAA	TERRA	ISS
6	25.4N	800	368	1	1	0.5
7	28.6N	800	491	1	1	1
8	18.5N	4500	102	0.1	0.2	0.2
9	20.7N	4500	248	0.1	0.2	0.1
10	22N	30	500	40	100	150
11	22N	100	200	10	17	20

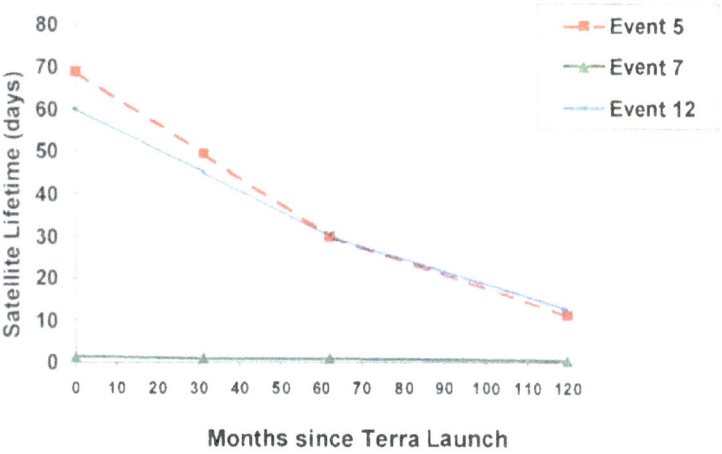

Figure III.23. TERRA satellite lifetime after a high altitude nuclear event vs. time since launch. (Two-times-natural hardening assumed for total dose.)

VIII.B.5.b Effects on GPS, GEO and HEO satellite

Results for detonations at high latitudes (events 18-21), presumably in an attempt to damage GPS or satellites in a geosynchronous orbit, produced no dramatic nuclear effects, both because satellites in GPS and GEO orbits are designed to operate in a far more robust natural space environment than are those in LEO, and because we followed the usual practice of assigning to each satellite its full two-times-natural radiation budget at the time of detonation. The result was a prediction of negligible damage to geosynchronous satellites, and a reduction of GPS satellite lifetime from ten years to seven years. The latter is a costly, but not immediate, effect.

However, the assumption of a full radiation budget is really only appropriate to satellites launched as replacements following a detonation. For a satellite near the end of its design lifetime, absorbed dose from a nuclear-pumped belt could cause prompt demise. If one considers that GPS satellites, for example, have a range of residual hardness due to their distribution of on-orbit ages, then the GPS constellation could be quite vulnerable to some special weapon events. Specifically, event 19, a 10 Mt burst (with 50% fission yield), would place a sufficient flux of fission electrons at GPS altitudes to significantly affect that constellation.

Table VIII.16 shows the current GPS constellation of 29 satellites (also known as the NAVSTAR constellation), with launch dates from June 10, 1989 to March 31, 2003, along with the natural radiation levels already accumulated on the satellites. We have taken the design lifetime to be ten years; most of these satellites have been in space for ten years or longer. If the satellites are assumed hardened to the two-times-natural specification, then each satellite can tolerate 1.1 megarad of radiation (equivalent to about twenty years of natural radiation) during its operational lifetime. In this case, the oldest satellite, NAVSTAR 14, has only about a third of its original radiation budget left due to its long exposure to the harsh natural radiation environment that exists at 20,000 km altitude. By contrast, if we apply a less stringent 1.5-times-natural specification for hardening, we find that six satellites have been reduced to less than a quarter of their original radiation budgets.

Figure VIII.24 shows the number of satellites remaining as a function of time under the assumptions of 1.5- and 2.0-times-natural hardening. The effect of the event-19 detonation is to expose the satellites to about five years' equivalent of natural radiation (varying somewhat among the different orbits) during a period of about a month (see Figure VIII.18). Here we see a large difference between the two hardening requirements. With two-times-natural hardening we lose relatively few satellites until nearly five years after the blast when the large number of satellites now ten years old (having endured ten years pre-blast plus five years equivalent from the blast plus five years post-blast) exceed their radiation budgets. By contrast, with 1.5-times-natural hardening the blast completes the radiation budget of the ten-year-old satellites, so that a large number of satellites fail promptly.

Satellite loss can be translated into impacts on users of the GPS constellation, insofar as it leads to substantial "blackouts" in precise navigation services (Figure VIII.25). For precise navigation, four satellites are normally required. As satellites drop out of the constellation, outage times gradually increase. Degradation is not continuous, but occurs at various times during the day. Some outages can last 30 minutes while others can be a few hours at a time.

If GPS satellites are hardened to twice the natural environment, the constellation has sufficient redundancy to keep major outages at bay for four years following the blast. If the satellites are hardened to only fifty percent above natural, then outage time increases rapidly, and the system is unavailable a majority of the time after ten months.

It must be emphasized that nuclear event 19 is a special event where an adversary desires to conduct an EMP attack while simultaneously attacking the GPS constellation. If the adversary's sole objective is to conduct an EMP attack, then it may be unlikely that the restricted conditions of weapon yield, height of burst, and burst location necessary to jeopardize the GPS constellation will occur.

Table III.16. GPS constellation radiation accumulation (rads) as of 23 May 2003.

Satellite	Launch Date				Total Dose				
	month	day	year	days in orbit	Accumulated to date	2X Natural Spec	rads remaining	1.5X Natural Spec	rads remaining
NAVSTAR 14	6	10	1989	5093	7.5×10^5	1.1×10^6	3.2×10^5	8.0×10^5	0.5×10^5
NAVSTAR 17	12	11	1989	4912	7.2×10^5	1.1×10^6	3.5×10^5	8.0×10^5	0.8×10^5
NAVSTAR 21	10	1	1990	4617	6.8×10^5	1.1×10^6	3.9×10^5	8.0×10^5	1.2×10^5
NAVSTAR 22	11	26	1990	4562	6.7×10^5	1.1×10^6	4.0×10^5	8.0×10^5	1.3×10^5
NAVSTAR 23	7	4	1991	4339	6.4×10^5	1.1×10^6	4.4×10^5	8.0×10^5	1.7×10^5
NAVSTAR 24	2	23	1992	4105	6.0×10^5	1.1×10^6	4.7×10^5	8.0×10^5	2.0×10^5
NAVSTAR 26	7	7	1992	3971	5.8×10^5	1.1×10^6	4.9×10^5	8.0×10^5	2.2×10^5
NAVSTAR 27	9	9	1992	3909	5.7×10^5	1.1×10^6	5.0×10^5	8.0×10^5	2.3×10^5

Satellite	Launch Date				Total Dose				
	month	day	year	days in orbit	Accumulated to date	2X Natural Spec	rads remaining	1.5X Natural Spec	rads remaining
NAVSTAR 28	11	22	1992	3836	5.6×10^5	1.1×10^6	5.1×10^5	8.0×10^5	2.4×10^5
NAVSTAR 29	12	18	1992	3810	5.6×10^5	1.1×10^6	5.1×10^5	8.0×10^5	2.4×10^5
NAVSTAR 30	2	3	1993	3760	5.5×10^5	1.1×10^6	5.2×10^5	8.0×10^5	2.5×10^5
NAVSTAR 31	3	30	1993	3703	5.4×10^5	1.1×10^6	5.3×10^5	8.0×10^5	2.6×10^5
NAVSTAR 32	5	13	1993	3660	5.4×10^5	1.1×10^6	5.3×10^5	8.0×10^5	2.6×10^5
NAVSTAR 33	6	26	1993	3617	5.3×10^5	1.1×10^6	5.4×10^5	8.0×10^5	2.7×10^5
NAVSTAR 34	8	30	1993	3553	5.2×10^5	1.1×10^6	5.5×10^5	8.0×10^5	2.8×10^5
NAVSTAR 35	10	26	1993	3497	5.1×10^5	1.1×10^6	5.6×10^5	8.0×10^5	2.8×10^5
NAVSTAR 36	3	10	1994	3358	4.9×10^5	1.1×10^6	5.8×10^5	8.0×10^5	3.1×10^5
NAVSTAR 37	3	28	1996	2610	3.8×10^5	1.1×10^6	6.9×10^5	8.0×10^5	4.2×10^5
NAVSTAR 38	7	16	1996	2502	3.7×10^5	1.1×10^6	7.1×10^5	8.0×10^5	4.3×10^5
NAVSTAR 39	9	12	1996	2446	3.6×10^5	1.1×10^6	7.1×10^5	8.0×10^5	4.4×10^5
NAVSTAR 43	7	23	1997	2130	3.1×10^5	1.1×10^6	7.6×10^5	8.0×10^5	4.9×10^5
NAVSTAR 44	11	6	1997	2027	3.0×10^5	1.1×10^6	7.8×10^5	8.0×10^5	5.0×10^5
NAVSTAR 46	10	7	1999	1326	1.9×10^5	1.1×10^6	8.8×10^5	8.0×10^5	6.1×10^5
NAVSTAR 47	5	11	2000	1107	1.6×10^5	1.1×10^6	9.1×10^5	8.0×10^5	6.4×10^5
NAVSTAR 48	7	16	2000	1042	1.5×10^5	1.1×10^6	9.2×10^5	8.0×10^5	6.5×10^5
NAVSTAR 49	11	10	2000	928	1.4×10^5	1.1×10^6	9.4×10^5	8.0×10^5	6.6×10^5
NAVSTAR 50	1	30	2001	843	1.2×10^5	1.1×10^6	9.5×10^5	8.0×10^5	6.6×10^5
NAVSTAR 51	1	29	2003	114	0.2×10^5	1.1×10^6	1.1×10^6	8.0×10^5	7.8×10^5
NAVSTAR 52	3	31	2003	52	0.1×10^5	1.1×10^6	1.1×10^6	8.0×10^5	7.9×10^5

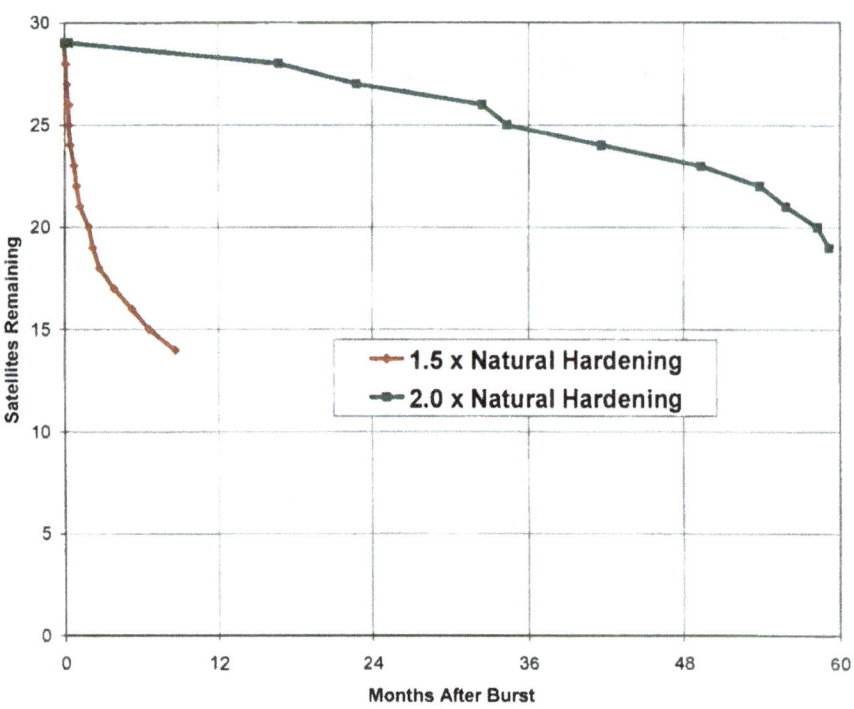

Figure III.24. GPS satellites remaining as a function of time following a 10 Mt blast (event 19). The two curves assume hardening to 50% above the natural environment (lower curve) and 100% above natural (upper curve).

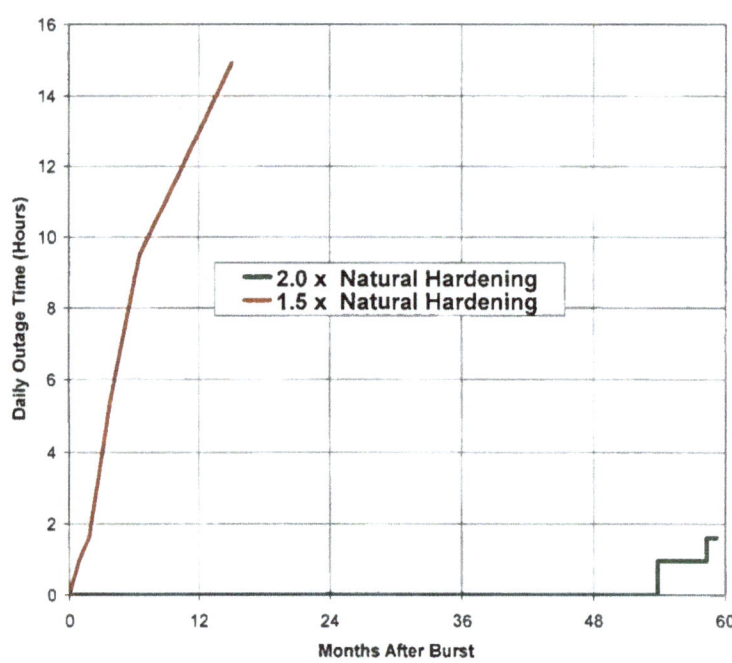

Figure III.25. GPS outage time in Baghdad after a 10 Mt burst (event 19).

HEO satellites already reside in orbits that are relatively challenging in terms of the natural radiation environment. Assuming these satellites are hardened to twice the natural dose they would normally accumulate in 15 years, a satellite's electronics would be hardened to approximately 325 krad behind a 100 mil (0.1 inch) semi-infinite slab of aluminum. With this level of hardness, one would expect these satellites would not be vulnerable to single, low-yield (~ 50 kt) Third-World type high-altitude bursts. SNRTACS calculations suggest this is indeed the case. These types of bursts have little effect on HEO assets from a total-ionizing-dose point of view. Substantially higher-yield bursts are required. Prompt radiations (X-rays, gamma rays, and neutrons) are also not an issue for Third-World-type bursts since HEO satellites of interest are at high altitudes over the Northern Hemisphere where such detonations are hypothesized to occur in our study.

Three large-yield events were investigated to see if they would present a threat to HEO satellites. Two of these events (events 11 and 21), would not present a total ionizing dose problem for a HEO satellite. Although event 21 is a 10 Mt burst, it has little effect on a HEO satellite because the trapped electrons are spread out over a large L-shell region extending to geosynchronous orbit with correspondingly small trapped electron flux levels. In addition, the lifetime of electrons trapped at high L shells is modeled to be relatively short. In contrast, a 100-kt burst such as event 11 does result in some detectable radiation accumulation on a HEO satellite as it passes through altitudes near perigee. This yield is, however, too low to present a threat to the satellite. A 5-Mt burst as in event 17, on the other hand, does present a substantial threat to HEO satellites given the hardening assumptions mentioned earlier. Figure VIII.26 shows that the assumed 2x natural hardening level of the satellite is exceeded about 36 days after event 17. The combination of high yield and relatively small volume of the low-L-shell magnetic flux tube in which the energetic electrons are trapped results in very high electron fluxes to which the HEO satellite is exposed near perigee.

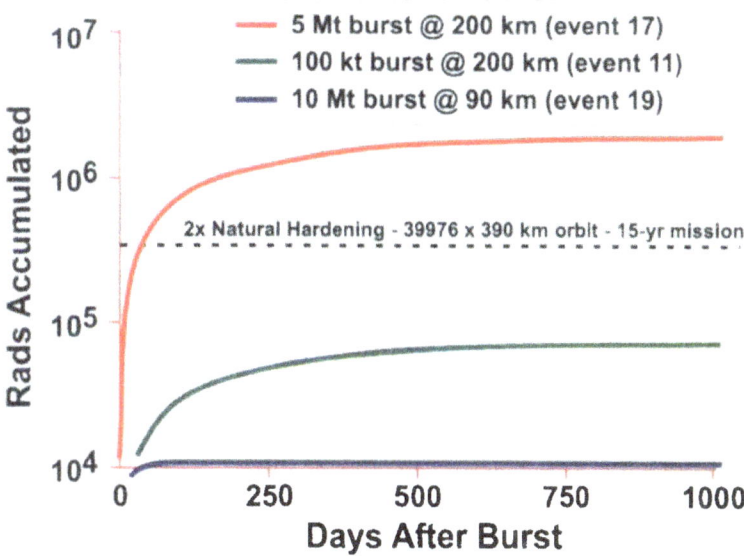

Figure VIII.26. HEO satellite exposure to trapped radiation produced by selected events.

VIII.C Discussion of Results

The worst-case exposure of a LEO satellite to direct X-radiation from a nuclear weapon may be lethal and, as shown in Section VI.1.b.iii, UV radiation may damage spacecraft surfaces in excess to its proportion of total photon fluence. However, the large distance between a detonation for an EMP attack and a satellite in MEO or GEO makes the probability of damage very low, at least for the cases analyzed. MEO and GEO satellites are already designed to operate in the relatively severe natural radiation environments at such altitudes.

Any nation with missile lift capability and sufficient technology in the requisite number of disciplines can directly attack and destroy a satellite, but significant damage to satellites in MEO or GEO cannot easily be accomplished with detonations at high latitudes. Electron fluxes in belts at high L-shells are not sufficiently intense to cause early demise of satellites in MEO or GEO.

Satellites in LEO are much more susceptible to damage from both direct and persistent radiations that result from an EMP attack, but severity is highly dependent on latitude/longitude, height of burst, and yield.

Line-of-sight exposure of research satellites such as ISS to energetic photons are estimated to cause significant damage to solar-array coverglass coatings for events 4, 6, 7, 9 and 19. While such exposures are thought statistically infrequent, in those instances where they do occur they will result in immediate loss or diminution of many of the ISS's power generating capacity and operational capabilities. Low energy trapped electron flux from fission beta decay and neutron beta decay exceeds the natural flux for high-yield events 8, 9, and 17. Low-energy beta-decay fluxes will cause electrostatic breakdown in certain types of thermal radiator coatings and external cables on NOAA, DMSP, and TERRA within the first few days following the burst.

CHAPTER IX
CONSEQUENCES OF FINDINGS

IX.A General Findings

In 2000 a Congressionally chartered Commission to Assess United States National Security Space Management and Organization conducted an assessment of space activities that support U.S. national security interests. As part of this study, the Commission concluded that space systems are vulnerable to a range of attacks due to their political, economic, and military value[13], and there was inadequate management and infrastructure within the U.S. to deal with the problem.

Direct attacks on space assets, although credible, are not within the scope of this study. Therefore, we must consider ramifications of satellite losses in concert with other losses resulting from an EMP attack. If an EMP attack is perpetrated over a military expeditionary force, or over a carrier battle group, those satellites in jeopardy could be unique in the service they provide or could be but one of a number of viable mission-fulfilling alternatives. For example, a military surveillance satellite may be unique in its image resolution capabilities, but civilian imaging satellites might credibly function as backups (if sufficiently hardened). It is possible that some missions nominally dependent on satellites could be performed by high-altitude long-endurance Un-crewed Aerial Vehicles (UAVs) provided the UAVs and their communications systems have been hardened against EMP and other nuclear effects.

From the analysis in Chapter VIII some inferences can be drawn on the consequences of the damage to satellites.

- Line-of-sight exposure to prompt radiations from a readily achievable high altitude detonation puts LEO satellites at risk, but their ephemerae cause them to be shadowed by the Earth most of the time in their orbit. Also, depending on satellite position at time of detonation, radiations may be attenuated by transport through portions of the atmosphere. Therefore, susceptibility assessment becomes statistical in nature. While worst-case radiation dose, as shown in the final column of Table VIII.1, may be dire, the probability of acquiring such a dose, or even a much lower "significant" dose, is fairly modest, as shown in the remainder of Table VIII.1 and in Figures VIII.1 to VIII.3. The nearest approach of a satellite to the direct X-radiation from a nuclear weapon can be lethal, but the large distance between a detonation for an EMP attack and a satellite in MEO or GEO makes the probability of damage to them very low. These satellites are already designed to operate in the relatively severe natural radiation environments that exist at such altitudes. Some military satellites are actually hardened against nuclear environments.

- An EMP attack over northern CONUS or Canada with a single weapon of yield less than ~ 1 Mt is unlikely to produce serious satellite damage from trapped beta-decay electrons because

---

[13] *"Report of the Commission to Assess United States National Security Space Management and Organization," January 11, 2001.*

explosions at higher latitudes will not inject sufficient trapped flux onto the magnetic field lines transited by LEO satellites to deliver a serious radiation dose. Therefore, catastrophic collateral damage to satellites from persistent trapped electron radiation, under these constraints, does not appear to be a factor in assessing effects of an EMP attack on the United States Infrastructure with a burst over Northern CONUS. However, this study has focused principally on satellite vehicles and not the overall satellite system. Ground stations are subject to the same EMP threats and effects as are other communications systems. Also, nuclear-disturbed environments through which radio transmissions take place could be disrupted for periods of hours.

- Damage to GPS and GEO satellites, for yields greater than 10 Mt can be serious. Below this yield the damage can be costly but not catastrophic. Most examinations of lifetime-in-orbit reduction by a nuclear detonation are based upon assumption of the satellite being new with very little accumulated natural radiation dose. Clearly, a relatively small nuclear radiation dose could seriously damage a satellite that is near its design lifetime. To conduct a more rigorous analysis the GPS constellation was examined, taking into account actual launch dates of individual satellites. Figures VIII.24 and VIII.25 indicate that the constellation of 29 GPS satellites of varying ages would still allow access with an acceptable outage time for an extended period.

- EMP attacks over parts of the world at lower latitudes than Northern CONUS are more likely to damage satellites in LEO by "pumping the electron belts", as indicated in Tables VIII.13 to VIII.15. Regrets associated with these losses are, of course, subjective.

- Detonations at high latitudes to target GPS and GEO satellites can inject beta-decay electrons at high L-values, but the incremental increase in flux will be too low to cause very early loss of assets.

- A major finding of this study stems from a more systematic examination of the ultraviolet radiation that emanates from a nuclear detonation and its effect upon exposed satellite components such as mirrors, filters, and baffles in optical systems and solar cells in power systems [Gurtman et al., 2003]. The very large material absorption cross-sections for UV photons make this threat potentially exceedingly lethal. Though the probability of direct line-of-sight exposure is low, regrets can be quite serious in terms of completion of a satellite's mission.

IX.B   Civilian Satellites

From an economic viewpoint, perhaps the greatest impact would result from loss of LEO weather satellites. These satellites provide unique meteorological services to the country, and to the world for that matter, by providing critical information on cloud moisture content, wind velocity, ocean temperatures and wave heights. All of these parameters are required for accurate weather prediction and cannot be remotely sensed at high latitudes with weather satellites at geosynchronous orbits. A study of economic benefits of the NOAA satellite [Hussey, 2002] states that industries that contribute $2.7 trillion to the U.S. Gross Domestic Product rely on accurate weather forecasting. Unfortunately, we could find no algorithm for estimating the loss to the U.S. GDP should satellite resources for weather prediction become inoperable. A more recent NOAA study [U.S. Dept. of Commerce, May 2002] provides quantitative data on annual savings to certain industries that has been summarized in Table IX.1. We conclude that there is a net annual savings of slightly over $5B, but regrets from the loss of the satellites for the GDP remain unclear to us.

Table IX.1. Economic Benefits of Weather Satellites.

Sector	Annual Savings, $ Million	Source
Marine Industry	400	<ul><li>Fuel from improved ship routing</li><li>Catch advantage for fishing industry</li><li>Increased offshore drilling safety and efficiency</li></ul>
Agriculture	1,500	<ul><li>Reduced weather related loss</li><li>Improved planting and harvesting decision making</li><li>Improved Resource management</li></ul>
Search and Rescue	500	<ul><li>Reduced search time</li></ul>
Construction	2,500	<ul><li>Reduced weather related loss</li><li>Improved activity scheduling</li><li>More efficient utilization of manpower and equipment</li></ul>
Utilities	60	<ul><li>Improved demand/load forecasting</li><li>Improved hydro-energy management</li></ul>
Aviation	200	<ul><li>Improved flight planning and fuel savings</li></ul>

These economic figures imply significant consequences, particularly for organizations that rely heavily on space assets. The Commission's assessment is that, while the cost of losing these space systems would be high, this loss by itself would not place at risk long-term functionality of American society.

For civilian communications satellites in LEO, countermeasure protection provisions can be made to divert satellite communications links to other media such as fiber optics. Thus, the loss may be acceptable [Anhalt, 2002], but this option must exist within a well-planned protocol in order to avoid an indeterminate period of chaos. Most civilian communications satellites are in GEO orbits and at these altitudes they should be much less susceptible to radiation from other than direct attacks.

If the means of communication between elements of a power distribution system (*e.g.*, substations) includes satellite telephone systems such as Globalstar, loss of satellite-based connectivity may not be compensated by terrestrial landlines that are also at risk to EMP attack. Loss of communications connectivity could seriously impact damage assessment and recovery. Previous studies [Parmentola, 2001] have found that Globalstar and Iridium are as much at risk from nuclear-enhanced radiation belts as the satellites analyzed in this study.

IX.C Military Communication and Intelligence Collection Satellites

Commercial LEO satellites used for military communications can be an important adjunct to military GEO Comsats. A rapidly moving expeditionary force may not have the luxury of exploiting fiber optics for increased communications capability and, without well-established alternative means that have been used in realistic exercises, they may be placed at an unacceptable disadvantage. In addition, handsets for LEO communications are less cumbersome than those for mobile GEO systems making them much more attractive for highly mobile special forces.

Similar arguments hold for intelligence collection. It is presently Presidential policy to exploit civilian Earth surveillance satellites to the maximum extent [NSPD, 2003]. If users of these assets are left with the impression that they will be available post attack, there may not be sufficient planning to exploit other options.

Satellites that employ optical systems for surveillance and target acquisition are highly subject to radiation effects. This particularly applies to missile defense components. Optical systems can be degraded or destroyed by UV or X-rays if the threatening missile is salvage fuzed or intended to open a path for subsequent missiles in the attack. Gamma radiation from nuclear weapon debris can raise the noise level in photodetectors, which is tantamount to blinding them. High X-ray and gamma fluxes can burn out signal processors and upset memories in a satellite.

IX.D Civilian Satellites to Support the Military

Sudden loss of most, if not all LEO commercial satellites would seriously impact U.S. national security as well as the American economy. A recent GAO report [GAO, 2002] recommends that commercial satellites (GEO and LEO) be identified as critical parts of the infrastructure and steps be taken to address security of these assets.

Low Earth Orbit intelligence-gathering assets are crucial for global monitoring of trouble spots around the world. This is especially true today as the US leads the War on Terrorism. As capable as National Geospatial-Intelligence Agency (NGA) assets are, they cannot be everywhere at all times, so commercial high-resolution space assets such as IKONOS, QUICKBIRD, OFEQ, etc. are becoming increasingly critical assets for the intelligence community [Clapper, 2003].

The President has directed [NSPD, 2003] that the United States Government will:

- Rely to the maximum practical extent on U.S. commercial remote sensing space capabilities for filling imagery and geospatial needs for military, intelligence, foreign policy, homeland security, and civil users;

- Focus United States Government remote sensing space systems on meeting needs that cannot be effectively, affordably, and reliably satisfied by commercial providers because of economic factors, civil mission needs, national security concerns, or foreign policy concerns;

- Develop a long-term, sustainable relationship between the United States Government and the U.S. commercial remote sensing space industry;

- Provide a timely and responsive regulatory environment for licensing the operations and exports of commercial remote sensing space systems; and

- Enable U.S. industry to compete successfully as a provider of remote sensing space capabilities for foreign governments and foreign commercial users, while ensuring appropriate measures are implemented to protect national security and foreign policy.

The Director of the Central Intelligence Agency has directed that the NGA use commercial imaging satellites to the "greatest extent possible," and commercial imagery should become the "primary source of data used for government mapping [Tenet, 2002]" The NGA announced in January 2003, that it will spend up to $500 million to purchase commercial imagery over the next 5 years[14]. Additional capabilities available through commercial satellite assets make it much more difficult for adversaries to conduct clandestine operations because areas in which they are operating are under surveillance more often than could be solely sustained with Federal resources. Another future capability that is likely to be exploited is hyper-spectral imagery satellites in LEO. These satellites will provide detailed observations of factories and nuclear facilities to determine, via aerosol emissions, what products/weapons are being produced.

There is danger that elements of the National infrastructure, both military and civilian, will be assumed—without careful analysis—to be functionally replaceable by other means nearly instantaneously to compensate for nuclear-burst-induced losses. This would always be a truly dangerous assumption.

---

[14] NGA Media Release OCRNP 03-16

CHAPTER X
UNCERTAINTIES AND CONFIDENCE ASSESSMENTS

X.A Overview of Uncertainties and Confidence

Analyses presented in preceding chapters represent best-available information about collateral effects on satellites from a high-altitude nuclear detonation utilized as an EMP attack. Differing threat events have been considered to provide representative ranges of weapon effects of import to satellites. There are, however, substantial uncertainties associated with our results. The reason for this is that best-available information does not automatically imply precision and accuracy, i.e.:

- An ensemble of identically made nuclear weapons will produce a distribution of prompt outputs with statistical deviation about mean characteristics,

- Aspects of physics governing induced nuclear-weapon environments are imprecisely known,

- Analyses in this paper are predicated on assumptions about military characteristics and related properties of threat weapons, locations of detonations, and space systems hardening technologies. Given the current state of knowledge, we regard these uncertainties, in the absence of focused technology programs, as irreducible.

Consequently, it is not sufficient to develop only baseline assessments of collateral effects on satellites from high-altitude nuclear detonations. The total assessment process must include, within current abilities, a quantitative appraisal of uncertainties and confidence in our baseline assessments. Due to interplays between certain of the nuclear influences and some of the many natural processes in space (e.g., naturally-occurring geomagnetically trapped radiation and nuclear-pumped radiation belts), uncertainty and confidence appraisals are further complicated by the need to span the realm of competing and cooperative effects, be they of natural or nuclear origins.

The majority of this section will be devoted to *uncertainties*. The reader will observe that this is an imprecise process, with uncertainty bounds often based in part on objective quantitative science and in part subjective qualitative reasoning. Our uncertainty estimates will have, to varying degrees, a less-than-hard-edged qualitative nature. Nevertheless, we hold these uncertainty estimates to be representative of the state of the art and leave the challenge of quantitative improvement to our successors. The later portion of this section will focus on *confidence* in a Bayesian statistical sense, i.e. confidence assessments are considered subjective, taken as a melding of the proponent's past experience and best technically-based intuition.

Uncertainty and confidence assessments provided below are a distillation of inherently complex phenomena. In attempting to strike a balance between completeness and brevity, at least for those situations that are reasonably understood, and in providing qualitative information for aspects that are less well understood, we find that in many respects the discussion is technically superficial. Uncertainties in nuclear weapon effects on satellites arise in no short supply from multiple sources, including: inherent variability of weapons of identical construction due to aging and stochastic phenomena in the exploding device; physics governing interactions between energies emitted by a detonation and the atmosphere, space environment, and satellite systems; physics describing the evolution of the nuclear-disturbed environment; and physics governing interactions between the nuclear-disturbed environment and satellite systems. Overriding many of these considerations are fundamental unknowns associated with the nuclear threat, i.e., what precisely are the characteristics of the threat weapon? Absent definitive knowledge, we can only estimate ranges of effects and apply physical principals to establish bounds on physically possible levels of effects.

Table X.1 summarizes estimates of expected levels of effects on satellites, along with approximate uncertainties and confidence assessments. (This may prove a useful shortcut for those who do not care to read this chapter in its entirety.) Although it is common practice for workers in the field to quote uncertainties as "x percent" or "a factor of x", where "x" is a multiplier, without specifying the statistical meaning of the definition, we have elected to interpret such pronouncements as indicative of one standard deviation about the expected mean value. No doubt this approach associates a greater degree of statistical significance than was originally intended, but we felt it necessary to place, at least conceptually, the mix of often ill-defined uncertainty estimates on a common footing.

Owing to the central role trapped radiation plays in hardening decisions that ultimately affect satellite lifetimes, vulnerability to nuclear explosions, sensitivity to environmentally induced upsets, and cost, the issue of uncertainties in trapped radiation of natural and nuclear origins is of special importance. Here uncertainties are exceptionally large, especially at L shells above ~ 3, primarily because the natural environment that regulates the distribution, intensity, and persistence of geomagnetically trapped electrons (natural and nuclear) is highly variable in response to solar activity that is expressed in the solar wind and interplanetary magnetic field. Furthermore, the initial dispersal of radioactive weapon debris from a high-altitude detonation and subsequent transport of debris during the period it is actively emitting beta-decay electrons, as modeled by the SNRTACS code used for satellite lifetime assessments in this report, is prone to very large uncertainties. Available trapped-radiation data from high-altitude nuclear tests are insufficient to provide (alone) definitive guidance to redress these large uncertainties.

Table X.1. Collateral Effects, Uncertainties, and Confidence for Satellites.

NUCLEAR ENVIRONMENT	Effects on Satellite	Uncertainty Factors	Uncertainty in Mean Level of Effects	Confidence
PRIMARY OUTPUTS				
X-rays	SGEMP; thermomechanical damage	X-ray spectrum, flux and fluence	± 10% for a well-characterized device and its surrounds; otherwise bounded by yield of device moderated by surrounding mass	Moderate: ideally characterized threat devices largely mirror U.S. designs and are analytical estimates
Gamma Rays	SGEMP / TREE	Gamma fluence and flux	± 15% for ideally characterized device; otherwise crudely bounded by fraction of device yield	Low ideally characterized threat devices largely mirror U.S. designs and are analytical estimates
Neutrons	Upsets & damage to electronics, power systems, & optics	Neutron fluence and energy spectrum; satellite components and construction		Low: ideally characterized threat devices largely mirror U.S. designs and are analytical estimates
Energetic Debris Ions and cosmic rays	Charging & ESD; upsets* & heavy-ion damage to electronics, power systems, & optics; implanted β & γ emitters. Single Event Upset (SEU) from cosmic rays	Competition between processes that generate UV, hydromagnetic waves, and energetic air ions	± 5x based on uncertainties in ion flux.	Moderate for bursts below ~ 250 km; Low for bursts above ~ 250 km
INDUCED EFFECTS				
Ultraviolet Fluence	Damage to solar power systems and optics	Atomic physics in blast wave; multiple factors for direct device-generated UV	± 2x to 3x	High for blast-wave generated UV; Low for direct device-generated UV
Trapped Radiation	Charging & ESD; upsets & damage to electronics, power systems, & optics	Dispersal of radioactive weapon debris; trapping efficiency of energetic electrons; transport processes for energetic electrons; persistence; electron energization	± 10x under best of circumstances; otherwise ± 100x or greater (crude estimate)	Very Low
Energetic Air Ions	Charging & ESD; upsets & heavy-ion damage to power systems, & optics	Shock energization of air ions vs. UV and wave-generation processes that compete for kinetic yield of weapon	± 10x	Low

X.B Uncertainties in Natural Radiation Environment

Two primary considerations enter into uncertainties in characterizations of energetic particle fluxes in the natural radiation belts: (i) the non-steady (fluctuating), quasi-random behavior of trapped-electron fluxes and (ii) inaccuracies in predictive models that arise from (a) combinations of incomplete, inaccurate, and non-physics-based model algorithms and (b) insufficient model input data for geospace factors (e.g., magnetospheric electromagnetic environment) that regulate the belts.

Natural belts of geomagnetically trapped energetic particles exist as a balance between processes that inject particles into the trapping region, processes that modify the trapped population (e.g., redistribute, energize, and de-energize), and processes that remove particles from the trapping region, as was illustrated by the "leaky bucket" analogy of Figure V.4. The non-steady, fluctuating character of natural trapped electron fluxes was illustrated by satellite data displayed in Figure V.3. These data indicate peak-to-peak fluctuations in trapped flux as large as four orders of magnitude (i.e., a factor of as much as 10,000 in the environment to which satellites are exposed). Long-term-average models (e.g., the commonly used AE-8 model [Vette, 1991]) eliminate this consideration by averaging trapped-particle data acquired over long intervals (e.g., many years on the order of a solar cycle), but as a consequence these models may err compared to measured instantaneous trapped-electron-flux values (and associated *dose rates* to sensitive components) by several orders of magnitude.

If a satellite is hardened sufficiently that irradiated components accumulate dose in a manner such that total dose is the dominant factor and dose rate is demonstrably inconsequential, then variability between differing long-term-average models (taken to be ~ 2x to 3x) appropriately characterizes the uncertainty in cumulative exposure hazard for that satellite system. Where dose rate is a factor, then uncertainties more properly derive from several-order-of-magnitude levels of variability versus L shell of Figure V.3.

The root cause of the variability seen in Figure V.3 is dynamic and fluctuating solar wind density and velocity, along with continuous changes in the interplanetary magnetic field (magnetic field torn from the Sun and carried by the solar wind). These properties regulate the coupling of solar-wind energy to the interior of the Earth's magnetosphere and the geomagnetic particle trapping region therein. To translate this qualitative statement into a quantitative measure, consider that geomagnetically trapped particle fluxes are often characterized by a phase-space-density function $f(r,p,t)$, where r represents spatial coordinates, p the conjugate momentum, and t time. Starting from the Liouville Equation $\mathcal{D}f = 0$ for conservation of phase-space density, where $\mathcal{D}$ represents the total time derivative, and allowing for linearized diffusion processes that modify the phase-space density (a simplifying assumption for what is inherently a nonlinear process), one arrives at a Fokker-Planck equation for f —

$$\frac{\partial f}{\partial t} = \nabla \cdot \overrightarrow{D} \cdot \nabla f + \ldots$$

where $\overrightarrow{D}$ represents diffusive processes that approximate in aggregate large numbers of infinitesimal particle scattering interactions (adiabatic invariants; see Walt [1994]). Elements of matrix $\overline{D}$ represent diffusion in phase space, including spatial diffusion, pitch-angle diffusion, etc. If we use the L-shell coordinate in this representation, then radial diffusion is represented by the D_{LL} element of $\overline{D}$. Uncertainties in the evolution of trapped-electron flux can be gauged, in part, by uncertainties in D_{LL}, as shown in Figure X.1. Solid curves in the figure represent radial diffusion coefficients derived from fitting various data sets to the diffusion equation. Dashed curves are various theoretical estimates of D_{LL}. The spread in experimentally-derived D_{LL} curves is indicative of the wide range of magnetospheric electromagnetic conditions that influence the behavior of trapped particles. The spread in theoretically-based D_{LL} curves in the figure arises primarily from differing assumptions about the power spectral density of the perturbation electromagnetic field in the trapping region of the magnetosphere. The important point here is that at all values of L the spread of experimentally and theoretically based D_{LL}'s is three to five orders of magnitude. That is, even in a linearized equation for the phase-space density of trapped electrons, there is a several-order-of-magnitude uncertainty. This observation is of paramount importance to uncertainties in the nuclear-pumped radiation problem we will discuss later because trapped energetic electrons originating from natural processes (with naturally occurring D_{LL}'s of Figure X.1) and trapped energetic electrons originating from a nuclear explosion are regulated by identically the same governing physics. Except for modifications to D_{LL} that may arise from the nuclear detonation, the range of D_{LL}'s (and the inherent uncertainties) of Figure X.1 applies to nuclear-pumped belts.

At present there are no suitable means to forecast *a priori* magnetospheric conditions in sufficient detail to predict D_{LL}. One might view this situation as stochastic, and there is some merit to this view, but the expectation is that accurate forecasts of solar wind plasma and magnetic field properties combined with a high-fidelity model of the magnetosphere could provide a deterministic aspect to the problem. At present solar wind plasma and magnetic field properties are not predictable based on observations of the Sun, but they are measurable by satellites such as the Advanced Composition Explorer (ACE) that orbit the L1 Lagrange point, about 1.5 million kilometers from Earth along the Earth-Sun axis.

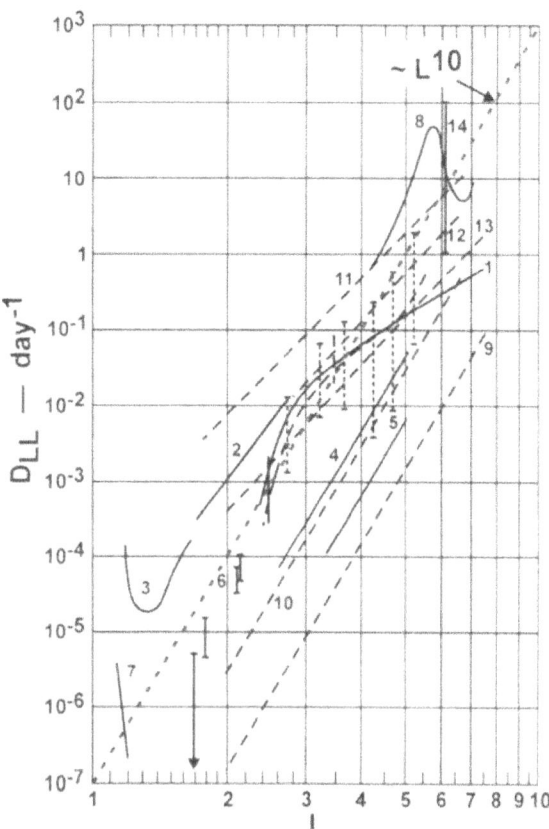

Figure X.1. Radial diffusion coefficients obtained by a variety of methods. Dashed lines are based on theory. Solid curves and points are based on fitting the diffusion equation to experimental values. (From M. Walt [1996].)

X.C Uncertainties in Environments Produced by High-Altitude Nuclear Detonations

In characterizing disturbed environments from nuclear explosions, the same convention as used in Section V will be followed:

- Prompt environments are those that arise from the detonation on time scale short compared to formation times for blast waves and fireballs

- Induced environments follow from the interaction of nuclear-burst energies with the atmosphere and geomagnetic field generally around the burst point. Some induced effects may be located half a world away, in the opposite hemisphere at the magnetic conjugate point, or may have the global extent of radiation belts that encircle the Earth.

X.C.1 Uncertainties in Prompt Nuclear Environments

Prompt nuclear environments consist of gamma-ray and neutron emissions from nuclear and thermonuclear reactions in an exploding weapon, X-rays emitted primarily by very-high-temperature materials of which the weapon was constructed, and energetic ions, electrons, and neutrons of weapon debris. Consequently, uncertainties in these characteristics of a nuclear burst are dominated by factors that influence the performance of weapon (e.g., design, materials, stochastic aspects such as inherent instabilities during the assembly of the critical core, aging of components, etc.), uncertain material properties under the extreme conditions within a detonating weapon, along with assumptions and approximations in weapon performance predictions that are common to modern computer-based weapon design (particularly for foreign weapons), and unknown materials that may shroud the weapon at the time of detonation. In the development of quantitative assessments of uncertainties, we assume the threat weapon in question is based on technology that mirrors a pre-1970's U.S. design. Alternatively, we can assume an analysis based on detailed design information for the threat weapon. Should neither of these assumptions apply, then uncertainty estimates described below are essentially unbounded, with an associated confidence approaching zero.

The most comprehensive assessment for which nuclear outputs were relatively thoroughly diagnosed was the TENABO test of 1990 [LLNL, 1999]. Data from this experiment have since become the principal metric by which the DOE's output community has calibrated its design tools and analysis techniques.

X.C.1.a Uncertainties in Prompt Gamma Environments

Uncertainty estimates for both gamma fluence and its time derivative, gamma-dot, are highly dependent on the degree to which a source has been characterized and predictive computer codes "tuned" to the device (generally with the aid of extensive experimental data). Such instances are rare, but for such a case uncertainties in both gamma fluence and its time derivative, gamma-dot, as quoted by sources at Lawrence Livermore National Laboratory (LLNL) based on recent predictive models, are on the order of ± 15% [Hoover, 2001; DiPeso, 2003]. What precisely is meant by this figure is somewhat vague, but as noted above we will assume it defines one standard deviation in the distribution about the mean.

As has been noted earlier in this report, prompt X-ray output of a weaponized nuclear device detonated in space could approach 80% of its total yield. Predictive capability of total yield is no better than about ± 10%. Weapons specifically designed to maximize either gamma or neutron radiation can lower this X-ray fraction substantially. Very large mass high-explosive designs can also lower the X-ray output by converting X-ray energy into internal and kinetic energy. The Nagasaki device, for example, emitted less than 1% of its energy as X-rays, approximately 1% as gamma rays and neutrons, and the remaining 98-99% of its nuclear energy as kinetic and internal energy [Tubbs et al., 1999].

X.C.1.b Uncertainties in X-Ray Environment

For total photon output, sources at LLNL again profess to an uncertainty of ± 15%, but with the caveat that this is integrated over the full photon spectrum from UV to gammas [Thomson, 2003]. X-ray spectral intensity measured in cal/cm^2-keV over relatively small energy ranges, say 1 keV, may be uncertain by an order of magnitude. This is particularly true for UV [Thomson, 2002] and in regions where photon energy is reduced several orders of magnitude from the spectral peak. While UV radiation affects only the exterior surfaces of a satellite, interior components may be particularly sensitive to relatively narrow portions of the high-energy photon spectrum, and thus damage may occur internally though the incident spectral fluence could be quite small.

X.C.1.c Uncertainties in Prompt Neutron and Debris-Ion Fluxes from Nuclear Detonations

Prompt neutron predictive capability, integrated over all neutron energies and again assuming that the weapon type is known *a priori* and well characterized, is thought to be uncertain to approximately ± 15%, but with the caveat that the weapon has not been designed to specifically boost gamma output.

Uncertainties in fluxes of energetic debris emanating from a nuclear detonation arise primarily from uncertainties in the three-dimensional weapon-disassembly mass and velocity distributions and charge state distributions of debris ions, each as modified by the aeroshell and any other materials in the vicinity of the burst. A secondary factor is the orientation of the weapon relative to the geomagnetic field at the time of detonation. For detonations below about 150 km altitude, short-range coupling (a combination of collisional and Larmor coupling) will efficiently extract the bulk of the initial kinetic energy from debris ions and convert it, through complex atomic-physics interactions, to UV photons. A fraction of the energetic debris-ion inventory may escape the coupling region, in the loss cones along the magnetic field, with little loss of kinetic energy. For bursts above ~ 100 km, this fraction may be a fraction of a percent or as high as ~ 30%, but it will depend on mass and velocity distributions relative to the geomagnetic field.

For detonations in the ~ 150 km to ~ 400-600 km altitude range with an assumed peak disassembly speed of ~ 2,000 km/s, interactions in the magnetically-dominated high-Alfvén-Mach-number blast wave transfer initial debris-ion kinetic energy to air ions that are overrun and swept up by the blast wave. This process competes with short-range coupling and the associated conversion of debris kinetic energy to UV photons, but above ~ 250 km altitude short-range coupling becomes inefficient, and the majority of debris kinetic energy appears outside the blast-wave region as kinetic energy of air ions and hot neutrals produced by charge-exchange reactions (see Section X.3.b.ii). At altitudes above ~ 400-600 km, or for detonations with substantially lower disassembly speeds, the Alfvén Mach number of the debris expansion is sufficiently low that a substantial fraction of the initial debris kinetic energy (up to ~ 55% according to current theoretical estimates) is thought to be radiated as hydromagnetic waves. Interactions between debris and the geomagnetic field are thought to direct the bulk of debris ion mass (~ 65% to 95%, depending of burst yield and altitude) upward to LEO and MEO altitudes, and beyond. One of the three low-yield ARGUS test shots above the South Atlantic may qualify as a detonation in this low-Alfvén-Mach-number regime, but no other tests, U.S., or Soviet, appear to qualify. The planned U.S. URACCA test was cancelled by President Kennedy following extensive damage to satellites by STARFISH PRIME, so we have no definitive data on which to base uncertainty estimates.

The net result of these considerations is that for bursts below ~ 150 km altitude, debris-ion fluxes are limited mainly to loss-cone fluxes with uncertainties dominated by weapon-design and exterior-mass-distribution considerations. Outside of the loss cone, debris energy is rapidly drained by the UV-radiating blast wave, so debris is largely contained inside the fireball. Uncertainties in energetic debris-ion fluxes are estimated at 10x for low flux values to 2x for cases with large loss cones. For detonations in the ~ 250 km to ~ 600 km altitude range, similar considerations apply, except that initial debris kinetic energy is drained by energization of air ions in the high-Alfvén-Mach-number blast wave. The residual debris-ion gas, the bulk of which is contained in the magnetic bubble, has mean energy on the order of 100 eV or less. For detonations above ~ 600 km altitude, one is left largely to theory alone. Conservatively, uncertainties must be pegged at 10x or greater.

X.C.2 Uncertainties in Induced Nuclear Environments

Induced environments are those resulting from interactions of energetic emissions (electromagnetic and particulate) with the atmospheric and space environment in which the detonation occurs. Consequently, to greater or lesser degrees uncertainties in induced environments reflect uncertainties in ill-defined statistical distributions of weapon characteristics, uncertainties in properties of the atmospheric and space environment at the time of detonation, and imprecise characterizations of physics underlying the important processes that produce significant effects on systems.

X.C.2.a Uncertainties in Induced Energetic Particle Fluxes

Induced energetic particle fluxes are composed of air ions (principally oxygen and nitrogen ions) that receive substantial kinetic energy during the early-time rapid expansion of weapon debris. For detonations below ~ 150 km altitude, most of the kinetic yield (kinetic energy carried by high-speed weapon debris) is converted to UV photons. For detonations above ~ 250 km and below ~ 600 km, an assumed 2,000 km/s debris expansion will produce a high-Alfvén-Mach-number blast wave that will shock heat air ions to high energies (tens of keV to ~ 100 keV). The majority of the kinetic yield of a weapon will be converted to energetic air ions and, through charge exchange of a fraction of the downward-direct portion of energetic ions, energetic air neutral species. For burst points above ~ 600 km, the Alfvén-Mach-number of the debris expansion decreases, so the conversion efficiency of debris kinetic energy to air ion kinetic energy decreases rapidly with increasing burst-point altitude. Thus, it is bursts in the ~ 250 km to ~ 600 km altitude window that are of primary importance to this sub-section.

Uncertainties in energetic air-ion and air-neutral fluxes are inferred indirectly from comparisons between STARFISH PRIME data and simulation results with the best-available model for STARFISH PRIME phenomenology [Kilb and Glenn, 1978; Hausman et al., 1992a; Hausman et al., 1992b] and a heavy dose of inference based on experience. On this (rather unsatisfying) basis one asserts the energetic fluxes of air species produced by STARFISH PRIME-like detonations is the aforementioned altitude range to be uncertain to ~ ±5x. Insofar as the team of technical experts that originally developed the analysis and modeling tools for this burst regime has long since been dispersed and work on the problem abandoned by the Defense Threat Reduction Agency, there is little expectation of reduced uncertainties in this and related aspects of STARFISH PRIME-like detonations.

X.C.2.b Uncertainties in Delayed Beta and Gamma Radiations

As noted in EM-1 [Kaul, 1990], delayed beta and gamma uncertainties are strongly affected by a weapon's yield, its total fission fraction, and the yield fractions of the various fissile materials used in its construction. Weapon characteristics that influence the energy and angular dependence of prompt neutron or gamma emissions, however, do not strongly affect the delayed radiation component. There is an additional uncertainty in specifying the delayed emission rate and fission product radiation for times of interest to satellite vulnerability. Wilson [1979] attributes a total ± 20% uncertainty to the delayed radiation output of a fission weapon, and ± 30% for that of a boosted thermonuclear or enhanced radiation device.

X.C.2.c Uncertainties in Nuclear-Pumping of Radiation Belts

Nuclear-pumped radiation belts are attributed to three mechanisms for generating high-energy electrons (tens of keV to tens of MeV): beta decay of radioactive weapon debris, free-space decay of neutrons, and shock acceleration of in-situ ionospheric electrons. Nuclear pumping of the radiation trapping region of space surrounding the Earth requires that energetic electrons from each of these sources be injected into the trapping region and be durably trapped for a period of time sufficient to cause concern for satellites (i.e., generally for a few days or more). Energetic electrons from these sources, once trapped, are governed by identically the same physics as regulates naturally occurring electrons in the radiation belts.

Uncertainties arise in the sources, injection efficiencies, evolving energy spectra, evolving spatial distributions, and lifetimes of electrons attributable to nuclear-burst sources. Each category of uncertainty is considered qualitatively in turn. An overarching consideration is that given the commonality of governing physics for trapped particles, be they of natural or nuclear origins, in conjunction with knowledge gaps and exceptionally large uncertainties in modeling of temporal and spatial properties of the natural radiation belts, we are in a poor position to characterize nuclear-pumped radiation belts as anything less than highly uncertain.

The dominant uncertainty in the beta-decay source involves the distribution and dispersal of radioactive weapon debris following a detonation. For detonations below ~ 200 km altitude, short-range coupling between debris and air keeps most of the debris within the fireball. Predictive capabilities for fireball plasma and debris densities are generally within a factor of three with uncertainty in spatial distribution localized within a fraction of a fireball dimension. This is about as good as it gets. For detonations such as STARFISH PRIME (burst point at 400 km altitude), we can account for perhaps 2/3 of the weapon debris inventory, with the fate of the remaining third remaining a mystery. For bursts above ~ 400-600 km (low-Alfvén-Mach-number regime), theory/modeling is our only guide, and theory/modeling for this category of detonations is in an embryonic state. Uncertainties in this regime for debris dispersal vs time are intuitively pegged at greater than a factor of ten for want of anything better.

Uncertainties associated with belt pumping by the decay of neutrons liberated in a detonation arise primarily from uncertainties in the neutron spectrum of the threat weapon and the current lack of careful neutron transport calculations under a variety of representative atmospheric density profiles. At least the latter of these can be rectified with some effort.

Parametric studies may be sufficient to bound uncertainties. At present this source is considered a relatively minor contributor, although investigations by Allen [2002] are underway.

Shock acceleration of in-situ ionospheric electrons by the blast wave from a detonation has been suggested by some as a means to generate energetic electrons to several MeV in energy. We have no direct evidence to support the concept of shock acceleration of electrons to MeV energies by a nuclear explosion. Data from STARFISH PRIME directly support shock acceleration of electrons to tens of keV energy. Under nominal solar wind conditions the bow shock of the Earth has an Alfvén Mach number comparable to the Alfvén Mach number of the debris expansion from the STARFISH PRIME nuclear test. Although the Earth's bow shock is enormously larger that the STARFISH PRIME blast wave, nominal solar wind conditions are observed to produce energetic electron fluxes in the 100 keV energy range. In the absence of definitive experimental evidence to the contrary, we do not regard shock acceleration in a nuclear explosion as a credible source of significant fluxes of MeV electrons and therefore cannot associate a meaningful uncertainty with it.

We next turn to uncertainties in the efficiency with which energetic electrons from a nuclear burst are injected into durable trapped orbits in the radiation belt region surrounding the Earth. Charged particles in a dipole magnetic field execute three types of motion simultaneously: gyration about magnetic field lines; repetitive bounce motion along magnetic field lines, centered about the magnetic equator; and drift motion about the Earth. These motions are illustrated in Figure X.2. Durably trapped radiation belt particles must execute these three motions while remaining high enough (nominally above ~ 100 km) to avoid being captured by the atmosphere while remaining on closed magnetic field lines (both ends in the Earth). The altitude of the "mirror points" (see Figure X.2) depends on a particle's pitch angle (angle between particle velocity vector and the geomagnetic field[15]); pitch angles near 90° cause particles to mirror near the magnetic equator while pitch angles near zero cause particles to mirror below the critical altitude for atmospheric capture.

Electrons become durably trapped in several scenarios. If a debris nucleus is above ~ 100 km in a region of space with closed magnetic field lines (both ends in the Earth) when it undergoes beta decay, and if the pitch angle of the emitted beta electron is such that the electron will mirror above ~ 100 km, then the electron will be trapped. Alternatively, in the same scenario if the beta electron is emitted with a pitch angle too small to mirror above ~ 100 km, then it will likely be absorbed by the atmosphere unless it is pitch-angle scattered to a larger pitch angle while above ~ 100 km. Collisions with atmospheric particles or wave-particle interactions can accomplish the required pitch-angle scattering. The same considerations apply to electrons emitted by the decay of free neutrons and to shock-accelerated electrons. Electron scattering and capture by the atmosphere is well in hand, with uncertainties originating primarily from the lack of a well-defined density profile in the upper atmosphere at the time of the detonation. This profile is subject to excursions as a result of variations in solar activity.

---

[15] By convention a charged particle's pitch angle is generally specified at the magnetic equator where the magnetic field strength along a field line is weakest and the instantaneous pitch angle is at its minimum. As a charged particle gyrates along a field line from the magnetic equator toward a mirror point, its instantaneous pitch angle increases until it reaches 90° at the mirror point, at which time it is reflected back toward the magnetic equator.

Similarly, the power spectrum of waves in the inner magnetosphere where particles are trapped is subject to large variations as a result of solar activity.

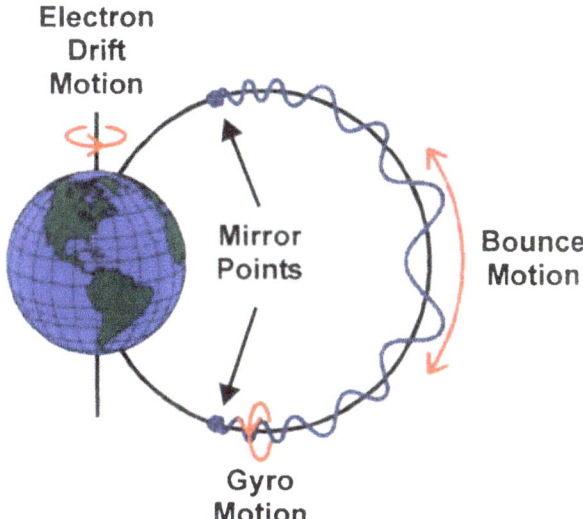

Figure X.2. Three simultaneous motions of geomagnetically trapped electrons are illustrated: gyration about magnetic field lines; bounce motion between magnetic mirror points, and drift around the Earth.

Electrons scattering is further complicated by the burst itself. High-altitude nuclear explosions convert a fraction of their kinetic yield to hydromagnetic and electromagnetic waves in the frequency range suitable to radially diffuse and to pitch-angle scatter energetic electrons. As burst altitude is raised, the fraction of the kinetic yield so converted increases, with a peak conversion fraction estimated at ~ 55% for some bursts in the low-Alfvén-Mach-number regime.

Overall, the electron injection process is highly non-linear and poorly characterized theoretically. Consequently, extrapolations of electron injection data from the very few high-altitude nuclear tests conducted by the U.S. and the Soviet Union are ill advised. Figure X.3 illustrates regions where nuclear test data pertinent to nuclear-pumped radiation belts are applicable and inapplicable. The key point of this figure is that for contemporary ballistic-missile-defense scenarios that involve contact fused or salvage-fused detonations upon intercept, available test data for nuclear-pumping of the radiation belts are in the wrong region of magnetic space. Observe that high-altitude detonations used in an EMP attack on CONUS would also occur within the red-shaded region. Extrapolation of nuclear test data of 1958 and 1962 to the region of magnetic space above CONUS is ill advised owing to the non-linear character of the governing physics. Modelers nevertheless rely heavily on these data, and that reliance introduces a large measure of uncertainty.

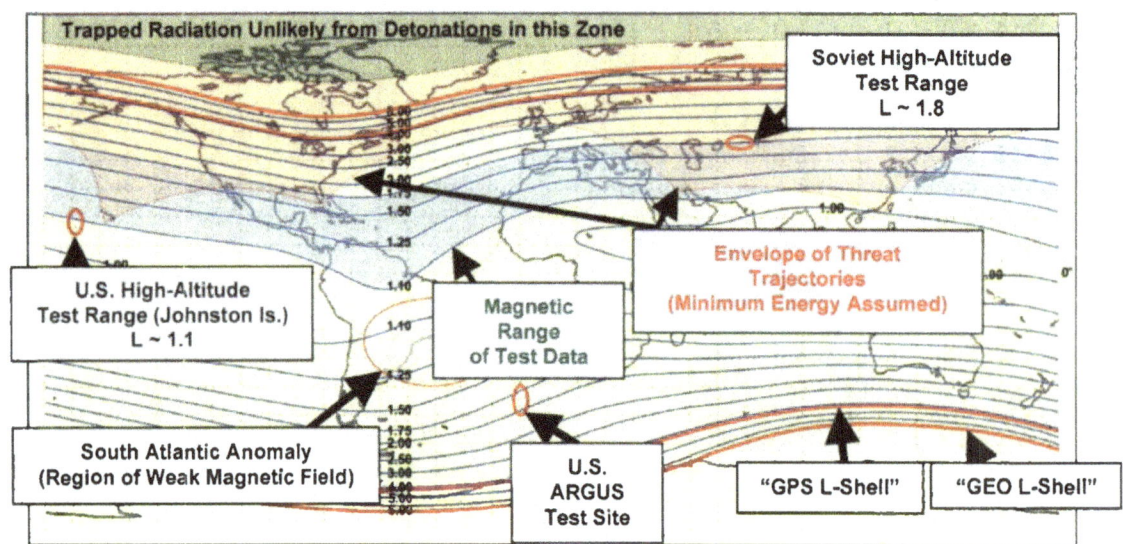

Figure X.3. Cylindrical map projection with overlaid contours of constant geomagnetic L shell values (blue lines) illustrates magnetic locations of U.S. and Soviet high-altitude nuclear tests of 1958 and 1962. L-shell contours would be straight, horizontal line if the geomagnetic field were an ideal geocentric dipole field, but displacement of the true field source from the Earth's center in combination with higher-order multipole moments in the true field result in the contours shown. The South Atlantic Anomaly is a region of weak field that permits trapped particles to mirror at lower-than-average altitudes, so it is a region where the atmospheric capture rate is above average. The principal U.S. and Soviet high-altitude test sites at L = 1.1 and L = 1.8, respectively, are indicated. These are the sites with magnetic properties for which the bulk of test data for nuclear-pumped radiation belts exists. The band of magnetic-shell space bounded by test-site L values is shaded in blue to indicate the portion of magnetic space for which the test data are deemed applicable. Extrapolation of nuclear test data to L values well removed from test sites is regarded, in the absence of reliable physics models, as highly questionable. To add contemporary context to this map, an ensemble of minimum-energy threat trajectories for ballistic missiles launched from a variety of Asian locations toward targets in the U.S. have been used to define the threat envelope indicated by the red shading. It is within the red-shaded region that one would expect high-altitude nuclear detonations that result from ballistic-missile-defense intercepts of threat RVs. Minimal overlap between red- and blue-shaded regions is indicative of the very limited applicability of belt-pumping data from past high-altitude nuclear tests.

The last elements that contribute to uncertainties—evolution of the energy spectrum and spatial distribution, along with lifetimes of energetic electrons of nuclear origin—can be addressed simultaneously. These are important aspects of the nuclear-pumped belts that are directly regulated by identically the same magnetospheric dynamics that govern the natural radiation belts. Consequently, one would expect that readily available data for dynamical evolution of the natural radiation belts could be used as a basis for evaluating nuclear-pumped belts. At a minimum, a model for nuclear-pumped belts should be able to reproduce the dynamical evolution of the natural belts. Data for the natural belts could then be used to validate important non-nuclear aspects of models for nuclear-pumped belts. Unfortunately, it is reported that the primary model available for estimating nuclear-pumped belt effects on satellites, the Air Force Research Laboratory SNRTACS code used for analyses supporting this paper, does not reproduce the dynamical evolution of the natural belts [Hilland, 2003]. With respect to uncertainties in SNRTACS predictions of the nuclear-pumped belt trapped flux environment, published assessments indicate "The overall uncertainty in environment code predictions is estimated to be at least a factor of 10" [Jakes, et al., 1993]. This estimate does not encompass bursts in the low-Alfvén-Mach-number regime (i.e., bursts above ~ 600 km altitude) because the physics of these bursts has not been incorporated into SNRTACS.

Overall, uncertainties in predictions of nuclear-pumped trapped radiation belts are unacceptably large. Owing to multiple non-linear aspects of the total process, there is at present no mathematically rigorous means to provide a definitive assessment of uncertainties. The best one can do is to provide a best estimate based on a melding of the above considerations. For any point in space subject to nuclear-pumping of the radiation belts at any time beyond an hour or two after a detonation, we estimate uncertainties in trapped electron flux to be not less than one to two orders of magnitude, bounded only by the available inventory of energetic electrons produced by the detonation.

X.C.2.d Uncertainties in Ultraviolet Photoemissions [16]

Nuclear detonations in the altitude range of ~ 90 km to ~ 250 km altitude produce a debris-air blast wave that is known to efficiently convert the kinetic yield of a nuclear device (i.e., kinetic energy initially carried by high-speed weapon debris as it expands away from the burst) to ionizing and non-ionizing ultraviolet (UV) photons. The conversion efficiency can be as high as about 80%. For a nominal weapon with kinetic yield equal to 25% of total yield, this translates into a UV yield that can be as much as 20% of the total device yield.

The production of ultraviolet radiation from the debris-air blast wave is primarily from inelastic collisions of atoms and ions with electrons. Such collisions excite discrete levels of the species, primarily O I - O VII (atomic O to O^{6+}) and N I - N VI (atomic N to N^{5+}), which in turn, emit UV line radiation. Continuum emission occurs via free-free (Bremsstrahlung) and free-bound (electron capture) processes. These latter processes can generally be computed with robust reliability. Below about 50 km thermal equilibration is rapid and discrete emissions can be calculated assuming thermodynamic equilibrium. At very high altitudes (>250 km), collision frequencies are sufficiently infrequent that energy is drained from the debris blast wave primarily by energization of air ions rather than by UV radiation. The transition altitudes in between are of most interest, and predictions must be based on individual transitions and rate equations; one cannot rely on a single equation-of-state. Generally, the transition energies (wavelengths) are well-known. Less well-known are the relative amplitudes of discrete excitation processes, aspects which lead to uncertainties in emission intensities. In computing rate coefficients for direct electron impact excitation, one generally assumes a Maxwellian electron velocity distribution. Electron-electron collision frequencies are generally sufficiently high for conditions of interest that this is likely a good assumption. Much of what is currently used in first-principles predictive modeling is summarized by Laher and Gilmore [1990].

The primary source of uncertainties in the prediction of UV emissions in this region is the paucity of either real test data on the congregate processes or valid experimental data on discrete electron impact excitation rates and quenching rates. Absent sufficient data on excitation rates, predictions rely on theoretical computations which, although becoming more reliable, retain inherent uncertainties [Abdallah, et al., 1988; Clark et al., 1988]. Quantifying such uncertainties is difficult since theoretical calculations do not produce error bars and the code developers seldom directly address the issue. It has been arguably claimed by some [Itikawa et al., 1985] that theoretical results have reliability factors (errors) of a factor of three or less. Some

---

[16] This section makes extensive use of information supplied by R. A. Armstrong [2003] and uses, directly and by paraphrasing, his descriptions of processes and uncertainties.

experimental data on electron impact excitation, with varying error bars, exist on atmospheric species with which to validate theoretical results and bound uncertainties. With a few exceptions, experimental data targets transitions in species of aeronomic interest. These do not include most of the higher-charged species and high-energy transitions of interest for UV blast wave predictions. Generally, for these experimental data sets, error bars range from ~10% to more than a factor of three, depending on experimental difficulties and age of the data. Exacerbating the dilemma of uncertainties, seldom are data available over the range of energies of interest, limiting our ability to comprehensively validate theoretical results. Where overlap of data and theoretical results do exist, the theoretical results generally lie within the error bars of the data. However, some exceptions occur where theoretical results are pathological, indicating complex coupling and interference of configurations in the calculations. For these, generating reliable excitation rates is problematic in the absence of real data. Generally speaking, computations of transitions that are hydrogenic in nature, either in highly charged species or transitions involving a single electron outside a closed shell are well behaved and yield reliable results. Transitions from open-shell configurations are less reliable but are arguably accurate to within about a factor of three. Producing accurate predictions of UV emissions is also predicated on models which are sufficiently inclusive of transitions to mimic "reality". In the past, such inclusive predictions were constrained by computer limitations. Such limitations have been lifted with current computer capabilities so efforts to expand the rate models can increase the reliability of UV emission predictions. It is possible that someone has written a review of cross section accuracies, but if they have, we did not find it in a literature search.

Cross sections are directly proportional to oscillator strength, so uncertainties can be estimated based on how close theoretical model values are to current NIST compilations, where NIST provides overlapping information. Most are within 50%, some are within factors of 2 - 3, and a few are so far off that their meaning is unclear.

Two caveats apply: (1) oscillator strengths listed in the NIST compilations have their own estimate of accuracy from very good to very poor. (2) electron collision cross sections can result in mixing of the coupling terms, in which case relying on oscillator strength alone can be dangerous.

Operationally, one finds that careful first-principles modeling of UV generation in the blast wave results in fireball electron density, size, and related properties that agree with test data to within the error bars on the data. It is generally accepted that such results are within a factor of two to three of reality. By inference, we conclude that model predictions of UV generation by a debris-air blast wave are, in aggregate, uncertain to a factor of two to three. This statement does not mean that every spectral interval $\delta\lambda$ is of this level of accuracy, but rather it means that the total energy flux is thought accurate to this level.

X.D Uncertainties in Natural and Nuclear Effects on Satellites

The ultimate failure of a satellite subject to radiation exposure will be derived from an electrical, optical or thermal control malfunction. Those major satellite subsystems in jeopardy are:

- The power system:
    - Solar cells

- - Power management electronics
- Attitude control system electronics
- Communication systems
  - Antennas
  - Receiver/transmitters
- Surveillance systems
  - Passive optical components
  - Optical structural components
  - Spectral imaging
  - Focal plane detectors and processors
  - Information conditioners
- Information processing systems
  - Logic elements
  - Memories
- Thermal Control Systems
  - Radiator panels
  - Paints
  - Blankets
  - Louvers

Any temporary or permanent disruption of these subsystem functions might defeat the mission of the satellite. The electronic systems are controlled by semiconductor microcircuits that operate at low signal levels and have relatively low energy damage thresholds. Microcircuit active element density has increased astronomically over the past several decades to support high processor speeds and memory densities. Feature sizes have dramatically decreased, reducing the effects of charge trapping, but increasing sensitivity to single event effects.

A discussion of uncertainties in the response of a complete satellite or even some of its major components requires assumptions about particular technologies and materials used by manufacturers in fabrication. An assessment of hardness confidence can be the most accurate for the most basic module of the system i.e., a resistor or a simple bipolar transistor. As the size and complexity of a module grows, i.e., a microcircuit, a processor or a memory, the accuracy of the analysis becomes more uncertain. There are issues of manufacturing reproducibility, differences in chosen semiconductor technology, self-shielding and test radiation fidelity and uniformity. As the size of the module increases to a major subsystem or the complete satellite, a statistical analysis becomes meaningless. At that point one must resort to engineering judgment based on past testing experience and careful design.

The largest module ever tested was the STARSAT module that bore a close resemblance to a DSCS III satellite. This was an underground nuclear test called HURON KING that consisted of the nuclear device, buried at a depth of ~ 1000 ft, a pipe through which the radiation was brought to the ground surface, and the vacuum test chamber that contained the satellite (Figure IV.3). Performance of many of the active electronic subsystems was carefully monitored during the test. The only satellite malfunction observed occurred in an attitude control circuit. Post-test analysis and a subsequent test demonstrated that this malfunction was only an anomalous effect that occurred because of an environmental artifact. The major factor in the success of this test is attributable to a long history of testing of piece-parts and subsystems in laboratory simulators prior to actual nuclear testing. It is difficult to predict if satellites with contemporary technologies would respond in the same manner given that 25 years have passed since the HURON KING event. Contemporary satellites are constructed differently, with parts representative of current technologies. Furthermore, laboratory test facilities are different or non-existent.

Today there is no longer an underground test capability and many of the above-ground laboratory facilities are being closed. The lack of such facilities reduces the capability to test at the largest sizes of system integration, with remaining test capability down by several orders of complexity and materially decreased confidence in hardness.

Table X.2 shows current uncertainties in the response of satellites to the different radiation effects

Table X.2. Uncertainties in Nuclear Effects on Satellites.

Effect	Uncertainty	Description
ELECTRONICS		
TREE	Order of Magnitude	• Variation in device response comes from manufacturing rather than lack of understanding of radiation effects
SGEMP	Factor of 2-3 Factor of 4-6	• Bounding estimates of currents on a single wire • Coupling to wire in a complex system complex systems
ECEMP	Factor of 2-3	• Upper bound on magnitude of discharge
DEMP	Order of Magnitude	• Small effect in satellite hardened to SGEMP
OPTICS		
X rays	Factor of 2-3 Factor of 3-4 Order of magnitude	• Impulse from low temp X-rays • Deformation from heating in simple materials • Deformation from heating in complex materials

X.E Confidence Assessments in Light of Uncertainties

We have in this chapter cited uncertainties of as much as two orders of magnitude (or possibly more) in our ability to calculate the threat to a specific satellite of a specific detonation. To this we must add the three orders of magnitude (as measured by weapon yields from 10 kt to 10 Mt) or more spanned by the potential threat space. To proceed with a mitigation program, one must have confidence that a significant portion of the potential threat space (a) constitutes a serious hazard to important space assets, and (b) is not so severe as to make mitigation impossible (or prohibitively expensive).

To assess these criteria, we consider separately threats from "prompt" weapon outputs and from "induced" environments, including long-term trapped radiation ("pumped belts"). Prompt radiation represents a potential immediate threat to those satellites within line-of-sight of a detonation, in which case our uncertainty as to severity of the threat is due largely to lack of detailed knowledge of weapon outputs. By contrast, trapped radiation represents a potential long-term threat to all satellites in orbit at the time of burst, or launched for some period thereafter. Important components of uncertainty include beta-electron trapping efficiency and the rate of dispersion and decay of trapped fluxes via natural (or artificial remediation) processes.

The threat with smallest uncertainty is prompt X-ray fluence. Knowledge of the fluence is limited by uncertainty in weapon design and yield. Calculations supporting Table VIII.1 indicate (for postulated events) probabilities of X-ray induced latchup and burnout as high as 20%, based on the likelihood of a satellite being in proximity to the burst. For other orbits and larger yields, higher probabilities may obtain. If modifications to satellite designs were to increase thresholds for onset of damage, these probabilities (and associated uncertainties) would be reduced.

Other components of prompt radiation, including gamma rays, ultraviolet photons, and neutrons, carry greater uncertainty than do X-rays, both as to expected fluence and damage thresholds. Nonetheless, numerous radiation effects studies (including both underground weapon tests and tests using other radiation sources) have indicated that these effects do represent a hazard, at least at the high end of the threat spectrum. It would be prudent to continue to characterize these effects and to improve the ability of spacecraft to survive them.

Trapped radiation carries a larger degree of uncertainty, but represents a problem that is potentially far more serious because it threatens a large number of satellites currently in orbit as well as those launched for some time following the detonation. Confidence in the existence of a threat stems in large part from observed effects following the U.S. STARFISH PRIME test and three Soviet high-altitude tests. "Pumped belts" produced by STARFISH PRIME were anticipated, satellites were in place to measure the radiation, and teams of scientists were poised to analyze the results. The post-burst distribution of trapped radiation is known approximately, and resulting satellite failures are documented. Because STARFISH PRIME occurred at an altitude where the ambient environment is highly variable as a consequence of solar activity, and because dispersal of radioactive weapon debris is strongly influenced by ambient burst-point conditions, there is a distinct possibility that a modern-day burst similar to STARFISH PRIME in altitude, L-shell, and weapon output might lead to a significantly different trapped-radiation environment.

For purposes of this study, the SNRTACS code system was used to estimate satellite exposure to trapped radiation from nuclear bursts. As best we can determine, the trapped-radiation-environment module of the SNRTACS code system is tuned to reproduce estimates (circa 1970) of "pumped belts" produced by STARFISH PRIME and Soviet high-altitude tests, and to extrapolate to other burst parameters using limited models of relevant physical processes. Large uncertainties derive directly from extrapolation aspects of this computational process and from highly uncertain models of debris transport used in SNRTACS. Because confidence in SNRTACS predictions requires that the model reasonably predict trapped radiation along the satellite orbit over the lifetime of the satellite, one must recognize limitations inherent in current predictive capabilities as applied here.

Benefits of hardening can be nonlinear. Because peak trapped-radiation intensity drops rapidly over the first few days after detonation, a satellite orbiting through the peak-flux region might survive significantly longer if its radiation tolerance were doubled.

Radiation Belt Remediation (RBR) concepts currently under study *may* require several weeks to reduce significantly trapped-radiation fluxes. If so, RBR would likely not prolong lifetimes of satellites expected to fail within a few days after a detonation. RBR, if proved viable, may have a principal benefit in reducing the waiting time before replacing failed satellites.

In conclusion, despite very large uncertainties in our ability to predict trapped radiation resulting from a specific detonation, radiation hardening of satellite components will likely prolong LEO satellite survival times measurably. Outstanding questions revolve around relative costs versus benefits to be derived from an investment in hardening technology. Quantitative answers require better estimates of nuclear-pumped belt intensities and lifetimes.

GEO and MEO satellites require different considerations and have not been extensively evaluated here. Our baseline prediction is that only high-yield detonations will affect these satellites because (a) MEO and GEO satellites operate on average in more intense natural radiation environments than do LEO satellites, so are designed with inherently greater radiation tolerance, and (b) the magnetic volume extending to MEO and GEO altitudes that is "pumped" by a detonation is much larger and trapped fluxes are proportionately smaller.

X.F What Needs To Be Done

- **Phenomenology of Nuclear Detonations Above 600 km**

Consequences of a high-altitude nuclear detonation depend on just how high an altitude (i.e., consequences depend on burst-point air density and ionization state). The highest-altitude nuclear detonation for which reasonable data were collected was STARFISH PRIME at 400 km. STARFISH PRIME phenomenology is understood to be applicable from about 250 km to no higher than about 600 km altitude. The URACCA test planned in 1962 to be at ~ 1,200 km was cancelled by President Kennedy following STARFISH PRIME effects on satellites. In the absence of anything better, it has been common to predict effects of detonations above 600 km by extrapolating STARFISH PRIME phenomenology to higher altitudes. Until recently it has not been possible to quantify the magnitudes of errors that result from such extrapolations. However, recent improvements in analysis and modeling indicate the errors can be large. For example, for a 1 Mt detonation at 1,300 km, "cold" plasma electron density predictions based on extrapolation of STARFISH PRIME phenomenology are now indicated to be in error by two to three orders of magnitude.

Mid-course ballistic missile defense intercepts are posited up to ~ 1,500 km or more. Salvage-fused detonations resulting from BMD intercepts at altitudes above 600 km will likely create levels of nuclear environments and systems effects that are not reasonably predicted by many of the existing models that have not been modified to account for phenomenology of very high-altitude detonations. Consequently, BMD system elements and battle-management strategies may risk being designed on the basis of inappropriate levels of nuclear effects, at least for detonations in the upper half of the mid-course battle space.

A recent technical breakthrough permits preliminary assessments of environments, but a sustained program built around multi-fluid magnetohydrodynamics (MHD), augmented with plasma kinetic physics, is needed to quantify environments and system effects in a defensible manner.

- **Uncertainty Reduction for Nuclear-Pumped Radiation Belts**

Intensities of nuclear-pumped trapped radiation belts depend on several factors: nuclear yield; burst location; trapping efficiency of energetic particles; loss mechanisms of natural and nuclear origins. Each of these factors is subject to uncertainty, but from data one infers the latter two are subject to very wide variations that are neither adequately understood nor appropriately modeled. Uncertainties in trapped fluxes are plus or minus a few in the exponent! Trapped radiation from multiple high-altitude detonations is, for lack of anything better, treated by linear superposition, even though governing processes are highly nonlinear.

In the absence of a reliable predictive model for nuclear-pumped radiation belts, hardening criteria for nuclear-survivable space-qualified electronics for satellites, interceptors, and related applications are currently based on limited data and a healthy dose of conjecture. Planning for time-critical replenishment of important satellites that would be lost following a high-altitude detonation suffers from large uncertainties in estimates of radiation belt intensities and lifetimes.

Reliable predictive modeling of nuclear-pumped radiation belts is within reach. In the past 40+ years, considerable scientific understanding of natural radiation belts has accrued and numerous satellites now routinely report natural trapped-particle fluxes. Because nuclear-pumped radiation belts differ from natural belts only in their source, considerable model validation can be accomplished on the basis of readily available natural-belt data. Sophisticated modeling of the space environment that regulates radiation-belt behavior is available. It remains to combine available data resources, modern scientific understandings, and sophisticated modeling capabilities to resolve the nuclear-pumped radiation belt problem.

- **Space Environment for Natural and Nuclear Conditions**

The environment of near-Earth space in which satellites orbit and in which offensive missiles and defensive missile interceptors fly is governed by a combination of quiescent and eruptive phenomena of the Sun that propagate to the vicinity of the Earth as the solar wind and interplanetary magnetic field (IMF). Because the solar wind and IMF are highly variable, the environment of near-Earth space is highly variable. The frequent many-order-of-magnitude swings in fluxes of energetic electrons in the natural radiation belts are testimony to these effects. High-altitude nuclear explosions that may occur for any of many reasons would occur in this variable environment, would influence it, and would be subject to it.

As a means for providing accurate descriptions of the host environment for high-altitude nuclear explosions, as a basis for using natural energetic phenomena in space, and as a technology transfer effort toward utilization of advanced technologies in support of operations Air Force space forecast activities, DTRA applied modeling methodologies developed for high-altitude nuclear explosions to simulate the space environment. The effort has produced the Integrated Space Weather Prediction Model (ISM) that is without equal in capability and scope. Many benefits remain to be exploited. For example, ISM has proved capable of providing an advanced 3-D time-dependent description of the electromagnetic environment that maintains the radiation belts around the Earth, but the capability is going unexploited. The ISM program has been inordinately successful to date as a proof of concept, but considerable work remains to be done to realize its full potential.

The ISM currently lacks model components that are essential for an adequate description of the space environment under natural and nuclear-burst conditions. First-principles high-altitude nuclear burst effects need to be made an integral part of ISM.

- **Nuclear Detonations Between 30 to 90 km Altitude**

U.S. test experience with nuclear detonations in the 30 to 90 km altitude range is limited to a handful of shots. Limited effort has been expended to understand and model phenomenology of nuclear detonations in this altitude range, said phenomenology having unique aspects associated with entrainment and turbulent mixing, fireball dynamics, electron density profiles, optical phenomena, and transport of radioactive weapon debris. Based on sparse nuclear test data we conclude shots above ~ 45 to 50 km are capable of creating trapped radiation belts, but mechanisms for belt creation have not been demonstrated to be understood. In the natural atmosphere, this altitude regime is difficult to characterize in terms of chemical dynamics and transport processes because it is directly accessible primarily only by rocket probes and very large balloons. Necessary remote sensing is not highly developed.

Current understandings of nuclear detonations in the 30 to 90 km altitude range are not sufficient to support reliable analysis, hardening criteria, mitigation requirements, and battle management planning for ballistic missile defense systems.

A concerted effort is needed to understand nuclear detonations in the 30 to 90 km altitude range. Basic phenomenology, systems effects, and mitigation options need to be explored.

CHAPTER XI
THREAT MITIGATION

XI.A Introduction

There are several approaches to mitigation of the nuclear threat to space-based assets, including both satellites and their supporting ground stations. For satellites, mitigation techniques include:

- Shielding
- Hardening of critical circuitry
- Redundancy for the line-of-sight threat
- Possible remediation of pumped belts
- Possible change of orbit
- Deterrence

For ground stations the options are:

- Proliferation of ground stations
- EMP Shielding
- EMP hardening
- Deterrence

Shielding and/or hardening for both satellites and ground stations are mature engineering disciplines, and their application is determined by priorities set by the government or commercial customer. Project managers who make necessary decisions on the approach to system survivability must examine whether addressing only the satellite or only the ground station will still leave exploitable system vulnerability.

Commercial operators will probably choose not to protect their systems against acts of war. The cost effectiveness of hardening or shielding would be considered in terms of the competitive position of their system vis-à-vis other similar systems at the same risk.

For DoD satellites the cost-effectiveness of hardening and shielding must be measured against regrets of loss as well as fiscal and weight budgets of the system. Current studies, however, suggest that shielding may introduce only tens of pounds of weight penalty which is usually well within launch vehicle launch margins. Also, the addition of hardened parts in some areas of a spacecraft may add only a few percent to system cost [Webb et. al., March 1996]. There are ethical issues associated with choices made by a satellite operator that supports a military customer. If a conscious decision has been made not to harden or protect a satellite by some means, this should be made clear to all of organizations that use the satellite for intelligence, data acquisition, or communications purposes.

There is presently little protection against direct attack except some form of deterrence by threats of retaliation or economic sanctions. There can be other measures taken to prevent use of a "cheap shot". That is, have sufficient redundancy, reserve systems or alternative systems to make it very expensive for an attacker to kill more than one of a particular constellation or a total mission with only one shot. The feasibility of accelerating the decay of trapped nuclear radiation is currently under investigation and is described in the following section.

XI.B Remediation of Pumped Belts

A current Air Force project is studying the feasibility of using VLF transmissions, either ground-based or space-based, to remove trapped electrons from the radiation belts following a high altitude nuclear detonation. If successful, this would reduce the cumulative damage inflicted on orbiting spacecraft as well as reduce the delay in launch of replacement satellites.

Physical processes governing pitch-angle scattering (and thus lifetime) of trapped electrons have been reviewed by Abel and Thorne [1998]. These processes cause electron pitch angles to diffuse into the "loss cone", *i.e.*, electrons become sufficiently parallel to the magnetic field that their mirror points fall into the "sensible atmosphere" (usually cited as below 100 km altitude) at some longitude. Artificial VLF transmissions are believed to play an important role in limiting lifetimes of electrons with energies of 0.5 MeV or higher in the inner radiation belt. Interaction of VLF transmissions with trapped electrons has been seen in both ground-based and space-based observations. [Clilverd and Horne, 1996; Inan *et al.*, 1984; Koons *et al.*, 1981; Imhof *et al.*, 1981.] Note that since these transmitters have been active since the early 1950's, the "natural" radiation belts (*i.e.*, the belts when free from human interference) have never been observed.

Preliminary estimates suggest that six kilowatts of wave power near L=1.5 can reduce the lifetime of 1 MeV electrons at LEO from about a half-year to a half-month. If the antennas are about one-third efficient, this can be done with a few satellites. Further studies and proof-of-principle experiments are planned to refine these estimates, and to determine whether the transmitters are best located on high-altitude equatorial satellites, low-altitude polar satellites, or on the ground.

A recent review of this topic has been published by Inan *et al.* (2003).

An alternative proposal is to promote pitch-angle diffusion using electrostatic fields surrounding several high voltage tether arrays. [TUI, 2004] This concept is currently under study by DARPA. The system would consist of several long (up to 100 km) tether arrays maintained at high negative voltage (up to 100 kV). The plasma sheath around such a tether would be very large, perturbing a substantial volume of space. The tethers would be in elliptical orbit so as to pass through most of the inner belt L-shells. Proponents calculate that the proposed system "can reduce the MeV particle flux in the inner electron belt to 1% of its natural levels within about half a year."

XI.C Orbit Modification

It has been proposed that reduction of radiation exposure due to belt pumping may be accomplished by a change in orbit. A satellite would be lowered to a less hazardous altitude using propellant and hardware that was designed into the system for this purpose. This operation would potentially require an enormous amount of fuel and could only be available to specific satellite systems.

XI.D Ground Control Stations

Ground control stations can be an Achilles heel for satellite systems. They can be subject to any number of attacks on land by terrorists or special forces using any number of weapons. A station that is not EMP hardened can be shut down or seriously damaged by a HEMP attack. This in turn could defeat the satellite mission. Satellites in any orbit, LEO, MEO, GEO, or HEO, can only function for a finite time in an autonomous mode after which they may cease to operate.

CHAPTER XII
CONCLUSIONS AND RECOMMENDATIONS

XII.A Conclusions

The most outstanding findings from this and previous studies are the following:

- **All satellites, regardless of orbit, are vulnerable to direct attack.**

Though the question of direct attack is beyond the scope of this study, we feel compelled to admonish the intelligence community to be alert for signs of developing capabilities in missile lift, nuclear warhead development, electromagnetic and/or laser weaponry (jamming or burnout) or any other technology that can seriously impair satellite function.

- **Ground control stations for satellites are subject to direct attack by EMP or any other means.**

Satellites typically communicate with multiple ground antennas, but have only one or two ground control stations. If a satellite requires updated instructions from a ground station, it may not retain substantial autonomy for a only a limited period after ground stations are rendered inoperable. Vulnerability to the loss of a ground control station for satellites **in any orbit (LEO, MEO, GEO and HEO)** should therefore be examined regarding the hardness and multiplicity of ground stations as well as a satellite's ability to survive and function autonomously.

- **An attack on MEO or GEO satellites by high latitude detonations for the purpose of populating electron belts at those altitudes would require large yields ($\geq$ 10 Mt).**

The mean natural radiation level in these orbits is already high, as is its variability. Further, the volume of these outer-belt magnetic flux tubes (at L=4.0 to 6.6) is much larger than that of the flux tubes encountered by LEO satellites. A high-yield weapon would be required to significantly raise radiation intensity above natural levels. In addition, injected radiation would decay due to natural processes in a period of days to weeks, rather than the months-to-years persistence of the inner belt electrons.

- **Satellites in MEO or GEO are not at risk to immediate loss from radiation damage resulting from a credible EMP attack anywhere on Earth.**

The optimum altitudes for an EMP attack (below a few hundred km) are too far from these satellites (above 20,000 km) to pose a threat from prompt line-of-sight irradiation simply due to the inverse-square falloff of the radiation intensity.

- **All satellites in LEO are at risk to serious damage from line-of-sight or enhanced radiation belt exposure resulting from EMP attacks over many geographical locations of the Earth.**

Earth's atmosphere and the ephemerae of LEO satellites reduce the probability of line-of-sight irradiation to less than 20% for many threat scenarios, rendering the immediate loss of a few satellites a distinct possibility. The pumping of radiation belts constitutes a serious long-term hazard to all LEO satellites. Loss of LEO intelligence capabilities could seriously hamper any war effort, particularly in remote regions.

- **An EMP attack directly over CONUS or Canada of less than ~ 1 Mt does not place LEO satellites at risk to radiation damage because those countries are located at relatively high magnetic latitude.**

The magnetic flux tubes whose footprints fall in Northern CONUS or Canada extend beyond most LEO orbits. High inclination orbits only pass briefly through these flux tubes at high latitudes.

- **Uncertainties in numerical calculations of damaging nuclear-induced environments can be mitigated to some extent by current modeling efforts.**

Large uncertainties for predicted nuclear radiation belt intensities can, to some extent, be remedied. Recent scientific advances in the comprehension and interpretation of the physics governing high-altitude nuclear detonations, combined with vastly greater computer capability than that available in the late 1950s and early 1960s (at the time of U.S. and Soviet high-altitude nuclear tests), allows one to describe a nuclear explosion in greater technical detail and with greater certainty. At the same time, more than forty years of data and analysis of the natural radiation belts has advanced scientific understandings of basic radiation-belt physics. In combination, these advances offer an opportunity to reduce to tolerable levels currently large uncertainties in nuclear-pumped radiation belts and their consequences. Reductions in uncertainties would make current investments in radiation-hardened electronics more quantifiable and would optimize and economize hardening requirements as regards nuclear induced environments.

- **Recent more rigorous examination of the ultraviolet output of high altitude detonations indicates that this portion of the radiation spectrum is present in sufficient magnitude to be much more damaging to surface components than previously thought.**

The reexamination, conducted at LLNL at the request of Commission staff, reveals that the amount of UV fluence is sufficient to be a hazard to satellite surface components (optical and power) because of the very large absorption cross-sections for ultraviolet radiation.

XII.B Recommendations

It is recommended that the following measures be directed and implemented:

- Stringent nuclear hardening criteria should be placed on LEO satellites and control systems which serve intelligence missions. Their hardness should be a matter of record available to DOD management and the Congress.

- The JCS should review hardening specifications of all crucial satellite systems, including ground control stations, and establish consistent survivability criteria.

- Hardening measures and threat remediation tactics should have Secretariat or Congressional oversight.

- Hardening costs to civilian satellites that host intelligence functions should be borne by the U.S. Government.

- Mandated and fenced research programs in high-altitude nuclear effects should be adequately reviewed and funded to assure a better understanding of nuclear burst phenomena, a greater confidence in the quantitative prediction of their effects, and a substantial reduction in costs associated with present large hardening safety margins.

- Research and development into the feasibility of electron-Radiation-Belt Remediation technologies should be pursued with a greater sense of urgency to provide more options for survivability of critical satellites.

REFERENCES

Abdallah, J., Jr., R. E. H. Clark, and R. D. Cowan, Theoretical Atomic Physics Code Development I – CATS: Cowan Atomic Structure Code, Los Alamos National Laboratory, LA-11436-M, Vol 1, 1988.

Abel, B. and R. M. Thorne, "Electron scattering loss in Earth's inner magnetosphere 1. Dominant physical processes," Journal of Geophysical Research 103, 2385, 1998.

Adamson, "Alouette: Canada's record setting satellite", 29 Sept 2002, http://exn.ca/Stories/1999/05/14/52.asp

Allen, C., private communication, 2002.

Anderson, P.C., "Surface Charging in the Auroral Zone on the DMSP Spacecraft in LEO," 6th Spacecraft Charging Technology Conference, AFRL-VS-TR-20001578, 2000.

Armstrong, R. A., private communication, December 2003.

Astronautix.com

Bell, M., D. Breuner, P. Coakley, B. Stewart, M. Treadaway, J. Sperling, E. Wenaas, and A. Woods, "Capabilities of Nuclear Weapons (U) : EM-1, Chapter 22-Damage to Space Systems (U)", Defense Nuclear Agency Report, DNA-001-87-C-0275, November 1990. (SRD)

Biggs, F. and Lighthill, R." Analytical Approximations for X-Ray Cross Sections III", SANDIA Report SAND87-0070,UC-34, August 1988.

Birkeland, K., Expédition Norvegienne de 1899-1900 pour l'étude des aurores boréales, Vidensk. Skrifter I. Mat. Maturv. Kl. 1901, 1, 1901.

Birkeland, K., The Norwegian Aurora Polaris Expedition, 1902-1903, vol. 1, 1st and 2nd sections, Aschehoug, Christiana, 1908 and 1913.

Childs, W.H., "Thermophysical Properties of Selected Space-Related Materials", Aerospace Corp. Rept. No. TOR-0081 (6435-02)-1, Feb. 1981.

Christofolis, N.C., Proc. Nat. Acad. of Sci. U.S. 45, 000, 1959.

Christofolis, N.C., "Sources of Artificial Radiation Belts" in Radiation Trapped in the Earth's Magnetic Field, Proceedings of the Advanced Study Institute Held at the Chr. Michelsen Institute, Bergen, Norway, August 16-September 3, 1965, B. M. McCormac, ed., D. Reidel Publishing Company, Dordrecht, Holland, 1966.

Clapper, Jr. USAF (Ret), Lt. Gen. James R., Director, NGA, *State of the Agency*, Pathfinder, Sept./Oct. 2003

Clark, R. E. H., J. Abdallah, Jr., G. Csanak, J. B. Mann, and R. D. Cowan, Theoretical Physics Code Development II – ACE: Another Collisional Excitation Code, Los Alamos National Laboratory, LA-11436-M, Vol. II, 1988.

Clilverd, M. A., and R. B. Horne, "Ground-based evidence of latitude-dependent cyclotron absorption of whistler mode signals originating from VLF transmitters," Journal of Geophysical Research 101, 2355, 1996.

Comments on the Phillips Laboratory Exoatmospheric Nuclear Environment Models and Accuracy, Greaves, 25 Aug 1994.

Correlation Smart Data Manager, version 2.1, Jaycor, November 1999.

Croff, A.G., ORIGEN2: A Versatile Computer Code for Calculating the Nuclide Compositions and Characteristics of Nuclear Materials, Nuclear Technology, 62, 335-352, 1983.

DiPeso, G., "Current Output Calculation Results for NWM21-4 (U),", LLNL Report COPD-2003-039, February 2003 (SRD-CNWDI-NOFORN)

Evans, R.D., "The Atomic Nucleus", McGraw-Hill Book Co., 1955.

Fennell, J. et al., "Spacecraft Charging: Observations and Relationship to Satellite Anomalies," Proceedings of the 7th Spacecraft Charging Technology Conference, ESA-ESTEC, Noordwijk, The Netherlands, 23-27 April 2001.

Fischell, R.E., "Solar Cell Performance in the Artificial Radiation Belt", AIAA Journal, Vol 1, No 1, pp 242-245, Jan 1963.

Frederickson, A. R., and J. T. Bell, "Analytic Approximation for Charge Current and Deposition by 0.1 to 100 MeV Electrons in Thick Slabs," IEEE Transactions on Nuclear Science 42, 1910, 1995.

Gillmor, C.S., "The Formation and Early Studies of the Magnetosphere" in Discovery of the Magnetosphere, History of Geophysics Volume 7, American Geophysical Union, Washington, D.C., 1997.

Government Accounting Office, *Critical Infrastructure Protection – Commercial Satellite Security Should Be More Fully Addressed*, GAO-02-781, Aug 02.

Grimwood, James M., "Project Mercury: A Chronology", NASA Special Publication-4001.

Gurtman, G.A., M.J. Mandell, V.A. Davis, M.H. Rice, G.C. Kweder, W.W.White, and E.E. Conrad, "Satellite Surface Vulnerabilities to Exo-Atmospheric Nuclear Detonations", SAIC Report No. SAIC-03/2000, May.

Gurtman, G.A.and M.H. Rice, "Response of Silicon and GaAs Solar Cells to a Nuclear X-ray Environment", Maxwell Technologies Report MTSD-CDTM-98-16099, April 1998

Gurtman, G.A., M.J. Mandell, V.A. Davis, M.H. Rice, G.C. Kweder, W.W. White, and E.E. Conrad, "Satellite Surface Vulnerabilies to Exo-Atmospheric Nuclear Detonations", SAIC Report No. SAIC-03/2000, May 2003

Hausman, M. A., D. C. Terry, and R. W. Kilb, STARFISH PRIME Volume 1 - 3D-CMHD Fine-Grid Results (U), Mission Research Corporation, DNA-TR-91-174-V1, May 1992a. (Secret-Restricted Data)

Hausman, M. A., D. C. Terry, and R. W. Kilb, STARFISH PRIME Volume 2 - Detailed Graphical Results, Mission Research Corporation, DNA-TR-91-174-V2, May 1992b.

Hilland, D., AFRL, private communication, 2003.

Hoerlin, H., "United States High-Altitude Test Experiences," Los Alamos Scientific Laboratory report LA-6405, 1976.

Hoover, T., "Preliminary Output Results for NWM21-2 (U)," LLNL Report COPD-2001-039, December 2002, (SRD-CNWDI-NOFORN)

http://www.sputnik1.com/sput_history1.htm

Hussey, John W., "Economic Benefits of Operational Environmental Satellites," reprinted from A. Schnap (ed.), Monitoring Earth's Ocean, Land, and Atmosphere from Space-Sensors, Systems, and Applications, Vol. 97 of Progress in Astronautics series (Washington, D.C.: American Institute of Astronautics and Aeronautics, 1985).

Imhof, W. L., R. R. Anderson, J. B. Reagan and E. E. Gaines, "The significance of VLF transmitters in the precipitation of inner belt electrons," Journal of Geophysical Research 86, 11225, 1981.

Inan, U. S., Bell, T. F., Bortnik, J., Albert, J. M., "Controlled precipitation of radiation belt electrons", Journal of Geophysical Research 108, No. A5, SMP 6-1, May 2003.

Inan, U. S., H. C. Chang and R. A. Helliwell, "Electron precipitation zones around major ground-based VLF signal sources," Journal of Geophysical Research 89, 2891, 1984.

Itikawa, Y., S. Hara, T. Kato, S. Nakazaki, M. S. Pindzola, and D. H. Crandall, Electron Impact Cross Sections and Rate Coefficients for Excitations of Carbon and Oxygen Ions, *Atomic and Nuclear Data Tables, 33*, 149, 1985.

Jakes, E.M., K.J. Daul, and Robert Greaves, "Exoatmospheric Nuclear Radiation Environment Prediction and Shielding Codes," Report PL-TR-92-1056, Air Force Phillips Laboratory, March 1993.

Jakes, et. al., "Satellite Orbital Handbook for the Study of High Altitude Nuclear Tests", PL-TR-93-1051, May 1994

Johnson, M. H., and H. Kierein, J. Spacecraft and Rockets 29, No. 4, p 556-563, 1992.

Katz, I., V.A. Davis, M.J. Mandell, B.M. Gardner, J.M. Hilton, J. Minor, A.R. Fredrickson, D.L. Cooke, Interactive Spacecraft Charging Handbook with Integrated Updated Spacecraft Charging Models, AIAA 2000-0247, 2000.

Kaul, D.C., et al, "Capabilities of Nuclear Weapons, EM-1 (U); Chapter 8-Nuclear Radiation Phenomena (U)" DNA Report DNA-EM-1-CH-8 (AD CO 458900) March 1990 (SRD)

Kilb, R. W., and D. E. Glenn, "CMHD Simulations of Very High Altitude Nuclear Bursts from 0 to 1 Second (U)", Mission Research Corporation, DNA 4629F, June 1978. (Secret-Restricted Data)

Koons, H. C., B. C. Edgar and A. L. Vampola, "Precipitation of inner zone electrons by whistler mode waves from the VLF transmitters UMS and NWC," Journal of Geophysical Research 86, 640, 1981.

Laher, R.R. and F. R. Gilmore, Updated Excitation and Ionization Cross Sections for Electron Impact on Atomic Oxygen, *J. Phys. Chem. Ref. Data, 19(1)*, 277, 1990.

Li, X. and M. A. Temerin, The Electron Radiation Belt, Space Science Reviews, 95(1/2), 569, 2001a.

Li, X., D. N. Baker, S. G. Kanekal, M. Looper, and M. Temerin, SAMPEX Long Term Observations of MeV Electrons, Geophys. Res. Lett., 28, 3827, 2001b.

Lawrence Livermore National Laboratory, "TENABO Post-Operational Report (U)," LLNL Report COPD-99-10, 1999, SRD-CNWDI.

Longmire, C. L., On the electromagnetic pulse produced by nuclear explosions, IEEE Trans. on Antennas and Propagation 26, No. 1, 3, 1978

Mayo, J.S., et al "The Command System Malfunction of the Telstar Satellite"., Bell Systems Technical Journal 42 (4), 1631, 1963

McIlwain, C. E., J. Geophys. Res. 66, 3681, 1961.

Morrow-Jones, J., D. Krueger, D. Walters, B. Crevier, J. Henley, F. Varcolik, T. Cooke, B. Shaw, M. Vandersluis, K. Doughty, R. Goldflam, "Testable Hardware Toolkit V 2.0", 2001.

Mullen, E. G., private communication, Space Environmental Effects Working Group Workshop, The Aerospace Corporation, November 2003.

NASA, 2003. http://www.spaceflight.nasa.gov/station

National Security Presidential Directive (NSPD), U.S. Commercial Remote Sensing Policy, April 25, 2003

NOAA, 2003. http://dmsp.ngdc.noaa.gov/dmsp.html

Northrop, John, "Handbook of Nuclear Weapon Effects, Calculational Tool Extracted From EM-1". DSWA Publication, September 1996.

Parmentola, J., et al, *High Altitude Nuclear Detonations (HAND) Against Low Earth Orbit Satellites (HALEOS),* DTRA briefing, April 2001

Parrington, J. R., H. D. Knox, S. L. Breneman, E. M Baum, and F. Feiner, Nuclides and Isotopes, 15th Ed., published by General Electric Co. and KAPL, Inc., 1996.

Pickel, J.C., A.H. Kalma, and G.R. Hopkinson, " Radiation Effects on Photonic Imagers-A Historical Perspective", IEEE Transactions of Nuclear Science, VOL. 50,No. 3, June 2003.

Satellite Tool Kit (STK 4.0) Analytic Graphics, 1997.

russianspaceweb.com/tselina.html

Particle Data Group, "Review of Particle Properties," Physical Review D45, 1992.

Presidential Recordings Project, pg 36, "Kennedy Meets with his Advisors on the DOMINIC Nuclear Test Series", Fall 2001

Sappenfield, D. S., and T. H. McCartor, "A Comparison of Equilibrium and Non-equilibrium Calculations of the TEAK Fireball (U), Defense Nuclear Agency Report DAN 4022F, 1976 (Secret-Restricted Data).

Satellite Tool Kit (STK 4.0) Analytic Graphics, 1997.

Sawyer, D. and J. Vette, AP-8 trapped proton environment for solar maximum and solar minimum, National Space Science Data Center, Report 76-06, Greenbelt, Maryland, 1976.

Shelton, F. H., Reflections of a Nuclear Weaponeer, Shelton Enterprise, Inc., Colorado Springs, CO, 1988.

Solar-Terrestial Energy Program, April 1994, Vol.4, No.4

Space News, "U.S. Military Buys Airtime on Iridium Satellite System", 7 Dec 2000.

Stern, D. P., "A Brief History of Magnetospheric Physics before the Spaceflight Era", Reviews of Geophysics, vol. 27, 103-114, 1989.
See also the web page: http://www-istp.gsfc.nasa.gov/Education/whtrap1.html.

Störmer, C., Arch. Sci. phys. et naturelles 24, 317-364, 1907.

Tenet, George J., Director, Central Intelligence, *Expanded use of Commercial Space Imagery,* Memorandum to Director, National Imaging and Mapping Agency, June 7, 2002

Thompson, T.,"NWM21-9A Preliminary Results (U)", LLNL Report, COPD-2002-420, August 30, 2002, (Secret-FRD).

Thomson, T. and T. Hoover, Private conversation with E. Conrad and G. Gurtman, LLNL, 17 October 2003.

Triplett, J. R., K. Sweet and B. Shkoller, "XRTH User's Manual and Reference Guide", S-Cubed Report SSS-R-89-9891, November 1988.

Tubbs, D. L., et al., "Proliferant Nuclear-Weapon Modeling Handbook (U)," Los Alamos National Laboratory report, LA-CP-99-320, December 1999 (SRD-CNWDI-NOFORN).

TUI, 2004: http://www.tethers.com/HiVOLT.html.

U.S. Dept of Commerce, NOAA Office of Policy and Strategic Planning, NOAA Economic Statistics, May 2002.

Van Allen, J. A., Special Joint Meeting of National Academy of Sciences and American Physical Society, Washington, D.C., May 1, 1958a.

Van Allen, J. A., G. H. Ludwig, E. C. Ray, and C. E. McIlwain, Observations of high intensity radiation by satellites 1958 Alpha and Gamma, Jet Propul., 28, 588-592, 1958b.

Van Allen, J. A. and L. A. Frank, Radiation around the Earth to a radial distance of 107,400 km, Nature 183, 430, 1959.

Van Allen, J. A., "Energetic Particles in the Earth's External Magnetic Field" in Discovery of the Magnetosphere, History of Geophysics Volume 7, American Geophysical Union, 1997.

Vette, J., "The AE-8 trapped electron model environment," National Space Science Data Center, Report 91-24, Greenbelt, Maryland, 1991.

Walt, M., History of Artificial Radiation Belts, Section 6 in The Trapped Radiation Handbook, ed. J.B. Cladis, G. T. Davidson, and L.L. Newkirk, DNA 2524H, Defense Nuclear Agency, 1971, revised 1977.

Walt, M., Introduction to Geomagnetically Trapped Radiation, Cambridge University Press, Cambridge, Great Britain, 1994.

Walt, M., "Sources and Losses for Radiation Belt Particles", in Radiation Belts, Models and Standards, J. F. Lemaire, D. Heynderickx, and D. N. Baker, eds., Geophysical Monograph 97, American Geophysical Union, Washington, D.C.,1996.

Walters, D. "SGEMP Sensitivity Study", JAYCOR-Titan memorandum to G. Gurtman, 14 April 2003.

Webb, R.C., L.M. Cohn, J. Pierre, A. Costantine, "The Cost Differential to Radiation Harden DoD Space Assets, 27 March 1996

Weenas, E. P., "Spacecraft Charging Effects on Satellites Following STARFISH PRIME Event", RE-78-2044-057, 17 Feb 1978

White, W. W., "An Overview of Nuclear Explosions at Intermediate and High Altitudes (U)", in the 1986 DNA Atmospheric Nuclear Effects Summer Study (U); Volume 1 - series edited by D.R. McDaniel, DNA-TR-87-181-V1, SRI International, June 1987 (Secret-Restricted Data).

Wilson C.E., et al, DNA Nuclear Weapons Output Handbook (U)", DNA Report 3728H Rev. 1, August 1979 (SRD-CNWDI)

DISTRIBUTION LIST
DTRA-IR-10-22

DEPARTMENT OF DEFENSE

DEFENSE TECHNICAL
INFORMATION CENTER
8725 JOHN J. KINGMAN ROAD,
SUITE 0944
FT. BELVOIR, VA 22060-6201
2 CYS   ATTN: DTIC/OCA

DEPARTMENT OF DEFENSE CONTRACTORS

ITT INDUSTRIES
ITT SYSTEMS CORPORATION
1680 TEXAS STREET, SE
KIRTLAND AFB, NM 87117-5669
2 CYS   ATTN: DTRIAC

SCIENCE APPLICATIONS
INTERNATIONAL CORPORATION
10260 CAMPUS POINT DRIVE
M/S A-1
LA JOLLA, CA 92121
        ATTN: G. GURTMAN

SCIENCE APPLICATIONS
INTERNATIONAL CORPORATION
10260 CAMPUS POINT DRIVE
M/S A2A
LA JOLLA, CA 92121
        ATTN: M. MANDELL

OTHER

SENIOR CONSULTANT
7500 MARBURY ROAD
BETHESDA, MD 20817
2 CYS   ATTN: E. CONRAD

CONSULTANT
58 ARBOR LANE
HOLLIS, NH 03049
        ATTN: W. WHITE

CONSULTANT
224 NEVER ENDING DRIVE
OLD FIELDS, WV 26845
        ATTN: G. KWEDER

DL-1

www.ingramcontent.com/pod-product-compliance
Lightning Source LLC
Chambersburg PA
CBHW080735300426
44114CB00019B/2594